# Privacy in the Age of Big Data

# Privacy in the Age of Big Data

*Recognizing Threats, Defending Your Rights, and Protecting Your Family*

Theresa M. Payton
and Theodore Claypoole

Foreword by the Honorable Howard A. Schmidt

ROWMAN & LITTLEFIELD
Lanham • Boulder • New York • Toronto • Plymouth, UK

Published by Rowman & Littlefield
4501 Forbes Boulevard, Suite 200, Lanham, Maryland 20706
www.rowman.com

10 Thornbury Road, Plymouth PL6 7PP, United Kingdom

British Library Cataloguing in Publication Information Available

**Library of Congress Cataloging-in-Publication Data Available**

Payton, Theresa M.
Privacy in the age of big data : Recognizing threats, defending your rights, and protecting your family / by Theresa M. Payton and Theodore Claypoole.
p. cm.
Includes bibliographical references and index.
ISBN 978-1-4422-2545-9 (cloth : alk. paper) -- ISBN 978-1-4422-2546-6 (electronic)

♾™ The paper used in this publication meets the minimum requirements of American National Standard for Information Sciences Permanence of Paper for Printed Library Materials, ANSI/NISO Z39.48-1992.

Printed in the United States of America

# Contents

Foreword       vii

Introduction: Your Life on Technology       xi

1   The Intersection of Privacy, Law, and Technology       1

**Technology Section I: Ground Zero: Your Computer and the Internet**

2   Your Computer Is Watching You       19

3   How Government Follows Your Electronic Tracks       33

4   Chased Online by Criminals and Snoops       57

5   Just Hanging Out Online . . .       77

6   The Spy in Your Pocket       95

**Technology Section II: Risks in the Streets**

7   Cameras Everywhere       113

8   When Your Car Is Just Another Computer       127

9   When Your Own Body Gives You Away       139

10   DNA and Your Health Records       155

**Technology Section III: Home Is Where the Heart (of Surveillance) Is**

11   Home Sweet Home: Spies in Your Living Room       173

12   Risks of Computer and Phone Networks       195

**Technology Section IV: Where Do We Go from Here?**

13   The Future of Technology and Privacy       211

14   Laws and Regulations That Could Help Preserve Privacy       227

Index       243

About the Authors       259

# Foreword

As a partner in the strategic advisory firm Ridge Schmidt Cyber, I help senior executives from business and government develop strategies to deal with the increasing demands of cybersecurity, privacy, and big data decisions. We often talk about the importance of maintaining security while protecting privacy and enhancing business processes. When I served as special assistant to the president and the cybersecurity coordinator during President Obama's administration, we saw repeatedly that the choices were not easy—if they were would not still be wrestling with this issue. It's a challenge I saw on both sides of the table from my roles with the White House, Department of Homeland Security, US military, and law enforcement to my roles in the private sector at market leaders such as Microsoft Corporation and eBay.

Some experts have indicated that the volume of data in the world is rapidly growing and is perhaps doubling every eighteen months. A recent report published by Computer Sciences Corporation (CSC) stated that the creation of data will be forty-four times greater in 2020 than it was in 2009. IBM has said that 90 percent of the data in the world today was created in 2011–2012. This might be why the elusive tech term of "big data" is starting become more mainstream within your household or workplace. How we collect and use the growing data supply can impact our professional and personal lives. Big data—is it going to prove to be a boon or a bust to business bottom lines? Is it the answer to all of our national security needs, or will it undermine the key liberties we cherish? Just because we can collect massive amounts of data and analyze it at lightning speed, should we? Are companies designing big data with privacy and security in mind? Big data analysis can be used to spot security issues by pinpointing anomalous behaviors at lightning speed. Big data provides businesses and governments around the globe the capability to find the needle in the haystack—by analyzing and sorting through massive treasure troves of data to find the hidden patterns and correlations that human analysts alone might miss. At the present time, most organizations don't really understand the best way to design big data applications and analytics, which translates into massive data collection with a "just in case we need it" approach. Companies may collect everything without truly understanding the data-security and privacy ramifications.

As business and government collects and benefits from all of this data, capturing data becomes an end in itself. We must have more and more data to feed the insatiable appetite for more. And yet, we are not having a serious public discussion about what information is collected about each of us and how it is being used. This book starts the discussion in a provocative and fascinating manner.

Nearly every industrialized country has passed laws addressing use of personal data. Some such laws exist in the United States, but the US Congress has not passed a broad law limiting the collection or use of all sorts of personal data since before the Internet was introduced to the public. The technology to gather and exploit information has rapidly outpaced our government's willingness and ability to thoughtfully pass laws protecting both commerce and privacy, so that business does not know what it can do and citizens are left unprotected.

Around the globe, too many citizens are exposed to identity theft, businesses are struggling to deal with cyberespionage and theft of intellectual property, banks are increasingly fighting regular cyberdisruptions, and the list of malware and breaches continue to mount against social-media networks and Internet platforms.

Big data and analytics will revolutionize the way we live and work. Those incredible benefits could look small in comparison if we do not address the issues of security and privacy. The best way to achieve that is to be better informed and strike the right balance. The potential privacy and security issues from big data impact all citizens around the globe, not just within the United States. The issues within the United States regarding citizens' right to privacy and reasonable expectations for security cross political party lines in terms of what is at stake. Now is the time to for countries to discuss and design a consistent set of best practices to protect the privacy of their citizens. In the United States, we have not had meaningful significant legislation passed on cybersecurity in over a decade. Now is the time to join forces to defeat the possibility that any American's personal data could be compromised.

I have devoted my life's work to the issues of protecting people and our nation's most critical assets, and I know Theresa Payton and Ted Claypoole share my same passion for leveraging technology capabilities to their fullest while planning for the inevitable attacks against that same technology by cybercriminals and fraudsters.

This topic is complex and not easy to understand, but finally there is a guide written by cyberexperts, not for big data geeks or techies, but for the average person. This book addresses global concerns and will appeal to the business executive and the consumer. Even if you consider yourself a novice Internet user, this book is for you. Cybersecurity and privacy authorities Payton and Claypoole explain in plain language the benefits of big data, the downsides of big data, and how you can take the bull by the horns and own your privacy. This book simplifies complex and technical concepts about big data while giving you tips, and hope, that you can do something about the privacy and security concerns that the authors artfully highlight.

Theresa understands better than anyone that the specter of a massive cyberdisruption is the most urgent concern confronting the nation's information technology infrastructure today. She tackles this issue through the lens of years of experience in high-level private and public IT leadership roles, including when she served at the White House within the executive office of the president. She is a respected authority on Internet security, net crime, fraud mitigation, and technology implementation and currently lends her expertise to organizations, helping them improve their information technology systems against emerging, amorphous cyberthreats. Ted has also spent a long career in data management and privacy, including addressing computer crimes and data privacy with one of the world's largest Internet service providers in the early days of the web and helping secure information for an enormous financial institution. Ted currently helps businesses and governments of all kinds with information protection advice and data-breach counseling. His work on data privacy topics for the American Bar Association has highlighted some of the most difficult legal technology debates of our time, including geolocation tracking, biometric identification regimes, and gaps in protection of DNA privacy.

Each chapter of the book shows how your everyday activities, at home and work, are part of the big data collection. The authors highlight the benefits of the data collection and illustrate where the technologies could be used to compromise your privacy and security. Each chapter provides tips and remedies to the privacy issue, if those remedies exist.

The book opens with an introduction on why, like it or not, your life is dominated by technology. The book begins with a great write-up on the intersection of today's technology with the legal systems and privacy concerns in chapter 1, including the arresting answers to the very important questions: "Why should I care if government, business, or bad guys invade my privacy?" If you believe you are already well versed on the issues, jump ahead to chapters 13 ("The Future of Technology and Privacy") and 14 ("Laws and Regulations That Could Help Preserve Privacy").

Perhaps when Ken Olson, president of Digital Equipment Corporation, said in 1977, "There is no reason anyone in the right state of mind will want a computer in their home," he was onto something. Only now, we don't really notice the computers in the home, in our pockets, and even on our wrists.

The Honorable Howard A. Schmidt,
Partner of Ridge Schmidt Cyber,
previously the cybersecurity coordinator and special assistant
to President Barack Obama
and cyber advisor for President George W. Bush

# Introduction

## *Your Life on Technology*

Where is the most private place in your life? Your bedroom? Your bathroom? Your office? Can you count on carving out zones of privacy within these spaces? What about your car, your local pharmacy, your backyard, or deep in the woods walking by yourself? Can you just disappear for a while and do what you want to do without anyone knowing?

## CIRCLES OF PRIVACY

We can think of privacy in concentric circles with ourselves in the center. In the middle, held closest to us, are the secrets, thoughts, and rituals that we keep entirely to ourselves and share with no one. Further out are the conversations we have and the actions we take that involve others but that we expect to remain private. We also expect a measure of privacy toward the outer circles, as some issues are kept within the family or inside our company without further publication. Certain information we hide from the neighbors, some financial data we prefer to keep from the government, and there are certain things that our mothers-in-law have no business knowing.

Privacy is complex and personal. Yet no matter what each person's perception of privacy is, some invasions are so extreme that they raise an immediate cry from everyone who hears about them.

### *Spying on Teens*

Teenager Blake Robbins thought his bedroom was private. In 2009, Blake was a student at Berwin High School, in the Lower Merion School District near Philadelphia. The Lower Merion School District sponsored a laptop-computer-loan program, and Blake took advantage of it, borrowing one of the school's laptops to help him with his homework. On November 11, 2009, Blake arrived at school in the morning and was called to the office of Assistant Principal Lindy Matsko. She informed Blake that the school district believed he was engaging in improper behavior in his home, and cited as evidence a photograph from the webcam embedded in the laptop computer loaned to him.[1]

The school district later admitted remotely accessing school laptops to secretly snap pictures of students (and others) in their homes, to capture the students' chat logs, and to keep records of the websites that the students visited. The software used to spy on students was a remote capture program supposedly included on these systems to prevent theft or loss of the equipment (as if geolocation trackers would not be enough). School technologists sent the secret pictures to servers at the school, and school administrators reviewed and shared the pictures.

Blake was shown a picture of himself with hands full of pill-shaped objects, popping them in his mouth as if they were candy. The picture was taken in Blake's bedroom by the school-owned laptop computer. Individuals in the school administration believed these objects to be illegally obtained drugs, and that Blake was breaking the law. Blake claimed the pills were Mike and Ike brand candies and that he was simply relaxing in his own room. The school disciplined Blake, claiming the computer had surreptitiously captured pictures of Blake abusing pills in his bedroom.

According to a subsequent report following investigation by the school district, two members of the student counsel at another high school in the Lower Merion School District twice privately raised concerns with their school's principal, claiming that webcam's green activation light would occasionally flicker on their school-issued computers, signaling that the webcam had been turned on remotely. The students found this creepy, and the school district called it a "technical glitch,"

Blake's family sued the Lower Merion School District, as did the family of Jalil Hasan, whose school-issued computer had snapped more than a thousand pictures of Jalil over two months, including pictures taken in his bedroom. The school district settled the lawsuits, paying more than $350,000 to four students.

## Spying on You

Nearly all portable computers, including tablets like the iPad, are equipped with cameras, and software can be installed on the device that will allow nearly anyone to control those cameras from a distance over the Internet—even from halfway around the world. Remote monitoring software will notify the owner that the subject laptop or tablet computer is on and connected to the Internet, and that person can then activate the camera remotely, even if the local user hasn't opened a camera application. Computer owners can activate these remote cameras to investigate the loss or damage to their property. The remote-access cameras can also be used to watch teenagers undress in their own bedrooms or get information to perform identity theft or burglary.

The Lower Merion School District computer spying is not an isolated incident. On September 25, 2012, the US Federal Trade Commission

(FTC) released a statement[2] announcing a regulatory settlement with seven rent-to-own companies and a software design firm, settling charges that the companies spied on consumers using the webcams on rented computers. The rental companies captured screenshots of confidential and personal information of the consumers, and logged their computer keystrokes, all without notice to, or consent from, the consumers. The software used by these companies even used a fake software-program registration screen that tricked consumers into providing their personal contact information.

*Invaders Can See Inside Your House*

Blake and his high school classmates were apparently not aware that their school would be watching them inside their bedrooms. Why would they be? But many of today's technologies can give remote peeks into our lives. Not only laptops, but smartphones and stationary desktop computers can see and hear into our homes and broadcast that information to someone far away. With facial-recognition software, the remote receiver of this information could confirm exactly which people are in your home at any given time.

Certain videogame-playing consoles use this face-recognition technology to identify the people in the room and save their preferences and game levels, and then send the data out of your home over the Internet. Your cable company receives feedback from all of the televisions and set-top boxes in your house, and at least one television provider is experimenting with cameras installed in the television or controller to watch you as you watch television.

Even your power company can record and analyze the activity within your home. The latest "smart-grid" technology makes this data easier to collect and read.

## SOCIETY BENEFITS FROM TECHNOLOGY

This book is about how technological and scientific advances steal your privacy, sending your personal information to crooks and advertisers, police and politicians, your neighbors, and your boss. But for all the privacy-destroying uses and consequences of technology in our interconnected environment, there are also advantages offered by that technology.

New technology brings many benefits and conveniences. Economically, we are much more productive with the new machinery than we were without. Think about the old methods of typing a document and then making copies. Prior to digital documents, letters would be typed by hand, starting over if a major mistake was made, and typing over the minor ones. Copies came from smelly, messy carbon paper laid against the back of the original letter. The process was time-consuming, and the product was inconsistent and often subpar. If the letter was stained or lost, the process would start over from the beginning. With digital word-processing programs, mistakes are eliminated quickly, and dictionary and thesaurus programs help us to make a better product, which is saved on a hard drive to make unlimited copies. The metadata attached to the document allows us to index the letter and find it more easily later. Aside from the emotionally satisfying clack of an old Royal typewriter, there was nothing better about the precomputer method of producing documents.

In some ways, our personal lives are even more improved by connected computing power than our work lives. Not long ago, you would have to wait for a weekday to check on the money in your bank accounts and to move funds from one account into another. In the past five years, smartphones and tablets have become ubiquitous, with millions of people carrying a powerful computer in their pockets that provides maps and information on demand, takes pictures, records sound, and quickly connects us to anyone we care about. There is no going back. This world is infinitely better than the one it replaced. But this does not mean that we should ignore the troubling issues raised by all of these technological wonders.

People can enjoy all the new conveniences and still protect their personal data, but it often takes an understanding of how that data is being used. The point of this book is not to create new-age luddites, who overlook the advances in machinery for the evil it can be harnessed to perform. Rather, the point of this book is to create a dialogue about some of the important but elusive values lost when we embrace this technology to its fullest, and to inspire users of tech to be mindful when providing information that may be used against them.

## WHERE DO WE GO FROM HERE?

Maintaining your privacy is important to your freedom to live your life as you like and important for protecting your constitutional rights, and yet the law in the United States does not stretch far to protect you. When you look closely at the laws of even the most privacy-protective countries, they also have flaws.

No one can protect your privacy without your help. Before you can help yourself, you need to understand the new technologies, what benefits they provide and what tradeoffs they require. Some of those tradeoffs—privacy for convenience—could be softened by our own behavior or be reduced by legislation if we fight for it.

This book analyzes why privacy is important to all of us, and it describes the technologies that place your privacy most at risk, starting with modern computing and the Internet. We examine the miracles provided by having the world at our fingertips, and the intrusions these computers make part of our daily lives. We describe the various parties—governmental, commercial, personal, and criminal—who want to learn more about you and use your computing habits to do so. We talk about the greater risks of taking your computing devices on the road, and what you can do to protect yourself.

You are not always carrying the largest threat to your privacy in your pocket or computer case, and so we analyze the privacy threats that blink at every street corner, those that fly overhead, and those that you park in your driveway at night. Each of these technologies is useful for us and for society, but they all also threaten your privacy as you move around in the world.

Another set of threats resides in your home as you unwittingly provide information to utility companies that have installed their lines in your house and you tape everything that moves on security cameras. All the companies with a current stake in importing power, entertainment, or phone access into your house also want to pull data out and use that data for purposes that might make you uncomfortable.

Your own body can also be used against you. The science of biometric measurements has grown over the past years with everyone from your bank to Disney taking the measure of your body parts and using that information for their own purposes. You may present your best face to the world, but that face can tell your name to local businesses. In addition, you may leave behind your DNA wherever you go, and it can then be used by police and others for identification and much more. DNA is the most essential building block in our bodies, but it can be easily captured and interpreted to our detriment. Do you own your own DNA, and if not, who does?

Finally, we look into the future and see what it holds for technology and for privacy. Scientists can already read and interpret brain signals from our heads. What happens when police and used car salesmen can do the same? Will we find that it becomes easy to manipulate another person when you know his or her thoughts?

Any of these issues can be addressed by regulation and legislation, but it may take the cumulative voices of people like us to turn the tide on entrenched interests that love the murky status quo. We talk at the end of the book about steps that could be taken by society to enjoy the fruits of our brilliant technology without substantially trading away our privacy.

But first you have to understand the scope of the problem. Let's lift up the covers and look inside, shall we?

## NOTES

1. See the pleadings and rulings in the case of *Robbins v. Lower Merion School District*, Case No. 10-0665 (E.D. Pa 20, filed February 11, 2010), and *Hassan v. Lower Merion School District*, Case No. 10- 3663 (E.D. Pa July 27, 2010). See also the many news stories covering the accusations against the Lower Merion School District and the court cases that arose from them, including, for example, David Kravets, "School District Halts Webcam Surveillance," *Wired*, February 19, 2010; Gregg Keizer, "Federal Judge Orders Pa. Schools to Stop Laptop Spying," *Computerworld*, February 23, 2010.

2. "FTC Halts Computer Spying; Secretly Installed Software on Rented Computers Collected Information, Took Pictures of Consumers in Their Homes, Tracked Consumers' Locations," press release of administrative settlement by FTC, February 25, 2012, available at this writing on FTC website at www.ftc.gov/opa/2012/09/designer-ware.shtm.

# ONE

# The Intersection of Privacy, Law, and Technology

Privacy is crucial to protect and support the many freedoms and responsibilities that we possess in a democracy. The law is society's primary method of protecting and enforcing our ability to exercise our rights—if a basic human right is denied, then the law should provide recourse to reinstate it. Unfortunately, our society has reached a point at which the law cannot keep up with the advancement of technology and the constant change technology brings to our lives. Those technological changes are important and helpful in many ways, but they are overwhelming our system, and our privacy is the canary in our technological coal mine. If the law can't keep up to protect our privacy, then the technology whirlwind may affect many of our important rights.

## WHY IS PRIVACY IMPORTANT?

Although it seems that every day fewer people care about their privacy, the ability to maintain parts of our life as private remains crucial to our democracy, our economy, and our personal well-being. Many people expose their deepest thoughts and barest body parts every day, leading pundits to decry that privacy is passé. Others suggest that the only people who would care if the government, the press, or even their neighbors are watching them are those people who are behaving badly.

These positions entirely miss the point of privacy. Privacy is not about embarrassment or bad behavior; privacy is about choice. In many cases people who expose their ideas or their derrieres online choose to do so. In those cases in which people were exposed through someone else's choice, such as a reporter, the people exposed felt that their privacy was violated.

1

Similarly, when the government watches your every move, sooner or later it is likely to find something objectionable.

Over time, the government and society change their definitions of what is acceptable and what is not, so staying on the right side of the law and society's standards is not always as easy as it seems. Recently, a car insurance company has been advertising a service in which it provides a small monitor to record and analyze the way that its insurance customers drive every second that the customer is in the car. The company markets this technology as a "cool" advance that allows good drivers to benefit from reduced rates. However, the company never promises to use consistent standards for what it considers "good driving," it never promises in its commercials not to turn its customers in to the police for speeding or running red lights or driving in restricted areas—all actions that could now be recorded and analyzed. The company never promises that the device's information will not be used against a customer in a trial following an auto accident, by the other driver, or by the insurance company itself. The company doesn't discuss whether it will find one incident of questionable driving behavior—maybe during the time the customer's car was loaned to her brother—and make broad generalizations about the customer's driving habits that affect her insurance prices, her ability to be insured at all, or even her freedom if the technology decides she was driving while impaired. In short, there are dozens of unexplained downsides likely to arise from a technology that watches our every move, even if the technology only reports the results to your insurance company initially.

*Losing Anonymity*

In this book we do not attempt to provide a definitive interpretation of the nebulous concept of privacy. However, we address the importance of maintaining your choices for what you wish to keep private. Your home, your body, your thoughts and beliefs are all within the control of their owner, and they are easier to hold private. Your finances, your relationships, and your sexuality are areas that most of us would consider private, although additional parties—your bank, your best friend, your sexual partner—hold information concerning these private matters, so privacy is expected, though absolute control is not possible. You may travel places on the public streets and therefore not expect absolute privacy, but you still expect to be relatively anonymous either in a crowd or a place where no one knows you.

In this case, you would lose a measure of independence if everyone knew you everywhere you went and could tie together information about this trip with other information they knew about your shopping habits, your family history, and whose company you enjoy. Once your movements in space are recorded and added into the general base of knowledge without your permission, your freedom is limited. With the pervasive technology discussed in the following chapters, loss of anonymity is rapidly increasing and the basic loss of ability to keep secrets is in jeopardy.

*Privacy Protects Freedom of Choice*

When your privacy is protected, you are free to choose how much of your sensitive information to expose, to whom you will expose it, and, in some cases, how others can use the information. Philosophers such as John Locke thought that private information is a type of property, and, as with other property, we have the choice about how it can be used and whether to profit from it.

When you have no control over your private information, you have less freedom of choice. When a person understands that everyone will hear his opinion, then his opinion tends to be expressed in a way that is more acceptable to his neighbors, his boss, or the local police. If your living room is being watched by video, you are less likely to walk around in your underwear or eat that block of cheddar on the couch in front of the television, even if that's the way you like to spend an evening.

You might refrain from arguing with your spouse, kids, or parents if you believe people are watching you. We all behave differently when we know we are being watched and listened to, and the resulting change in behavior is simply a loss of freedom—the freedom to behave in a private and comfortable fashion; the freedom to allow the less socially careful branches of our personalities to flower. Loss of privacy reduces the spectrum of choices we can make about the most important aspects of our lives.

By providing a broader range of choices, and by freeing our choices from immediate review and censure from society, privacy enables us to be creative and to make decisions about ourselves that are outside the mainstream. Privacy grants us the room to be as creative and thought-provoking as we want to be. British scholar and law dean Timothy Macklem succinctly argues that the "isolating shield of privacy enables people to develop and exchange ideas, or to foster and share activities, that the presence or even awareness of other people might stifle. For better and for worse, then, privacy is a sponsor and guardian to the creative and the subversive."[1]

Our economy thrives on creativity and new thinking, which in turn are nurtured by privacy of information. Without this privacy, the pace of invention and change slows because our ability to stay ahead of competitors sputters. Privacy is an important lubricant of free thought and free enterprise.

*Privacy Secures Our Human Dignity*

The wrongheaded notion that privacy is only important for people who are misbehaving ignores the fundamental aspect of privacy as protector of our essential human dignity. Civilized people tend to shield from view the activities and attributes that most remind us of our animal natures. Eating in public is taboo in many societies, and nearly every society contains unwritten rules about what is an acceptable manner of eating around other people. While some societies honor the naked body, people in the Western world cover themselves at all times in public and can be arrested in the United States for doing otherwise.

All animals must dispose of bodily waste, and people in the modern age find the act to be private and prefer to engage in it far from the public eye. Likewise, the entirely natural act of childbirth and the sexual acts that lead to it are considered to be personal and sensitive matters by our society, and basic human dignity requires that people be allowed to choose privacy in these matters. None of these subjects necessarily arouses a question of whether a person is behaving properly, but polite and civilized behavior dictates that people are allowed privacy in acting naturally. Privacy is important for maintaining our status as respected members of society.

Many intrusions on privacy can harm our dignity. In a landmark law review article on the nature of privacy under the law, Professor Edward Bloustein wrote in 1964 about a famous American court case limiting press access:

> When a newspaper publishes a picture of a newborn deformed child, its parents are not disturbed about any possible loss of reputation as a result. They are rather mortified and insulted that the world should be witness to their private tragedy. The hospital and the newspaper have no right to intrude in this manner upon a private life. . . . The wrong is in replacing personal anonymity by notoriety, in turning a private life into a public spectacle.[2]

Professor Bloustein defined this act as an imposition upon and an affront to the plaintiff's human dignity. Fifty years later, the concept of privacy as a protector of personal dignity seems somehow quaint, as game show contestants fight to heap more humiliation upon each other, and an entire class of reality television is based on exposing the ignorance and boorish behavior of happily compliant citizens. But this is a choice that these people make to grab their fifteen minutes of fame, maybe more, as some profit handsomely by exposing themselves to ridicule. Just because television producers can find people who will trade their dignity for silver or spotlights does not mean that dignity isn't important to the vast majority of us, or that privacy choices should be limited in any way.

Privacy is important for protecting personal dignity, not only because it shields our animal natures and our personal misfortunes from publicity. Privacy also allows us to think, talk, and behave as we like in seclusion but still be treated with basic respect accorded all members of our society. If everyone knew how each person behaved in her personal "down time," then their understanding of a person who drools in her sleep, is addicted to daytime soap operas, or can't cook could tarnish the professional and personal respect that they have toward her.

## Seeking Normal

No human is perfect, and it can be considered pathological to try too hard to be perfect. We all have our foibles and eccentricities. It seems that the only people who are not somehow strange are the people you don't know very well. But we try to seem "normal" in the ways that are important to each of us, and we present a face to the public that shows our best side. Privacy allows us the dignity to present ourselves as we want the world to see us, the freedom to make mistakes, be clumsy, and display socially unattractive behavior without fear of judgment.

In 1987, President Reagan nominated Judge Robert Bork for the Supreme Court seat vacated by Justice Lewis Powell's retirement. Bork was a controversial figure with strong views on nearly all legal topics, and his nomination engendered much opposition. During the battle for his confirmation, Judge Bork's video-rental history was leaked to the press and used as fodder by some reporters.

While the video history did not seem to affect the confirmation hearings, its introduction into the public consciousness led directly to one of the first federal privacy laws in the United States, the Video Privacy Protection Act of 1988. In this act, Congress recognized that video-rental databases contain private records that, if widely publicized, could negatively affect the ways that people viewed each other.

In a rare, quick act of protection of human dignity, Congress determined that information about the videos that you watch is nobody's business. The introduction of reading material, television-viewing history, video rentals, or Internet-surfing records into a public debate about a political figure allows the public to see a private side that is likely to be completely irrelevant to a person's performance in office, and it allows the public to chuckle at the silly, stupid, or offensive material a public figure consumes in private.

We are afforded less dignity and basic respect when people know the human foibles and odd preferences of our private lives. Privacy in the personal space allows us to maintain that core level of respect that all of us deserve.

*Privacy Protects People from Coercion*

Why would someone want to intrude on your privacy? Simply because the more he knows about you, the more he can influence your decisions. We have described privacy as a preserver of choices, and therefore freedom. The more choices you have, the freer you are to live your life in the way you prefer. Limiting that freedom can drive you to make the choices that someone else wants you to make.

The most severe example of this coercion through limited privacy was the police state of East Germany during the Cold War. Some estimates claim that the Stasi, the East German secret police, had over half a million informers within the state itself. Informants included many children and teens who were expected to inform on the activities of their parents and teachers, so that no citizen of the East German state could expect privacy from government snooping in any aspect of their lives.

This knowledge allowed the secret police and the government media to coerce the "appropriate" decisions from all citizens on the important aspects of political and economic life. East German citizens were afraid to express opinions or take actions that the government would find offensive, so they toed the party line or suffered serious consequences. Government in a police state first strips its citizens of privacy so that it may exert controlling influence on the large and small decisions of its citizens. Complete destruction of privacy leads to coercion on personal choices.

This ability to influence personal choices need not be so dramatic as to destroy your privacy. For example, a company that knows much about your private choices can influence your future choices. An apparently benign example of this influence is the subtle pull of Amazon.com's recommendations after you make a purchase. You bought a book about kite-flying and then you are presented with a list of similar books on the same topic that might appeal to you. Have you considered the new music by that singer whose previous three sets of mp3s are in your collection? Amazon fully expects that it will be rewarded for making these suggestions by your purchase of additional items from its store.

## THE ROLE OF DATA IN LOSS OF PRIVACY

Two practices made possible by technology are data mining and Big Data. Data mining systematically gathers information, while Big Data involves the prediction of trends based on that data.

*Data Mining: Your Privacy Is the Mine*

An invasive example of data mining is the story reported in the *New York Times* in 2011 about discount department store Target's use of data mining to increase sales.[3] The *Times* reported that Target had discovered that one of the few points in a person's life in which she is open to overhauling her shopping habits is after the birth of a baby, and Target realized that, because the birth of a baby is a public announcement, many companies attempted to influence shopping habits at this time. Target decided to try to learn when its customers were pregnant, so it could make an advanced play for that crucial baby business, breaking customers away from shopping at smaller stores for discrete items and moving them into shopping at Target for all of their needs. The store hired statisticians who identified several items, such as prenatal vitamins and purses big enough to hold diapers, that women purchased when they were pregnant. Target then sent coupons to those identified mothers-to-be to encourage them to increase Target purchases.

The store has been so successful using this strategy that its managers eventually realized that they shouldn't send pregnancy-only coupon packets to targeted customers, because the thought that their discount retailer knew their medical condition unsettled the young mothers-to-be and their families. Now Target sends the pregnancy-related coupons camouflaged in packages of unrelated items so as to not tip its hand that the store is working to influence purchases based on its knowledge of private customer information.

## Big Data

An entire new field of technology called "Big Data" has appeared on the scene recently. Big Data refers to the practice of companies collecting millions of facts about customers and using those facts to predict trends and develop better sales and marketing strategies. A store could consider that the technology is simply providing ways to serve its customers better; in reality the store is trying to influence spending decisions by analyzing the often-private information they gather about their customers.

Others besides government and business are interested in influencing your decisions, and so they learn as much about you as possible. For example, the two major political parties in the United States brag about the sophistication of their "voter-identification efforts," which dig up information on all registered voters and send propaganda to those voters to influence them on Election Day.

Certain charities buy the names and phone numbers of people who donate to other charitable causes, so that they have a list of soft hearts who might loosen the purse strings when given a nonprofit pitch. Particularly valuable lists include people who have previously committed money over the phone, because that means that the person is likely to be influenced by a persistent charity marketing representative. The more these people know about a prospective contributor, the easier it will be to push the buttons that lead to a donation. The less they know about you, the more you can protect yourself from a barrage of soliciting calls and letters. If you can keep your information private, you can defend yourself from those who would influence your actions and take your money.

Of course, your privacy is a target of thieves, as well. The more a criminal gang knows about your money, your possessions, your travel habits, your security, and your vulnerabilities, the easier it will be to rob you. Choosing to post all of this information on the Internet or otherwise tell everyone about your private business makes you more vulnerable to many types of theft and scam.

One of the most popular current scams involves finding a young person who broadcasts her life on Facebook and waiting until that young person goes on a trip. Then the thieves will call the person's grandparents, claiming to be police who have arrested the granddaughter in the vacation location that they learned about on Facebook. The grandparents believe that only the family knew this information. The thieves use all types of emotional manipulations to convince the grandparents to send money to bail their grandchild out of jail. They use information such as pet names and other family information. The more seemingly innocuous information they reap from Facebook, the easier it is to scam worried grandparents. Choosing more privacy online can guard against this type of scam. So privacy helps protect us from criminals hoping to "influence us" to part with our money.

## BUT DON'T I HAVE A RIGHT TO PRIVACY?

The way governments view privacy and the laws and regulations that govern privacy are important to understanding your own rights.

### Location, Location, Location

Because privacy is a subjective and changing concept, your rights to privacy depend on where you live. For example, in the European Union (EU) and Canada, governments have established that it is the human right of every citizen to direct control of business's and government's use of their personal data. Both jurisdictions have created large bureaucracies of privacy-protection forces that regulate the way personal data is collected and shared. Though regulations may be effective at protecting some data from use in certain business and government settings, they can't stop people from blurting out information on social media.

Many other countries, such as Israel, Switzerland, and Japan, have solid data-protection regimes based on privacy protected as a human right. Other countries, such as India and Mexico, have protective laws in place but may not have a mature enforcement infrastructure to truly protect their people as Canada can.

Conversely, the US federal government only protects certain classes of personal information. The United States does not take the position that the ability to direct how business and government use personal information is a human right. In the United States, state laws protect against exposure of customer data through having systems hacked. However, these laws are inconsistent and usually are only relevant after the data has been lost because they address how a business must notify customers, patients, or employees when data has been exposed.

In short, while many countries in the world protect private information in many ways, you still must be vigilant to protect your own private data. Even in Canada and the European Union, much of the information that you voluntarily expose through social media and in other media is beyond the government's protection. But in the United States and other countries, even the private information that is unknowingly provided to business and government is not necessarily protected by law, and even US constitutional protections only assure citizens that a certain process will be undertaken before their lives can be interrupted by surveillance. While the government may sympathize with your need for privacy, no government will protect you as well as you can protect yourself. In chapter 13, we discuss different ways that society can change its laws to further protect privacy.

*Looking at Your Constitutional Rights*

The US Constitution does not mention privacy, although the Supreme Court has read privacy protections into the rights underlying the Fourth Amendment and has read anonymity protections into the rights underlying the First Amendment. This means that certain privacy rights against the government will be recognized by US courts. However, keep in mind that a person's protection under the US Constitution tends not to be an absolute right against the government. Instead, privacy is often a process right in the United States—a citizen will have the right to due process before the person's privacy or property is breached by law enforcement. In other words, where you have a privacy interest protected by the Fourth Amendment of the Constitution, the government may be forced to secure a subpoena or other relevant court order before violating your privacy.

For example, let's say the government convinces a judge that there is probable cause to believe that you broke the law, and that the investigation that the police want to do is reasonably calculated to discover evidence that will prove that you broke the law. At that point a judge may issue a subpoena for the requested information or allow a procedure—such as tracking your car or bugging your workplace—to find the relevant information. So, even in the most generous reading of US privacy law, your privacy rights against law enforcement will last only as long as there is no probable cause to believe that you committed a crime.

This means that at some point in the midst of a criminal enterprise or a terrorist plot, a person may lose his right to privacy, though US law defines a process to determine this and precisely what "loss of privacy" means. Can the government bug your phone calls or put a camera in your home? A judge will decide this based on the wisdom of precedent and well-considered examples.

*Technology as Game Changer*

The torrid pace of technological change has outraced legal precedent. Should the police be able to see your mobile smartphone's geolocation signals to trace your steps over the past month? Should the police be allowed to take your DNA sample and hold it in the FBI database? Should the FBI activate the camera on your iPad or home computer to watch your most intimate moments? These are all relatively new questions with little precedent for a court to consult. Courts are encountering the new technologies but don't yet know how to make rulings concerning them.

New law in the United States is often decided based on analogy to previous similar circumstances. Should DNA, the core building block of life, be the most private information about you? Or should DNA, which you leave in a public place when a hair falls out or you leave saliva on a cup in the trash, be treated as public? Is cell phone geolocation-tracking data the same as landline telephone records (and therefore automatically available to the police), or is it closer to spying on your activities nonstop for a month, which requires a warrant? Requiring the legal system to answer these questions will decide whether the new technology can be used against you by law enforcement, or whether the new information unearthed by computers is protected as private data.

## HOW INFORMATION BECAME KING

The deeper technology becomes embedded into our lives, the more it threatens our privacy. Technology, such as location trackers that are built into every smartphone and new car being sold today, allows a new window into our routines that wasn't available before. There was virtually no way to follow your regular movements until you started carrying and driving computers that reported location data.

Sometimes the simple fact that we are using technology creates information that was never available before. For example, when you open a browser and sign onto the Internet, you are creating a type of record of your thoughts and actions that simply did not exist twenty-five years ago. When you sit on your couch and shop for shoes, watch funny videos on YouTube, check the weather in Vancouver for your trip, and then find a recipe for peach cobbler, you have just created insight into your personality (and travel destinations and shopping habits) that no one would have been able to collect prior to the Internet's pervasive acceptance.

*We Collect and Store Much More Data Than in the Past*

One of the first technology advances that made these methods of tracking possible is the "datamization" of our world. Over the past fifty years, we have moved from a society where we lived our lives in relative freedom from record or comment to a world where data is collected and stored about nearly every move we make.

Think about the information that you might be able to find about your great-great-great grandmother. There may have been paper records of birth, childbirth, and death, some of them kept only in a family Bible. Wedding announcements and arrests were recorded in newspapers and local records. Property records were often kept in official locations, whether your relative owned property or whether she was considered to be the property of somebody else. Immigration or travel overseas may have left a record. If various pieces of paper have been saved, it is quite likely that, short of personal letters, only three to ten data points exist that speak to the entire life of that person you are researching.

Your life can generate three to ten data points a second. In one mobile online purchase of concert tickets, many different companies—your phone company, your mobile commerce application provider, the company that provides the software ecosystem for your phone (Apple, Google, BlackBerry, or Microsoft), the ticket seller, the company putting on the performance, your bank, the ticket seller's bank, and others—make note of many possible data points. These points might include the item you bought, your time of purchase, your location when you made the purchase, the fact that the purchase was made on a smartphone, the type of smartphone and software you are using, the amount you paid and your method of payment, where you will be the night of the concert, and how many people you plan to bring with you.

Many of these data-capturing companies sell this information to other companies interested in one particular data point from your purchase. Don't be surprised when you see an advertisement or receive an email from a restaurant close to the concert venue offering you free parking if you eat with them on your night out. These businesses have learned the value of data and are using it to their advantage, which is why everything you do is a target of data collection.

Governments are also collectors of all this new data. Thanks to the Edward Snowden disclosures and other recent revelations, we also know that the U.S. National Security Agency (NSA) is capturing and preserving the information about the mobile phone calls of people all over the world, including Americans. News reports based on government documents have shown that the NSA paid hundreds of millions of dollars to private telephone companies for access to personal data, it has demanded or coerced private Internet companies to provide personal communications and search data, and it has hacked into encryption used to protect private data for millions of people. According to a recent report from a German newspaper, the NSA has the ability to tap into all major br4ands of smart phones, including email, texts, contacts, and even location information

## *Data Sources Are Proliferating and Interconnected*

The growth of personal computing devices has been mind-boggling, especially in the past twenty years. In the mid-1970s, there was less than one computer per one thousand people in the United States. By 1995, there was one computer for every three people in the United States.[4] The explosive increase in the number of computers gathering data, creating data, storing data, and analyzing data has enabled technology to invade your privacy. The more data-collection points record the minutiae of your activities, the more information will be available for anyone who wants to learn about you.

In 2012, the United States accounted for nearly 20 percent of all personal computers in the world. In fact, the United States had more computers than people in that year, with 321 million computers in use at the start of 2012.[5] According to Cisco Systems' research and projections, the number of *handheld* computer devices alone in 2012 exceeded the number of human beings not just in the United States, but on the entire planet.[6] The same report showed that mobile data traffic grew by more than 70 percent in 2012 and that mobile network connection speeds more than doubled that same year.

In the past twenty years, we have progressed from a world where only a lucky few people owned a home computer to a world where many of us have a work computer and at least one smartphone or tablet computer, maybe a separate PC at home or a laptop to take on the road. And soon, as you'll read later in this book, the "Internet of Things" will allow our cars, our appliances, and even our clothes with embedded radio-frequency identification (RFID) tags to become new data points on the Internet, sharing information with each other with their makers, and maybe with the NSA.

Computer networks, such as IBM's SABRE airline-reservation system, have been around since the 1960s. The Internet was born in the 1980s and rocketed into all of our homes through the 1990s and early 2000s, becoming a necessity of life for many, including nearly everyone under age thirty in the industrialized world.

The networking of computers also contributed to our current invasive technological environment. Nearly all of the computing devices that we use in our everyday life are connected, sharing data with other devices and with mother-computers around the world. This connectedness allows information collection devices to send the information they collect into massive databases managed by businesses and governments. Interconnectivity is what allows you the convenience of shopping for dog food and prom dresses from home, but it also allows the grocery store's database to connect to the department store's database and to send records of your purchases to anyone who can claim a need for them.

## *Databases Are Searched for Meaningful Information*

Data about financial transactions has been collected and saved for many years, but that data is becoming even more useful to businesses. Because it can collect data about you, your supermarket is willing to offer you a special discount on food items if you use your loyalty card, allowing the store to keep a running list of all the purchases you make.

Other types of companies are collecting data that few would have considered useful years ago, and this data can be tied directly to you. For example, locations that demand passcard access, such as parking garages, gyms, offices, and even automated commuter lanes on the highway are recording your location and the time you were there. Even your cell phone—smartphone or otherwise—is recording the cell towers that you pass.

As we discuss in greater detail in chapter 3, a recent study by MIT and Universite Catholique de Louvain in Belgium has demonstrated that their researchers can identify 95 percent of cell phone users by name using just four data points. These points are culled from hourly updates of a user's location tracked by pings from their mobile phone to nearby cell towers as users changed locations or made and received calls and text messages.[7] A company looking at your cell phone movements and a data set that Google, Apple, and others admit collecting can easily infer your identity.

Not so long ago, even the most important records kept about you were written on paper and housed in back rooms or warehouses: your medical records stayed at your doctor's office, your property records gathered dust in the county recorder's basement, even your wedding announcement was stored at the newspaper's morgue in back issues of old editions. Now all of those records and much, much more are kept in searchable databases that can locate your name immediately when someone performs a search.

The vast library of data about you is being supplemented all the time. This advance was made possible by computers that can capture and store all of this data, and especially by the precipitous drop in the price of data-storage capacity through the early 2000s. But computers have also allowed other changes that increase your vulnerability and the value of information about you. Not only is this new data stored electronically but it also resides in searchable databases that allow collectors to make useful lists of the types of data that interest them. It is easy to see a list of all advance ticket purchasers for the concert next Saturday, or who checked into the gym on Saturday, and then to further process this list by gender, age, income level, or zip code to find exactly the class of person you seek.

Your computing device can ID you as well. If you can tie a large volume of data to one account or device identification number, it is easier to find a name that matches the data you collected. Many of our privacy laws and regulations rely on a concept called "Personally Identifiable Information," often defined as a financial account number that is tied to a person's name, address, phone number, or other clearly identifiable bit of data. It turns out that "personally identifiable information" is simply a matter of mathematics. The more data I have about an account or device, the easier it will be for me to accurately tie a name to that account or device.

The ability to process, search, sort, sift, and categorize information within databases has led to a rush to collect more data about you and a push to understand how all this data can be used. Recently published studies have shown that a researcher who only knows your birth date, zip code, and gender can identify you by name 87 percent of the time.[8] If three points of data are that effective at proving your identity, imagine how simple that would be for a company like Google that collects thousands or millions of data points on your account and your device. Using several data points to work backward and find a name seems impossible, but with the right software, it can be easy.

The year 2013 was a banner year for public admission of computer shenanigans. The US government not only finally admitted that the Chinese government sponsored attacks on American computer systems but was forced to admit that US law enforcement had been building huge databases of phone records and Internet email traffic. Many people suspected these data collections and analyses were taking place, but a leak brought a fuller picture to light. Clearly the massive amount of data concerning our habits is interesting to the government.

*Advances in Social Science Help Derive Meaning from Data*

Our society may be moving forward, backward, or not at all, but science clearly progresses. Humans learn more every year about the universe, about manipulating tiny elements, and about the ways our bodies and minds work. The growing body of knowledge allows marketers and governments to interpret your actions and to make connections between today's behaviors and tomorrow's actions.

If you move from the city to the suburbs, for example, you will surely want new furniture to fill the larger spaces, and you will need a dry cleaner and hair stylist close to home. You may also change your voting habits because you are now a property owner, or you may buy a different car to carry your new dog and gardening supplies from the DIY store. This scientific growth of knowledge about human nature and correlations is just one example of how the advance of science can encroach upon our privacy.

As new technologies gather more seemingly innocuous data about our daily habits and desires, the new social science makes it easier for businesses, governments, and criminals to analyze and interpret this data, drawing a profile of you from a sea of basic facts. For example, researchers for Microsoft have determined that people who chat with each other are more likely to share personal characteristics than people who do not.[9] This may not seem like a surprising or significant fact, but it can encourage businesses to capture networks of people's regular contacts, knowing that they are likely to share personal characteristics, including those that made the original subject a good customer. As companies learn more about how human minds and human networks function, they collect and process data to draw conclusions that help them identify prospects who will buy what they're selling. This allows further targeting of individuals, not just for traits they have established, but for traits that marketers believe the individuals will demonstrate in certain situations.

Such research is often used to target marketing and advertising efforts, but it can have more significant effects on people's lives. For example, University of Pennsylvania professor Richard Berk made practical use of recent human behavioral research when he created software that is being used in Baltimore and Philadelphia to predict which people on parole or probation are most likely to commit murder in the future.[10] The software is currently assisting in defining a level of supervision for inmates on parole, replacing supervision decisions based on less scientific reasoning. The software is based on an analysis of more than sixty thousand crimes and an applied algorithm that can identify a subset of people much more likely to commit homicide when paroled or probated. On one hand, this software allows prison officials to take active steps that could reduce the murder rate. On the other hand, an entire class of people has been singled out for law-enforcement attention based on nothing more than a predictive computer algorithm, and essentially penalized for possible future behavior.

This is the double edge of the behavioral analysis sword. We can more accurately predict behavior, but people are classified into behavior categories before they even act in the predicted fashion. With the growth in the amount of data collected about you and advancements in analysis of that data, you are currently being classified and targeted by businesses and governments. Statistics are much better at providing correlation than prediction, but we can continue to use them for both.

The growth of social science analysis and understanding is the ultimate step in the chain of data described in this section. We are collecting more data, about more people, from more sources than ever before. We connect these data sources into networks and aggregate the information into huge databases. We have developed newly sophisticated ways to combine, comb, and sort these databases to provide information that relates to subjects of interest. Finally, we have discovered new correlations between personality traits and behaviors; between actions in the past and predicting actions in the future; between our daily habits and our shopping, saving, and voting habits, so that all of this data can be turned into productive advertising campaigns, voter turnout leaflets, and neighborhood policing efforts.

## NOTES

1. Timothy Macklem, *Independence of Mind* (Oxford: Oxford University Press, 2006), 36.

2. Edward Bloustein, *Privacy as an Aspect of Human Dignity: An Answer to Dean Prosser*, 39 N.Y.U.L. Rev. 962, 1964, referencing *Bazemore v. Savannah Hospital*, 171 Georgia 257 (1930) and *Douglas v. Stokes*, 149 Kentucky 506 (1912).

3. Charles Duhigg, "How Companies Learn Your Secrets," *New York Times*, February 12, 2012.

4. Press release, Computer Industry Almanac, Inc., April 28, 1995.

5. Press release, Computer Industry Almanac, Inc., February 1, 2012.

6. Cisco's Visual Networking Index (VNI) Global Mobile Data Traffic Forecast Update for 2012–2117, www.cisco.com/en/US/solutions/collateral/ns341/ns525/ns537/ns705/ns827/white_paper_c11-520862.html.

7. Kim Zetter, "Anonymized Phone Location Data Not So Anonymous, Researchers Find," *Wired*, March 27, 2013.

8. Jonathan Shaw, "Exposed: The Erosion of Privacy in the Internet Era," *Harvard Magazine*, September–October 2009.

9. Parag Singla and Matthew Richardson, "Yes, There is a Correlation—From Social Networks to Personal Behavior on the Web," International World Wide Web Conference Committee, 2008, research.microsoft.com/en-us/um/people/mattri/papers/www2008/SocialNetworksAndSearch.pdf.

10. Eric Bland, "Software Predicts Criminal Behavior," *ABC World News*, August 22, 2010, abcnews.go.com/Technology/software-predicts-criminal-behavior/story?id=11448231.

# Ground Zero:
# Your Computer and the Internet

The role that personal computers play in our lives may be the most dramatic shift in the way most people in industrialized countries live, work, and interact. Thirty years ago, computers were for hobbyists and big business, and now most of us carry one in our pockets and have others at home or at the office. Bringing this new device deep into our daily routines has also provided a tool that outside parties use to watch and record our lives. They can capture nearly every significant decision we make, from when we drive to work to how we pay our bills.

The following chapters examine how your dependable window on the world can become a window for others to look into your life. Whether the peeping Tom is Uncle Sam, a thief, or an investigator hired by your spouse, clues to our everyday lives are waiting patiently on our computers for someone to find them. A computer with a camera can see our lives as they happen, and someone can take control of that device. A visit to our bank's website may give a nosey thief the information he needs to rob you. A smartphone carried in our pocket will report our location frequently, and people can read and record our travels this way. This section explores the personal technology we use every day, and how it can steal our privacy.

# TWO

## Your Computer Is Watching You

For more than a quarter century, personal computers have been ubiquitous fixtures in our homes and lives. Many of us grew up in houses with a PC or a Mac in the den, and the rest of us have learned to incorporate computing and the Internet in every aspect of our lives. We use computers for business, social interactions, and personal contacts, reading the latest news, booking hotels, discovering pad Thai recipes, educating our children, and finding groomers for our pets. We invited these machines into our homes and have profited from their presence. But our computers are also watching us, recording our activities, and saving or transmitting that information so that others can learn about us, too.

In this chapter, we focus on the computer box itself: the information portals it offers into your home and your life, and what people do to take advantage of the information that can be gathered from you. Electronic home-invasion techniques that involve taking information out of your home through power lines, the cable box, home gaming systems, or other intrusive technology are covered in chapter 11.

### NOW ANYONE CAN BE A PRIVATE EYE

Software that turns your personal computer into a spy device is easy to procure and use, especially by those who live in your home. Once loaded, the software can be used to spy on the computer activity of anyone who operates the machine, such as a spouse, child, or parent.

For example, in Greenville, Tennessee, a third-generation owner of a successful lumber yard was in the midst of a divorce from his wife in 2011. Suspecting the husband of having an affair, his wife bought and installed a software package that provided do-it-yourself spyware on the husband's two work computers. According to the magistrate judge's opinion and news reports, "Evidence at trial suggested that [the wife] not only intercepted his email with the spyware, but also altered some of the emails to make it look like [her husband] had been unfaithful."[1] The magistrate judge ordered the wife to pay $20,000 in direct and punitive damages for violating federal and state wiretap laws by using spyware to incept her husband's email.

Despite the fact that the act of placing surveillance software on a spouse's computer can be considered a violation of federal and state law, leading to criminal and civil penalties, tens of thousands of spyware devices and software are sold to private individuals each year.

We tend to see our computers as private reserves. To a certain extent, the law will support us in this view, especially when it comes to using computers in personal communications, such as with Skype calls, text and instant messaging, and email. But the home computer can reveal a great deal about a person without ever monitoring who that person is talking to and what they are discussing.

## *Our Computers Reflect Our Lives*

By observing a computer user's Internet surfing habits, you can learn what stores she visits, where she banks, what she reads, and what topics interest her enough to search for them. You are likely to find travel plans, restaurant delivery orders, and information about the computer user's religion on her system.

Personal finances also rest comfortably in the home computer. Government websites state that over one hundred million people filed their US federal income taxes online last year, so finding income information on a home computer can be easy. Many people build their entire work lives on computer, which means documents and spreadsheets that relate to business can be found there as well.

On most home computers, you can probably find all of the most recent family pictures, and maybe any paintings and music created by the computer's owner. You will find the videos that the person likes to see, the songs he likes to play, and the radio/podcasts that he finds worth listening to. You might already know many of these things about the people who live in your household, but learning their computer activities provides a much deeper glimpse into their psyches.

## *Be Upfront about Monitoring in the Home*

Spying on your own home computers can be both productive and problematic. By looking deeply into the activity on any home computer, you are almost always likely to learn something you didn't know about your housemate or family member. And yet we all deserve a certain amount of privacy, even from our parents and spouses. Often this narrow band of privacy is the bulwark of strong relationships.

Tearing away the curtain on computer privacy can hurt many relationships and some people's psychological well-being. If you take advantage of the many tools available for learning about the activities on computers used by others, you not only risk violating the antieavesdropping laws, you can also hurt everyone involved. Search your ethical boundaries before undertaking such actions. Also, decide whether you are willing and able to withstand the likely practical consequences.

One way to undertake a computer review without creating enormous interpersonal problems is to tell your spouse, roommate, or children that you will be installing spyware, or monitoring software, on the computer before you do so, so that no one is surprised. This works particularly well with older children. While you may be resented for limiting your kids' freedom of action on the family computer, at least you are straightforward with them about how you intend to monitor their activity. The breach of trust engendered by stealth monitoring and its eventual discovery can be much more painful than limits announced ahead of time and enforced consistently.

---

**TOOLBOX**

Many types of tools exist to monitor your computers at home. For example, VNC, or Virtual Network Computing, allows one computer to control another remotely over a network. Full, open source versions of VNC are downloadable over the Internet. VNC facilitates remote screen control of another computer, so you can see what is being written and searched on the target machine. If the "Inputs" screen on the VNC controller is set so that none of the input boxes are checked, then the user of the target computer will not be notified when a controlling computer is monitoring the target's activity.

---

## HOW YOUR COMPUTER CAN BE TURNED AGAINST YOU

If reading about all the various tools and tricks that you can use to take control of computers in your household makes you uneasy, then you are probably thinking about how these and other tools can be used against you by those outside your home.

Years ago, it was not easy for an outsider to see into your home and create a mental picture of the activity taking place there. Who is watching television, and what are they watching? Who is in the kitchen, and what appliances are they using? Is the dog asleep? Are the kids playing video games or doing their homework? To spy on your home activities, a person had to break into your home, watch through windows with binoculars, or perhaps sit in a tree and listen for voices.

Today, we have all built electronic windows into our homes, and someone who wants to know about our household activities can simply open those windows from anywhere in the world. With connected computing, a peeping Tom or someone interested in your family life does not need to be in the vicinity of your house to spy on what you do there.

## *Surveillance for Fun and Profit*

If your computer is ever the target of a scheme to study your behavior, the threat most likely will come from a commercial spyware package that wants nothing more than to learn about your web-surfing habits to advertise to you, sell your name and contact data to spammers and salespeople, or sell you products such as cut-rate pharmaceuticals or software of questionable value.

Commercial spyware is malicious or sometimes just annoying software that resides on your machine to serve and profit another master. This annoyance can be simple adware that burrows deep into your computer's processes, hides and protects itself, then promotes its products and services every time you turn on your machine or open a web browser.

A specialized category of adware called *scareware* presents itself to you through official-looking pop-ups that seem to come from your computer's security software. The pop-ups warn that your computer has been infected and you need to pay $89.99 to download a computer-cleaning program that will rid you of this infection. Of course, the scareware doesn't tell you that the only infection it has detected in your computer is the scareware itself. If you pay the money to download its "solution" software, the program will hide the scareware messages until later, in hopes of repeating its sale. In addition, the company serving the scareware places your name and your machine on a list of "suckers" who are vulnerable to scams, assuring that you will continue to be the target of future attacks. These tactics include fake warnings from the FBI. The warnings are so dire and believable that the FBI had to post a statement for PC users in 2012 and as recently as July 2013 issued a warning for Mac users. The scam artists for the fake FBI warnings infected links on websites and then used that to push their "ransomware" to the computer. Once the ransomware is pushed, the user is prompted to provide a credit card to "unlock" the computer. The savvy cybercriminals even use "FBI.gov" within the URL to make the scam appear more legitimate.

Companies that track your habits with commercial spyware sell this information to advertisers who want to present you with targeted advertising. Some spyware hijacks your Internet browser, takes you to its desired sites, opens up a cascade of windows with advertised sites on each window, or even redirects your browser's homepage to the spyware site. Spyware is often connected to advertising for disreputable businesses such as pay-for-pornography sites or cheap knockoffs of popular drugs.

The most sophisticated spyware embeds itself in several places within your computer and contains more natural defenses than a porcupine. These programs can avoid being listed among the programs in your computer and can disable the tools you would need to remove them. Some have even seeded the Internet with fake "information" sites where fake "consumers" sing the praises of the program that just invaded your system. This is to make it seem as if other people found it to be a legitimate and helpful program with a function beyond telling your secrets and replicating itself. You can view much commercial spyware as parasitic worms with no other purpose than to enter your system by any means necessary, feed themselves, and then find a way to spread to other people's systems.

### To Keep Clean, Watch Where You Click

These basic rules of thumb can help you practice good computer and Internet hygiene, keeping your machine as clean and healthy as possible.

- Stay away from free software downloads, as they are often loaded with commercial adware.
- Do no open attachments in emails from anyone that you do not know and trust.
- Even if you trust the person, do not open email attachments when the text of the email is confusing or unexpected. For example, if your child's teacher suddenly sends you a new song from Justin Beiber or a raunchy comedy video, you can bet that the teacher's email has been infected with spyware or something worse. Simply delete all correspondence from that address.
- Do not click on buttons inside pop-up windows that invite you to close the window. Click on the "x" in the corner of the box to close it.

### Practice Browser Safety

Most web traffic is conducted using Microsoft's Internet Explorer, and so most browser-activated spyware is written to thrive on weaknesses in this browser. You can reduce the number of attacks aimed at your computer by using a different browser to travel the Internet, such as Google Chrome or Mozilla's Firefox.

All major browsers contain security settings. The higher you set these features, the less exposure you will have to spyware. You can set your computer's firewall and often even your operating system defenses to resist spyware or stop it from sending information about you out to the Internet. You may also want to consider disabling Java in your web browser to prevent cybercriminals from planting software on your computer stealthily when you visit a site that they have infected.

You can seek out and install spyware monitoring tools such as PestPatrol or Spybot—Search and Destroy. These programs isolate spyware as it attempts to load itself and can prevent the spyware from installing on your computer. The free Spybot program is an exception to the rule of avoiding free software downloads.

## When Your Devices Become Keyholes into Your Home

Using your computer to perceive activity inside your home is relatively easy, and tools exist to allow anyone with basic hacking skills to do it.

For example, in 1998 the "Back Orifice" software was created and distributed by a hacker's collective called the Cult of the Dead Cow, also known as cDc Communications. They issued a press release claiming to have created the software as a tool demonstrating the inadequacy of Microsoft Windows security. Back Orifice allows a third party to take total control of your computer, acting with system administration access to all of your computer's tools. That means the person controlling your computer can turn on the camera attached or built into your device and watch wherever the computer is aimed. If you keep your desktop in the family room or your laptop in your bedroom, a hacker using this software can see into those rooms and can take video or still pictures from the camera.

The Back Orifice software, and similar spyware such as Poison Ivy and Spynet, can be delivered to your computer by a Trojan horse program or other method of download.

The technique is so pervasive that the security industry has termed the people who infect computers as "Ratters." These are the people that use Remote Administration Tools (RAT) to infect computers and then control the audio, video, and even files on the computer to grab pieces of your life.

If a picture is worth a thousand words, then adding sound to the picture is even better. Nearly all modern personal computers contain microphones. When activated, these microphones can be used to listen into conversations, hear you singing in the shower, or otherwise tap into the mood of anyone operating the computer. A hacker who has taken over your computer can turn on the microphone to tell how many people are in the room and hear discussions taking place around the computer. Though most computer cameras light up when activated, most computer microphones have no visual or other display that tell when it is listening or recording. For that reason, the microphone can be the stealthiest way to spy on people through their computers.

*Peeking into Your Computer Box's Every Room*

While cameras and microphones attached to computers can help a hacker invade the physical world of his victim, he may find what he needs without ever leaving the confines of the computer box itself. Many people keep pictures on their computers and share them over email, text, chat functions, or even video conversations. Computer spyware can pull these pictures out of the machine or off of the correspondence. In addition, the emails and instant messages themselves can be racy, thought provoking, personal, or embarrassing to both sender and recipient, so access to messages may be all a hacker needs to spy on a victim.

PC surveillance software such as the Webwatcher brand can remotely operate to monitor email, instant messages, chat, and social-media activity conducted from a target computer. Using Webwatcher, the remote user can see every webpage visited by the person using the target computer and the duration of each website visit. Webwatcher works in both the Windows and the Mac operating systems.

*Case Study: Hacking for Extortion*

Luis Mijangos, a Mexican citizen living in Santa Ana, California, was sentenced to six years in prison for his behavior in taking control of over one hundred computers. Mijangos, who pled guilty to one count each of computer hacking and wiretapping, planted malware disguised as popular songs or video files. When his victims downloaded the files, Mijangos took control of their computers.[2]

According to court documents and news reports, Mijangos was known for the "sextortion" of his female victims. "If he obtained access to a woman's computer, he searched for incriminating photos and video—or accessed the webcam and tried to take some of his own."[3] If Mijangos accessed a man's computer, he impersonated the man and asked the man's girlfriend for nude photographs. Once he obtained nude photos of women, Mijangos approached the women for additional pictures, threatening to post their pictures on social media for the world to see. He would also hijack the email and text messaging from a woman's computer and punish her if she told anyone about his threats or if she approached the police.

His victims felt trapped because, for young people whose entire lives were tied up in their computers, Mijangos seemed omniscient. He could look into their rooms. He had intimate pictures of them and could listen into their conversations from the microphone on their computers. He could read their emails and other messages to the outside world. He knew all the material on their computers. If you only know that someone can see and hear into your room, and seems to know all of your communications, then you can feel totally surrounded by the attacker.

At sentencing, the judge noted the "psychological warfare" carried out by Mijangos and his "sustained effort to terrorize victims." When one woman refused to accede to his demands, Mijangos posted naked pictures of her on the MySpace pages of her friends. He could send out messages from his victims' email accounts so that they seemed to be written by the victims themselves. Mijangos is not the only person to be caught manipulating others through control of their computers. Fortunately, his case ended in a public trial and a long prison sentence.

## MONITORING YOUR EVERY KEYSTROKE

Using keystroke-capture spyware, a spy computer can record all of the keys typed by the target computer, an invaluable tool for anyone seeking passwords to personal accounts and messages in encrypted chat rooms. Those who want to spy on a computer while leaving minimum software on the machine use a keystroke *logger*. With a logger, they can simply piece together all the messages sent from the machine without exposing the target to substantial software that controls everything and is at greater risk of being detected.

### *Keystroke Monitoring on Both Sides of the Law*

Keystroke monitoring is important to law enforcement as the most direct method of capturing messages and signals at the point of entry, before they can become masked or overridden. When drug dealers or gangsters encrypt their electronic messages to comrades, a keystroke monitor can capture data outside the encryption scheme while it is still understandable, including the address of emails and the entire communication stream.

The FBI used keystroke-monitoring software to obtain the encryption passphrase of Nicodemo Scarfo Jr., son of reputed Philadelphia organized crime boss Nicodemo Scarfo. With access to the passphrase, law enforcement could decrypt and read an important electronic message from the Scarfo family.[4] Apparently, the FBI has developed proprietary keystroke-logging software built into a covert delivery system called "Magic Lantern" that will allow the agency to monitor messages outside of encryption programs. According to news reports, Magic Lantern was created by the FBI's electronic tools laboratory, which built the famous "Carnivore" program for Internet surveillance.[5]

But of course the bad guys like to deploy keyloggers as well, because the tool can grant them access into financial and brokerage accounts. Keystroke loggers allow cyberthieves to capture account passwords and interfere with the input of security information between your computer and your bank, brokerage, credit union, or other institution holding your valuable resources. Once the security passwords are taken, the thief no longer needs to linger on your computer and can access your online banking or brokerage accounts from any computer anywhere in the world.

## Is the Boss Watching Your Keystrokes?

The workplace is a fertile arena for the use of keylogging software. In the United Kingdom, Canada, and much of the United States, local laws permit employers to monitor their employees in this fashion as long as the employees are told how they are being monitored. Employers often use hardware-based keylogging platforms, which are small devices that can be plugged into the system between a keyboard and the computer it is serving. The devices work with keyboards connected by cords and those with a wireless receptor at the computer, but not with keyboards that are built into the computer itself.

Hardware keyloggers are not necessarily dependent on the target's operating system, and they will not interfere with programs running on the target computer. They are more commonly used in employee monitoring rather than in identity-theft situations, because the user must have physical access to the target computer system to install and later retrieve the loggers.

Thus far, courts in the United States have not held that workplace keystroke monitoring violates federal law. For example, a federal court in Indiana heard a case in which an employer had installed keylogger software on employees' machines, and management obtained passwords to at least one employee's personal accounts. They viewed the passwords, forwarded them, and discussed having access to the passwords among themselves, but they never used the passwords to access the employee's accounts. The court dismissed the employee's case based on the Federal Wiretap Act, but they allowed it proceed under the Stored Communications Act and the Indiana Wiretap Act.[6]

The case of Larry Ropp developed out of a reversal of the usual workplace situation. Mr. Ropp installed a keystroke-logging program onto the computer of a secretary at work in order to gain information against his employer, so he could blow the whistle against the employer's allegedly illegal acts. While Ropp was indicted by a grand jury for criminal violations of the federal wiretap statutes, a federal district court in California dismissed the indictment against Mr. Ropp. This court held, as others had in the past, that captured keystrokes were not analogous to wiretapped data because they were taken on the original computer before the information travelled over a network.[7]

Other countries may be more protective of an individual's privacy in the workplace. For example, the Alberta Provincial Privacy Commissioner found that the Parkland Regional Library did not have authority under the Canadian Freedom of Information and Protection of Privacy Act to install keystroke-logging software on the computer of one of its employees, and that the library should have used less intrusive means to collect the information it sought.[8]

## When Monitoring Keystrokes Is All in the Family

Like the story of Crystal Goan that opens this chapter, many of the keystroke-logging devices sold in the world today are purchased in connection with domestic concerns of infidelity and hiding family money. And like Ms. Goan, those who use these methods without telling a spouse or other interested party whose computer activity is being monitored could be in trouble. They run the significant risk of being found in violation of a state or federal eavesdropping statute, and of being fined for the activity, or worse. This is especially true where keystroke monitors are used to avoid a spouse's encryption of messages or to access financial accounts through captured passwords.

Cases in this area are hard to predict. The states covered by some US Circuit Courts, including Florida, Colorado, Ohio, Virginia, and Missouri find that recording a spouse's information in the home violates federal wiretapping statutes, while the states covered by other US Circuit Courts, like New York and Texas, do not find such in-home recording violates federal law. Unless and until the US Supreme Court rules on whether the wiretap laws are actionable in divorce situations, the rules are likely to apply differently depending on which federal circuit has jurisdiction over the case.

## IS SOMEONE SPYING ON YOU?

Two separate and similar categories of software go by the term "spyware." One category is commercial spyware, which tries to discover commercially valuable information about you and influence your purchasing decisions. The other category is targeted spyware used by someone you know—your spouse, your parents, a work rival, an ex-roommate, your boss, or law enforcement. This second category is more likely to target personal information and activities than commercial benefits. Both types of programs take over your system, cause problems with system functionality, and can pretend to be you when sending out email or texts under your name. Both will gather information about you. Both are trouble, and both can turn your computer against you.

The importance of communicating through computers and the explosion of spyware devices that allow police, thieves, employers, parents, and spouses to turn your home computer into a surveillance station have spawned a spyware backlash. You can now buy an arsenal of counter-measures designed to find and resist spyware, making your computer safe again for business, banking, and personal use. You can hire private detectives who will install spyware on a computer in the morning and sweep computers to clean them of spyware all afternoon. Technology consultants search for and discover spyware as a cornerstone service, along with repairing other damage that various versions of malware can inflict upon your computer. You can also purchase tools that will do this job for you, so that no one else needs to know that you were looking.

*How You Can Tell If Your Computer Watches You*

If you are suspicious that your computer has been turned into a surveillance tool, the best way to determine its safety is to hire a technologist you trust to scan it with professional tools. Your computer's appearance and behavior can give you clues that might indicate whether it is infected with spyware:

- If someone is watching you through the camera connected to your computer, a light on the camera will usually (but not always) activate to show that the camera is in use. If the light is on and you have not done anything to activate it, then it is likely that someone else is watching you through remote activation.
- The same is true for microphones on some models of computer. If the computer shows the microphone as presently activated, but you are not running any software that calls for microphone input, then a third party may be remotely activating the computer's microphone and listening to the room.
- You should be able to check to see whether any of your computer's sensors are turned on and functioning. That way, you can tell if the computer is operating some of the sensors without your knowledge and input. Some spyware masks the input displays, so this is not a foolproof plan to confirm that you are being watched or bugged, but checking the sensor activity is a good first place to start.
- Look at the connections between your input devices and the computer. Certain hardware-related spyware is noticeable from outside the computer. Is there a finger-sized extra connector plugged into the wires where your keyboard hooks into your computer? If so, then you likely have a hardware keylogger attached to your system. Did someone questionable offer you an improved keyboard or mouse, or did one just appear at your office without your requesting it? If so, you may have a keystroke or mouse-click monitor built into the new accessory equipment. Are there any strange or new jumpdrives attached to the USB ports on your computer? If so, they may be siphoning information from the system or downloading

spyware into the computer. Look for unusual hardware changes and you may find your bug.

- Much modern spyware is cleverly designed to mask itself and not trigger signals that will notify you of its presence. Some spyware also goes to great lengths to hide itself within your computer and keep its presence hidden from all the normal methods that you would use to find and remove unwanted programs from your computer. However, if a remote user has taken control of your computer, then the computer will continue to account for that user's activity as if it was your activity. So you can check for actions that your computer is logging that you did not undertake yourself.

- You may notice emails being sent without you even opening the email software, files moved or copied, or strange websites appearing in the search history of your web browser. Check for unusual activity from your email or instant messaging features, because a remote user of your computer may try to send himself items from your computer—pictures, files, correspondence, or passwords. You can even check the "recent items" folder in your Windows start menu to see if files have been recently opened or manipulated without your knowledge.

- The way the spyware program interacts with the rest of the computer provides many telltale signs of the infection. Your computer's performance may slow considerably. As spyware accumulates, the software pulls resources from your computer by performing tasks that you would find unnecessary. This includes a longer startup cycle, because the spyware has to start up at the same time as your computer.

- The programs that protect your computer from spyware, viruses, or other attacks may stop working properly, because much of the current sophisticated commercial spyware protects itself by first attacking your computer's defenses. Your computer's security program may seem to launch in a normal fashion, only to quickly shut down again.

- You may not be able to access the task manager on your computer, because many spyware variants disable the task manager so that its processes cannot be manually ended by the user of the target computer. Similarly, the spyware may disable the Windows registry editor and the folder options under the My Computer tools tab.

- Spyware on your home computer may also push the usage numbers of your computer's Central Processing Unit (CPU) toward 100 percent as long as the computer is running. Your settings may change, and you can't switch them back to the way they were. New items become part of your "favorites" list, and those items keep reappearing as favorites after you delete them. A new search toolbar appears in your browser and you don't know how it arrived or installed itself.

- And of course, a steady stream of pop-up advertisements that you have never seen before is a strong indicator that adware has taken hold of your computer.

### Extracting the Problem

Once you know that you have a spyware problem, act quickly to free your computer from this menace. When removing spyware, use only trusted sources. Spyware has existed long enough that its developers tend to be very careful and sophisticated, and they have likely anticipated the actions that most regular computer users would take to fight spyware tools. Some spyware creators even provide their own "spyware removal" tools that either install more and better spyware on your system or remove competitor's products but leave their own intact.

So this is one instance where it would be a good idea to request assistance from IBM, Cisco, Apple, Microsoft, Dell, McAfee, Symantec, Norton, Kaspersky, Google, or any other big technology or security company with a reason to provide support to your system. Just make sure that you are truly finding the company you seek, as some scammers and spyware makers also plant fake sites using famous names.

Another clear method of protection is to call the Geek Squad, your employer's tech support people, or other trusted technologists and simply pay them to help you remove the spyware from your system.

Sometimes commercial spyware identifies itself, or sometimes you can tell what specific spyware product has invaded your computer by reading the woeful tales of others with similar computer maladies and comparing them to your own problems. In these cases, you can often find a commercial fix for the problem online or through the company that makes your browser, security software, or your computer's operating system. Other times you can detect the precise enemy that has taken over your machine and remove it with a generic spyware removal program acquired from a trusted source.

However, when your computer is infected by professional spyware installed by law enforcement or by a private investigator, you are probably best off hiring a trusted tech guru to dig into your system and search out the bugs. You would not want to run the risk that any of the spyware was left in your system.

If nothing else works, there is always the nuclear option—purchase a new machine and take the old computer offline. Make certain that anti-spyware programs are properly installed in the new machine so you don't accumulate the same set of problems after buying fresh hardware. Then lock your new computer, shutting it down each time you leave and enabling a hardware password so that only you can log onto it. This will minimize the chances that a roommate, spouse, parent, or stalker will install more spyware while you are away from the machine.

For Vista and Windows 7, Microsoft offers a suite of spyware protection tools called Microsoft Security Essentials, which can be downloaded at no cost. The Windows Defender of Windows 8 is more advanced than Microsoft Security Essentials. If your computer is so compromised that it will not even allow you to download these security programs directly, then you can download the products offline and ask your Microsoft support professional how to inject them into your system.

While much less spyware and malware are written for the Apple platform than the Windows operating system, anyone with directly physical access to your Apple computer can install problem software. If you are concerned about spyware, take the time to run the MacScan product. While it will likely scare you with the number of legitimate software tools it finds that could be used against you, MacScan is likely to find the problem software as well.

Friedrich Nietzsche famously wrote that "when you look long into the abyss, the abyss also looks back into you." Our home computers have opened windows to the world, but they also open a window from which the world can peer back at us. To maintain our privacy, it is best to pull the shades on this window. Know what intrusion into your life is possible, and then guard against it. Knowledge and watchfulness are often the best protections we can exercise.

## NOTES

1. Anne Youderian, "Ex-Wife Owes $20K for Spyware Divorce Scheme," *Courthouse News Service*, July 25, 2012.

2. Greg Risling, "Luis Mijangos Sentenced to 6 Years for 'Sextortion,'" Associated Press as reported in the *Huffington Post*, September 1, 2011.

3. Nate Anderson, "How an Omniscient Internet "Sextortionist" Ruined the Lives of Teen Girls," *ARS Technica*, September 7, 2011.

4. Mark Rasch, "Break the Scarfo Silence," *Bloomberg Businessweek*, September 3, 2001.

5. Associated Press, "FBI's Secret Cyber-Monitor," as reported on *CBS News*, February 11, 2009.

6. *Rene v. G.F. Fishers, Inc.*, 2011 U.S. Dist. LEXIS 105202 (S.D. Ind. Sept. 16, 2011).

7. *United States v. Ropp*, 347 F.Supp.2d 831, Central Dist. CA (2004).

8. Order F2005-003, Office of Information and Privacy Commissioner, Edmonton, Alberta.

# THREE

## How Government Follows Your Electronic Tracks

Imagine a man who has just committed a crime running home to leave a note for his wife, pack his bags, and flee the country. He's pretty sure he wasn't followed because he took precautions—no texting about his whereabouts, no phone calls, and no social media updates. He drives his car home, checks the weather on his phone, and when he gets home he automatically turns on the air conditioner to cool the house down. Within minutes, there's a knock on the door and a warning to "come out with your hands up." The man surrenders, asking his captors "How did you find me?" The arresting officer tells him, "Your car's safety system let us know you were in the car, you checked the weather on your cell phone which required tracking your location, and your house is connected to the smart grid so we knew somebody was home when the A/C kicked on." This isn't a real story, but it could be.

In this chapter you get a peek at what governments are doing that could be considered invasive of personal privacy. Much of these activities are done to thwart criminals and terrorists, but the privacy of your personal information may at risk.

### FREE . . . AT A COST

Many of the social-media platforms, Internet services, and helpful tools that are integrated into our work and personal lives are offered free of charge. When a product or service is free, those who provide it need to make money and they don't make it all from annoying ads that pop into view when you log into the service. In most instances, when you use free services, what's really for sale is you and all the digital data nuggets you provide when you use the service.

Even the services that you pay for that claim they provide efficiency or safety features are tracking you in some way. Every time you visit or use one of these sites, they collect information about you and in many cases, know exactly where you are (give or take three hundred feet) and even digitally follow you around on the web after you leave their site. The information and digital data points collected are considered important indicators about your whereabouts, preferences, likes and dislikes, and habits.

The ability to know where you have been, both online and offline, can help clever marketers predict your next step so they can sell you a targeted product or service. Marketers are not the only ones taking advantage of this treasure trove of data: governments have realized that active and passive data collection and monitoring on the web is an important part of intelligence operations. They love it when you use these free services because it adds another dimension to you that public records do not offer.

## The Government Agenda

The United States and other countries' governments want you to be part of their data collection, aggregation, and analysis efforts. But don't expect them to ask your permission. You shouldn't expect an offer to "opt out or into" this program. Most citizens of the world are already in the mix without even knowing it.

The Google transparency report is an annual accounting for requests by global law-enforcement agencies and global governments for information about private citizens. The report stratifies the requests by country and reports the percentage of requests that are granted. Privacy International, a rights group based in the United Kingdom, reviewed the most recent Google transparency report and reacted to its statistics.

Privacy International stated that "Google, Facebook, and Twitter are highly vulnerable to government intrusion." In order to proactively deflect attacks or respond quickly during an attack, intelligence and counterintelligence are a vital part of government and law enforcement operations. It is natural for citizens of any country to expect their government to provide protection. Around the globe, citizens expect protection from foreign and homegrown terrorists, protection from organized crime, and efforts by their country's military and local governments to fight the bad guys.

What many citizens, especially those in democratic forms of government, may not realize is that much of the intelligence gathered today in an effort to thwart evil doing is collected for everyone—the innocent, the not-so-innocent, and those accused of wrongdoing. Many citizens across the globe appreciate the fact that data collection is handled proactively and comment that the price of security is worth the loss of privacy. You may read this and think, "I have nothing to hide. My life is pretty boring. Search away." However, many of the protections that citizens across the globe have put into place to prevent their own government from spying on them are eroding day by day.

Take, for example, citizens of the United States. Though the government cannot wiretap citizens without a warrant from a court, law enforcement and the government have a legal means to snoop on you without a warrant. A subpoena to your cell-phone provider or email provider will result in a treasure trove of information obtained without your knowledge and without a warrant.

*Smartphones Expose You Big Time*

Consider this: Your smartphone remembers more about where you were last week than you do and a recent scientific study proves it.

MIT and other groups came together to see if they could take data from phones and, without knowing who owned the phone, somehow track it back to an individual. They tracked where the phone went every day. Most people are predictable: they wake up, head to work, go to the gym, go to a soccer field, and so on. Most people have a pattern to their whereabouts. They found that they could identify a person by tracking his or her cell phone.[1] The study tracked 1.5 million people for a little over a year. The researchers compared their study to the way that law enforcement tracks valid and verified fingerprints, where it takes twelve data points to track a fingerprint down to an individual. In this study, the researchers said they only needed four data points to guess who the cell-phone owner was within 95 percent accuracy.[2] The researchers pulled hourly updates on the phone's whereabouts from mobile cell-phone towers. Over time, they could compare past tracking to current data and work backward to obtain a person's identity over 90 percent of the time.

Tracking cell-phone owners could be a good thing, especially if a person goes missing. However, in the wrong hands, this ability could get creepy and become an invasion of your privacy. It's important to understand that it used to be that only a mobile-phone company had this information. Now, this location information is widely shared with cell phone "partners" and manufacturers of all those fun and handy apps you just cannot live without.

Consider this staggering statistic: of cell-phone purchases made last year, 65.5 billion of associated payments were geotagged, meaning that somebody knows where each purchaser was when that payment was made.[3]

## GOVERNMENTS WATCHING THEIR CITIZENS

Many governments in a post–9/11 world have embarked on national security schemes or citizen-safety programs, deploying sophisticated digital surveillance methods abroad and at home. Governments across the
globe say that surveillance capabilities are essential to fighting home-
based crime rings, terrorism, and international crimes against their citizens.

Much of today's surveillance is done without James Bond or even the
use of video cameras. Governments are collecting and storing your
phone calls, purchases, emails, texts, web-based searches, social-networking interactions, doctors' visits, employment history, large bank deposits,
and even travel records. Name an activity and it's probably being
tracked, stored, and collated for future use. Cell-phone towers track the
movement of your phone and hence, you. Connecting through cell towers, an Internet service, or a Wi-Fi network using your digital devices and
phones, also gives your location away. Facial-recognition technology advances make it easier to spot and track you via photos and video feeds.

When you use your computers or digital devices to connect with the
web, you may assume that your online conversations, posts, whims of
the moment, thoughts, photos, and videos are protected by your Internet
services provider at home or work, your cell-phone company, or your
email-account provider. These companies do take your privacy seriously
but they also take regulations and international laws seriously. When the
police or a government agent asks a provider for your information or for
a large dataset that contains your data, whether you are innocent or not,
according to the Electronic Frontier Foundation (EFF) 2012 report, most
of those service providers turn your data over without notifying you or
putting up much of a fight. Companies such as Yahoo, Microsoft, Facebook, and Google have recently gone on the record stating that they
would like to tell consumers the extent they were asked to comply with
demands from law enforcement and the National Security Agency
(NSA).[4] When the CEO of Yahoo, Marissa Mayer, was asked during a
conference to explain why Yahoo did not protect its users' privacy, she
explained that Yahoo did what it felt it could do to protect their users but
also admitted that "if you don't comply, it is treason."[5] However,
through advocacy and awareness by groups like EFF, there have been
improvements. The best companies for notifying users about demands
for their data are LinkedIn, Google, Dropbox, Sonic.net, Spider Oak, and
Twitter. The EFF also gives high marks to companies such as Amazon,
Apple, AT and T, Comcast, loopt, Microsoft, and Yahoo because these
companies are seen as fighting for user privacy either through the court
system and/or through lobbying Congress and other legal bodies around
the globe.[6]

Uncle Sam or Peeping Tom?

According to Google's annual transparency report,[7] governments across the globe made over forty-two thousand requests for personal data on their systems alone in 2012. Google's report also indicates that the US government is the most active in requesting information, followed by India and France.

> **The value of any piece of information is only known when you can connect it with something else that arrives at a future point in time. . . . Since you can't connect dots you don't have, it drives us into a mode of, we fundamentally try to collect everything and hang onto it forever.**[8]
> **—Ira Gus Hunt, the CIA's chief technology officer at the GigaOM's data conference in New York City, March 2013**

First consider the security efforts of the United States, starting with big data. *Big data* refers to very large sets of data that can be used to spot trends such as disease or crime patterns in a society. In the United States, companies and government organizations have begun to use big data to solve a variety of problems and challenges. For companies, such big data projects might have a business goal, such as streamlined marketing and product development. Several security departments that we talked with while conducting research for the book see their big data as something that has to be protected but also as a tool to help them predict and react to cyber security threats.

The US federal government also has big data projects underway to handle a variety of analysis needs. This information, which is collected, collated, and analyzed at lightning speed, has been credited with proactively thwarting attacks on US soil and abroad and is being used overseas in investigations into incidents such as the Benghazi embassy attack or attacks on our allies. Information that is collected about US citizens and foreign persons of interest is being stored in many cases, indefinitely.[9]

The US government has various layers of checks and balances in place to help protect US citizens from illegal snooping. For example, when the NSA wants to track US citizens, they have to go through the Foreign Intelligence Surveillance Act ( FISA) court. This secret court has the authority to review special cases of national security and grant a federal department or agency the ability to track information without a warrant.[10]

Citizens of the United States and the United Kingdom learned in June 2013 that the NSA was collecting more information than originally understood and that the NSA was sharing the information gathered under their program with the UK's equivalent agency, Government Communications Headquarters or GCHQ. James Clapper, director of National Intelligence in the United States, confirmed reports by the *Guardian* and the *Washington Post* that the NSA is tracking phone records through cellular companies and tracking Internet traffic such as emails, videos, and photos stored on sites such as Google, Facebook, YouTube, Microsoft, and Apple. Think of an old-fashioned snail mail envelope. By looking at the envelope you can tell who sent the note and who the note is going to, and you can track it by the postmark's city and date. It's not until the note is opened that you truly know the contents of that communication. US officials have explained that they can see the sender, receiver, and some other information but not the contents unless they request a court order or go through a pre-defined legal process.[11] Assume for a moment that you trust the US and the UK governments to apply a sense of responsibility and respect for privacy to the data troves collected. In this scenario, this massive collection of data about private citizens is put at risk the moment someone decides to steal, attack, or otherwise compromise the data elements collected. Even if you assume the best of intentions, you cannot assume that this data cannot be hacked or stolen. For example, NSA contractor Edward Snowden allegedly took classified information and downloaded it to thumb drives and laptops and walked out of his employer's building with that information, fleeing the United States before sharing the information with the *Guardian* and the *Washington Post* newspapers.[12]

Though the US Fourth Amendment[13] recognizes that police and security forces protect citizens best if they assume that the citizens are all innocent until proven guilty, privacy watchdogs in the United States are increasingly concerned that the ongoing, unlimited collection of data for an undefined, future use undermines our Constitutional rights. The US government cannot listen in on your phone calls without a warrant, but currently they can request and receive the numbers you called, dates and times when you made calls, a list of incoming calls, and more from phone carriers.

The US government only needs to provide a subpoena and not a warrant (which indicates that a crime may have been committed) to cellphone companies if they want to view text messages that are 181 days old or older. If you store data online at services such as Google Drive or Dropbox, government agents can get at that data using a subpoena and without your consent. When served with a subpoena, Facebook will hand over your email address, IP addresses that your account was accessed from, and some other information without your knowledge.

The US government and law enforcement find that people often post information about their whereabouts without the need for a subpoena or a warrant. In fact, some security platforms depend upon you being free and open with your information. Raytheon is developing a platform called RIOT (Rapid Information Overlay Technology) that can sift through various social media sites across the globe to track a person of interest and in some cases predict his next move.[14] Jared Adams of Raytheon said in an interview with the *Guardian* newspaper that RIOT is "a big data analytics system design we are working on with industry, national labs and commercial partners to help turn massive amounts of data into usable information to help meet our nation's rapidly changing security needs."[15] The system will display a person of interest's interactions with others via a visual spider diagram. It will mine sites such as Twitter and Facebook, and it will dig for the GPS information hidden in the geocodes of photos, and more.

FBI Director Mueller, in his testimony on March 30, 2011[16] to the Senate Judiciary Committee, mentions that in the fight against crime and terrorists, one of their tools is a large database, built as part of their technological improvements program that has "past emails and future ones as they come in so it does not require an individualized search." Translated into layman's terms, this means that everyone, innocents included, will be tracked for posterity and just in case we need to investigate you in the future.

In the desert of Utah many say that the United States is building an enormous data-collection and digital surveillance cyber-security program called the "Utah Data Center,"[17] also known as the NSA's new intelligence cloud. *Wired* magazine claims to have details on this program, including the fact that it will contain four twenty-five-thousand-square-foot halls that will be completely outfitted for racks of data servers.[18]

*Surveillance Going Global*

These trends in surveillance aren't just happening in the United States. Here's a rundown of how some countries use information about citizens' digital lives:

**Live in Syria?** If you are one of the five million Internet users in Syria, your 3G Internet traffic might be routed through the Syrian Computer Society or the Syrian Telecommunications Establishment. The Syrian Internet infrastructure was updated recently to provide the government with the ability to scan the network for national security purposes. The government can also cut off connections if necessary to control civil unrest or criminal activities.[19] On November 29, 2012, the network security firm Renesys reported that seventy-seven networks were down in Syria, representing roughly 92 percent of the country's Internet traffic.[20] Internet-services provider Akamai reported similar outages. News reporters and security researchers believe that the Syrian government was behind the effort, perhaps in an effort to control Syrian in-fighting and the messages going outside of the country to the rest of the world. Google's "Transparency Report" shows various outages around the world and suspected causes. Google noted that in May of 2013, Syria experienced two service disruptions on May 7–8 and May 15.[21]

**Big Brother in the UK.** The British government has also wrestled with the challenge of increasing security while maintaining privacy for its citizens. It has built a plan to leverage the telecommunications infrastructure to intercept and sift through traffic as it flows through the digital pipeline. That traffic could include text messages or email as well as Facebook posts or website visits. The technique, also known as "deep packet inspection," allows surveillance devices to track information from the origination point to the data's destination point. Computer programs allow analysts to look inside the packet at details such as what is being transported (text, video, photo). In a report by Parliament's Intelligence and Security Committee, MI5 Chief Jonathan Evans said, "Access to communications data of one sort or another is very important indeed. It's part of the backbone of the way in which we would approach investigations . . . I think I would be accurate in saying there are no significant investigations that we undertake across the service that don't use communications data because of its ability to tell you the who and the when and the where of your target's activities."[22] In an effort to fight cybercrime, when the new plan is implemented MI5 and GCHQ cyber analysts will work with the private sector to comb through data. The cyber security information sharing partnership, or CISP, will have roughly twelve to fifteen analysts working on leads. This will require the collection, retention, and analysis of key data elements across the public and private sectors in the name of better security. An unnamed senior official in the UK said, "What we are trying to do is get that better intelligence picture and push it out to industry in a way that they can take action on, so it is very action-orientated."[23]

**Chinese checkers.** Those working and living in China know that their Internet activities might fall under the watchful eye of the "Great firewall of China," the nickname for all the filters and monitors on Chinese Internet connections. In the 2013 Business Climate Survey,[24] non-Chinese firms that conduct business in China made clear how they felt about Chinese Internet surveillance: 55 percent see China's current Internet surveillance and censorship as negatively impacting their ability to conduct business transactions there; 62 percent responded that the blockage of or impediments to accessing popular search engines such as BING or Google make it difficult or nearly impossible to keep up with the latest, real-time information. James McGregor, a contributor for *Quartz* digital news magazine, reported that international corporations are so concerned about Internet surveillance and spying in China that they were flying any China-based executives to South Korea for important phone calls to avoid tracking or eavesdropping.[25] According to a new report from National Public Radio (NPR), the Chinese government has built a cybersecurity program called "Skynet" and has also installed more than twenty million surveillance cameras in less than ten years. Cameras are mounted in every public setting imaginable, from taxis to public parks. It is believed that the combination of tracking using cameras, website visits, and traffic to social-media sites helps protect the government from outside threats and threats from their own citizens. According to one citizen, the benefit of this surveillance is a sense of security: "Before, when I parked my tricycle in neighborhoods, thieves always stole things. . . . Now they rarely steal. I feel a sense of safety."[26] However, there is the danger that surveillance and redefining what a "threat" actually is could infringe upon innocent citizens' rights. According to NPR's report, Chinese state security agents told them off the record that they can turn citizen cell phones into spy gear, recording and relaying audio to them.[27]

**German data paparazzi.** Malte Spitz, a German politician, requested his cell records while undergoing a legal proceeding. What the cell company sent him back was an astounding set of digital tracks that would make the most vigilant political paparazzi look like a slacker. He received roughly thirty-six thousand records. He plotted the cell-phone interaction on a map and saw his own life in great detail. His phone basically showed all his movements, which could include calls made or information accessed while riding a train or going shopping.[28]

**Afghanistan protections.** In Afghanistan, the law states that, "(1) Confidentiality and freedom of correspondence and communication whether in the form of letters or through telephone, telegraph and other means, are immune from invasion. The state does not have the right to inspect personal correspondence and communication unless authorized by the provisions of law."[29]

**Collaborative efforts.** The European Union (EU) recently released their plan to create a new collaboration of international police forces to fight cybercrime and to give all EU members new powers to request digital information from service providers in the name of improved security.[30] The European Network and Information Security Agency (ENISA) will be the coordination point for security agencies across the EU. If an EU member country suspects an EU company or person of a crime, it can request disclosure of that person or company. The plan, if fully approved and implemented, would supersede existing, country-based privacy laws. For example, they could force Spain, if the persons or companies of interest resided there, to provide police records, Google records, Facebook records, emails, and more for an EU investigation brought forth to ENISA.

According to Listverse, the Committee to Protect Journalists (CPJ) tracks the penchant for a government to conduct Internet surveillance of citizens, especially journalists. The top five on their list includes: North Korea, Burma, Cuba, Saudi Arabia, and Iran.[31]

# HOW GOVERNMENTS TRACK YOU ONLINE

**Many Facebook comments are public and people don't realize they're publishing to the world.**
                              **—Jim Killock, Open Rights Group** [32]

There are very few facts about our lives that are not tracked online in some way. How did you check the weather this morning: via cable TV, the printed daily newspaper, or your smartphone or computer? Once you realize that such information is tracked you might ask, who cares? Because we see much of this information as mundane and of little interest to others, we may not care that it's being tracked.

But consider for a moment that your digital tracks and patterns leave imprints online that can be tracked by governments for various purposes. Governments use different methods to track their citizens online. Some governments have complete control over their local telecommunications so they can insert the rules and technologies they feel they need to protect their sovereignty. Other governments have rules in place that implement checks and balances on when law enforcement can intercept and review the messages of private citizens.

*What Governments Can Grab*

Practices employed by global government and law enforcement can include, but aren't limited to:

- Deep packet sniffing. This is the practice of reviewing packets of information coming across the Internet to determine the type of content within the packets. This practice might not involve the specific review of a message (for example, watching a video contained in a packet), but packet sniffing may tell the reviewer that the message contains a music video about cats playing the piano, for example.
- Storage of voice communications traffic. The cell-phone towers or Wi-Fi a cell is talking to, the numbers called and connected, the length of time connected, and perhaps even voice mails may be available from stored data.
- Storage of photos and videos. These items may be intercepted and stored for a future access.
- Collection of online purchases and money transfers. Monetary transactions that hit certain thresholds may be collected and stored by a government or obtained by a subpoena sent to an online service requesting that information.
- Interactions with the government itself. Transactions with the government can include paying taxes, purchasing licenses, registering property, marriages, divorces, births, and adoptions.

- Interception of voice over IP phone calls and cell-phone calls. When your phone call takes place over the Internet through a cell-phone network or an Internet connection, the same techniques that can be used to watch traffic are applied to record, listen to, and store data about your call. Important data elements are tracked, such as location, number of the phone originating the call, the number dialed, and duration of call. If you leave a voice mail, that recording may also be stored and listened to at a later date.
- Interception of Internet-based phone or video conferencing systems. Conferences from services such as AOL's, Hotmail's, or Yahoo's chat/messaging platforms, Google Chat, Skype or Apple's FaceTime may be accessible.
- Traveler data. Hotel registrations, airline bookings, train reservations, or any type of travel information could be used to ascertain your digital whereabouts.
- Internet scans. The Library of Congress and The National Archives Records Administration (NARA) in the United States are storing every tweet that's made.[33] In the UK, libraries announced they will archive millions of web pages from roughly 4.8 million websites as part of their library project to include blogs, newspapers, Facebook posts, and tweets from libraries in Scotland, Wales, Ireland, and England.[34]

*When the Government Makes an Example of You*

There are times where it makes sense to publicize a threat to society. There have been a variety of ways to do that in the physical world — posting wanted posters, reviewing cases and alleged criminals on TV or radio, or publishing lists online or in print. It is critical to have that information in real time to share across law enforcement agencies as well as with the general public. In the past, if you did something wrong, your community might have put up a wanted poster at the post office or published your name in the newspaper. Those methods still exist but have also been extended to new digital halls of shame at Facebook, Twitter, MySpace, and other highly visible sites.

## LISTS YOU DON'T WANT TO BE ON: GOVERNMENTS TRACKING OF BAD GUYS AND GOOD GUYS

Could an email to a friend land you on a wanted list? "Sorry, I'm going to be late for our lunch, we have a service disruption and now the metro is late. LOL. Maybe a DDOS caused it or some kind of worm." Sounds farfetched but the italicized words in this fictitious email might trigger an investigation. According to the response to a Freedom of Information Act

(FOIA) request that the US Department of Homeland Security (DHS) responded to, certain words in an email might trigger an alert. DHS has a manual for their security analysts' use called the "Analyst's Desktop Binder"; using key words in that binder might trigger an alert to review someone's communications a little more closely.[35]

The former head of the NSA's global digital data program, William Binney, says you cannot avoid being on the wrong list just by being a good person. "If you ever get on their enemies list . . . then you can be drawn into that surveillance."[36]

There are a lot of practical reasons why governments create lists of "most wanted" or hardened criminals to help the general public with overall safety. Agencies keep a variety of lists, including:

- Scotland Yard. This UK law-enforcement agency now releases photos and information from their most-wanted lists in an attempt to capture criminals.[37]
- The FBI's Sex Offender Registry. This website (www.fbi.gov/scams-safety/registry), accessible only by law enforcement, is coordinated by the Department of Justice. The list can be searched to find the latest sex offender information for all fifty states, Puerto Rico, Guam, Indian tribal reservations, and the District of Columbia.
- US State-based Registers. This data is based on geography and the law that sexual offenders must register locally, and can be searched by citizens using name or address.
- The International Criminal Court. The court lists any offenders indicted under this independent international organization. Eighteen cases and eight other incidents, as of the writing this book, have been brought before this court and the details of each case and incident reviewed are published atwww.icc-cpi.int/Pages/default.aspx.
- The Terrorist Watch List. This list is compiled by the FBI from the Terrorist Screening Database, or TSDB.[38] The over one million records help contribute to other lists such as the "No-fly list" and the INTERPOL Terrorism Watch List (www.interpol.int/Wanted-Persons). INTERPOL is considered the world's largest international police organization, counting more than 190 countries as key members.
- Canadian Legal Records. Canada allows online access to court records as well judgments across its provinces at the Canadian Legal Information Institute's website called CANLII (www.canlii.org/en/index.html).
- The SAR List Maintained by the FBI. The FBI also operates the nationwide Suspicious Activity Reporting Initiative (SAR) that collects information from locally run law-enforcement groups. The SAR files submitted by local law enforcement have hundreds of

thousands of profiles of US citizens and visitors, even if they have not committed a crime. You need only act suspicious to be put on the list.

Finally, are you hosting a foreign exchange student? You could land on a list. It seems ideal to host a foreign exchange student. You open your home to a stranger but usually through a program that you learned about. You get exposure to new cultures and perhaps make a new friend who you can visit overseas. Watch what you sign up for, though, because depending upon the agency organizing the visit and the country the student is from, you may end up on a list at the DHS or the National Counterterrorism Center (NCTC).

### They Won't Track Me Unless I'm Suspicious, Right? Wrong!

The legal system is struggling to keep up with our privacy rights in this digital age, so don't assume that because you are a law-abiding citizen your data is protected. Even when laws are in place they are not always successful. When William Binney, a former intelligence analyst for the US government, was asked by *Russia Today*'s reporter how the US government places filters on emails so they don't read information of innocent citizens Binney responded, "I don't think they are filtering it. They are just storing it. I think it's just a matter of selecting when they want it. So, if they want to target you, they would take your attributes, go into that database and pull out all your data."[39]

With communications, emails, documents, photos, videos, video chats, and more moving to cloud services, if laws don't keep up officials may not have access to cloud content, which could stall their enforcement efforts. In the United States, CALEA, or the Communications Assistance for Law Enforcement Act, established a protocol for phone companies and Internet providers to capture and store information deemed critical by law enforcement. However, every time we create a new service or a new law we have to also be concerned with how to protect privacy while improving security.

One area of privacy law that will continue to evolve is whether or not your past can be used to judge your future acts. Most people have school records, work records, and references. But what happens to past indiscretions? Could those stop an employer from hiring you? The answer depends upon where you live in the world and the latest court ruling on how that information can be retained and disclosed. The European Court of Human Rights (ECtHR), for example, ruled in late 2012 that disclosure of police records to potential employers was not compatible with the Human Rights European Convention. This was considered a positive development in establishing what law enforcement can retain and disclose about private citizens without their consent.[40] The final verdict on whether police records can continue to be a part of the employment process is a case that is still under review at this time.

## *Why Your Travels Say So Much about You*

> **The right to travel is a part of the "liberty" of which the citizen cannot be deprived without due process of law under the Fifth Amendment. . . . Freedom of movement across frontiers in either direction, and inside frontiers as well, was a part of our heritage.**
> —**Justice William O. Douglas,** *Kent v. Dulles* **(1958)** [41]

Both noncitizens and citizens who fly anywhere in the United States are tracked electronically. The automatically integrated electronic capture and dissemination of information to the federal government started around 2002; prior to that, analysts looked at computer-generated lists and paper reports. The records stored in the US federal government's database are pretty benign: name, contact details, how the ticket was purchased, origination and destination cities, and dates and times. This tracking may also capture the travel agency used, if any, and the Internet address of the computer used to purchase the ticket. All of that information is used in DHS's Advanced Passenger Information system. [42]

Starting back in 2009, a similar procedure was instituted in the United Kingdom. Any passenger who departs the UK by air, sea, or land has his or her trip recorded. The information is kept on file with the UK Border Agency for roughly a decade. The UK Border Agency, as of writing this book, was debating data-collection procedures while also going through organizational restructuring.

If you are a citizen of the EU or flying through any country within the EU headed to America, Australia, or Canada, your PNR (Person, Name, Record) will be made available to authorities in those countries, if they request it. The EU insists this is a vital activity to keep citizens safe and that PNR sharing stops bad guys from getting away. British Conservative MEP Timothy Kirkhope said the data has "led to the capture of dozens of murderers, paedophiles, and rapists . . . 95% of all drug captures in Belgium and 85% in Sweden are caught using PNR data." [43]

When it comes to your privacy, remember that cell-phone communications aren't always secure. Have you passed by a "stingray" lately? We're not referring to marine life but to a technology that can track your everyday whereabouts. A stingray is a nickname for the technology that mimics a cell-phone tower but is actually a tracking device. A stingray can detect and locate a cell phone even when the phone's owner is not making a call. Investigators are leveraging this technology and laws have not kept up. Stingrays don't currently fit in any category under the rules that allow law enforcement to gather evidence without a warrant. It's also not clear whether stingray technology is more appropriately managed through subpoenas or a warrant.

One example is the case of Daniel David Rigmaiden, which is making its way through the US court system as of this writing.[44] Authorities say that Rigmaiden, who also goes by the name of Steven Travis,[45] ran a major tax-return fraud ring. Law enforcement had some help from an informant who passed along electronic communications from Daniel David that included the IP address in the communications. He used a wireless air card through a cell-phone provider to access the Internet. The current legal case against him considers whether or not stingray technology was used to help authorities pinpoint Rigmaiden's exact location via a wireless air card and whether that technology was used properly.

## EXPANDED CAPABILITIES OF THE NATIONAL COUNTERTERRORISM CENTER

Attorney General Eric Holder recently expanded the capabilities of the NCTC. Under these expanded capabilities, the NCTC may collect data about innocent US citizens for future analysis "for possible criminal behavior, even if there is no reason to suspect them. . . . NCTC can copy entire government databases—flight records, casino-employee lists, the names of Americans hosting foreign-exchange students and many others."[46] The storage limitation on this data is five years, unless the NCTC believes they have linked information to terrorism, in which case they may retain the data indefinitely. This information could be used to study patterns for any behavior that might be related to terrorism.

Just what kind of information might be of interest? Read on.

### What Online Radicalization Has to Do with Your Everyday Habits

Sometimes just reading the news online and visiting certain suspicious websites can make you look like a terrorist or a sympathizer. In France, President Nicolas Sarkozy announced that "Anyone who regularly consults Internet sites which promote terror or hatred or violence will be sentenced to prison. . . . Don't tell me it's not possible. What is possible for pedophiles should be possible for trainee terrorists and their supporters, too."[47] Although many have asked why the FBI was not tracking the Internet activities of the April 15, 2013 Boston Marathon bombers, caution warns us that just because someone follows links provided by a news site does not make that person a terrorist nor should it make it seem like he or she is being radicalized. This could be a case where a tragedy leads to an overreach by government.

*What Are the TIDE Files?*

TIDE is the acronym for the Terrorist Identities Datamart Environment. This database is made up of information about mostly non-US
citizens. The database contains more than seven hundred thousand identities and is growing. The profiles stored in the TIDE database are believed to be linked somehow to terrorists. Not everyone in the database is
a terrorist, but they may have only a few degrees of separation from a
known or suspected terrorist.[48]

The US National Counterterrorism Center can submit names (full or
partial) to TIDE. Analysts will update the file on each person as they find
new evidence or links to other people. Some TIDE entries will be added
to a terrorist watch list. In the case of the Boston Marathon bombings that
occurred on April 15, 2013, one of the bombers, Tamerlan Tsarnaev, was
on the list.[49] Who suggested he be on the list? The Federal Security Bureau (FSB) of Russia. The FSB notified the United States about him in
March 2011 and September 2011 because of their concerns that he had
been radicalized. Tsarnaev was a Chechen Russian immigrant who lived
in the Boston area. When the FSB sent the first notice in March 2011,
Tsarnaev and his family members were interviewed by the FBI but they
didn't find anything. It was only when the FSB notified the United States
again in late 2011 that Tsarnaev was added to TIDE database.[50]

*Does the Government Care about Celebrity Tweets?*

Here's a cautionary example of a celebrity tweeter and how the
government is treating her communications. Although most of Beyoncé's
tweets are for her fans, she recently posted some tweets and even an
Instagram for the fans of presidential hopeful Mitt Romney when she
posted on US election night, "Take that Mitches."[51] But that post is not
what will catch the attention of the nation's or the globe's data collectors.
All the tweets, posts, Facebook likes, web pages, and more of Beyoncé
and any other public celebrity or prominent figure are recorded for posterity. Why? It's considered part of the culture and potentially a part of
history. And who knows, today's Beyoncé's tweet could be tomorrow's
evidence.

*DHS Command Center and Others Monitor Popular Websites*

Are you a big user of social media? Watch what you "like," post, say,
and share because in the United States, the government and law enforcement are watching. Long past are the days when government and law
enforcement were blocked from accessing social media and other popular
"hang outs" to help them combat national security issues. In a show of
support for adding social-media and Internet searches to the everyday

surveillance job at the Department of Defense (DoD), the DoD posted this note on their portal: "Attention all Facebookers, Twitter tweeters and YouTubers: a new Defense Department policy authorizes you to access these and other Web 2.0 platforms from non-classified government computers, as long as it doesn't compromise operational security or involve prohibited activities or Web sites."[52]

It used to be the stuff of science fiction movies that a doctor in a lab could predict a pandemic and the ultimate geographic path it would take. Today the government plans to harness the power of social networking to look for trends in wellness around the globe. Leveraging a model that Google has perfected with their popular Flu Trends,[53] the government has been busily leveraging searches and social networks to predict issues that could impact national security. One test case is a DHS biosurveillance[54] program that will search across the most popular platforms looking for search terms, posts about going to the doctor, and other medical or illness-related incidents.

Here are a few other examples of government and financial groups that want to follow your social-media activities:

- The Pentagon is interested in leveraging new tools and approaches in the fight against cyber terrorists by searching through Facebook, Twitter, and other popular social-media sites. DARPA, the Defense Advanced Research Projects Agency, is creating the algorithms and search terms that will help the US military comb the Internet for social-media clues.[55]
- In the fight against gangs, the Chicago police department has installed technology and offered training to police officers so they can track gang members in real time on social media while working their beat.[56]
- The New York Federal Reserve bank started monitoring the web and determined that it must have a cohesive platform to target any hot spots of public opinion on the web at locations such as Facebook and Twitter. The Fed announced they want to review data to track how the messages they conveyed about monetary policy were perceived by the public.[57]
- The Fed issued a request for proposals asking companies to bid on a program to help them further their efforts to track any comments on the web. "The New York Fed is committed to improving its communications and engagement with the public in order to enhance and improve the public's understanding of its activities and the role it plays in supporting the U.S. economy. . . . To do that effectively, the New York Fed is interested in getting a better sense of the relevant concerns and discussions that are taking place in the public domain."[58]

- Countries like France and India are collecting information in the name of security. In France, the General Directorate for External Security collects Internet traffic, such as phone calls, emails, and social networking that flows in and out of France.[59] They keep the data on file in an effort to assist their police and security agencies in tracking trends, looking for criminal activity, and to help them in solving criminal cases.[60] In India, their program called the Centralized Monitoring System works in a similar way to France's, collecting data to help them with security. India's system appears to go a step further to record conversations via phone and email.[61]

## *Your Email and Social Sites Can Trigger an Investigation*

Think that nobody cares about your emails or what you post on social sites? Then ask the college students under FAA investigation if they ever dreamed that creating a Harlem Shake (a popular song that, when played, moves people to dance with abandon) video would trigger questions by the FAA. A group of students were on a flight to San Diego from Colorado Springs and started the Harlem Shake. They uploaded their video to YouTube and were surprised to have their school contacted by the FAA looking into whether or not the students violated flight safety rules.[62]

Watch what you post on sites like Instagram or Pinterest. Several police departments in the United States are now using the electronic billboard platform Pinterest to track down people on their most-wanted lists. Think of their approach as the old-fashioned wanted posters plastered on the entry hallway at your local post office.[63]

And now, if you are under investigation, law enforcement or the government can search deep into your social-media accounts if a "friend" connected to you provides permission. In one case, a federal judge ruled that it was legal for investigators to search a Facebook profile using a friend's account because they were given permission by the owner of the connected account. No subpoena or warrants necessary here! This ruling happened during the course of a racketeering trial in New York City. US District Judge William Pauley III stated that the accused person could not claim the Fourth Amendment to ask the court to ignore Facebook evidence that helped convince the court to indict him.[64] By getting access to someone's account who had friended the accused, investigators could look at messages that would not show up publicly due to privacy settings. Those messages, which included threats and details of former violent acts, were enough to get a search warrant for the case.

UNDERSTANDING THE ROLE OF THE NSA DATA CENTER

The more data we create, the larger the need to store the data and to figure out what happened in the past but also to try to predict future trends. The NSA is considered one of the world's leaders in collecting and analyzing data in a dynamic, stress-filled environment. It should be no surprise then that agencies such as the UK's MI5 and the United States' NSA are bursting at the seams in their current locations. According to a report in *Wired* magazine, the NSA has built a new data center for roughly $2 billion in Utah and that data center is to go online as of Fall 2013. The data center is reportedly to provide database storage for emails, cell-phone calls, Internet searches, travel itineraries, and any other digital data collected and stored for use in analysis.[65]

*In the Name of Safety, So Long Privacy*

> **Suppose twenty years ago Congress had proposed a law saying every citizen had to wear a radio transponder around his neck, all day and night, so the government could track him wherever he went. Can you imagine the outrage? But instead the citizens went right ahead and did it to themselves. In their pockets and purses, not around their necks, but the outcome is the same.**
> **—From the book *A Wanted Man* by Lee Child[66]**

In the quest for greater security, citizens of many countries are being tracked. This tracking is more complete and comprehensive than you can imagine. For example, the following types of information are commonly tracked by governments around the globe:

- Your digital tracks on the web—what you search, view, store, upload, download, and subscribe to.
- Your digital conversations—emails, texts, video chats, online chats and messaging, phone calls, and voice messages.
- Your digital whereabouts—where you sign in, visited Internet addresses, Wi-Fi locations, cell-phone locations.
- Public records such as births, real estate transactions, and deaths.
- Your face, eyes, voice, fingerprints, and handprints with vein patterns.

The well-known adage of Big Brother watching you has come into its own: all of that data is now collected daily by agencies that you might not even know about. Most of you may naturally think of the UK's MI5, Israel's Mossad, or the United States' FBI, CIA, or NSA. The data-collection owners are everywhere and several say their activities are justified because they are all in the name of better service or improved national security. Some agencies you may not even think of that are collecting data about you are the Veterans' Administration, Department of Education, Department of Transportation, Department of Health and Human Services, the Consumer Finance Protection Board, and the US Secret Service, or your country's equivalent if you are not a US citizen. Services such as Google and Amazon justify tracking you to provide you with a better user experience. Cybercriminals track you to exploit what they know about you for their own nefarious purposes.

According to *The National Biometrics Challenge* published by the national Science and Technology Council, "In response to the tragic events of September 11, 2011, the Department of State added a photograph repository and face recognition component to the Consular Consolidated Database (CCD) and began screening photos of visa applicants in 2004. CCD contains more than 110 million visa cases and nearly 90 million photographs . . . in 2004, the Department of Defense (DOD) deployed the Automated Biometric Identification system (ABIS) . . . adding palm print, face and iris matching . . . 6 million subjects and is increasing its transaction capacity from 8,000 to 20,000 per day."[67]

Data-collection technologies appear to be assisting the US government with tracking down bad guys, but at what price? Here are some cases where this technology did help thwart a bad event or apprehended someone wanted for allegedly committing a crime.

- One positive outcome came on May 27, 2011, when the DOD received a notice that an individual applied for US immigration benefits through DHS. Using the DOD ABIS system, they found that the individual was previously detained for stealing evidence during an investigation.[68]
- Tucson Border Patrol agents used the Integrated Automated Fingerprint Identification System (IAFIS) to access criminal records and stopped sexual predators from crossing the border into the United States on four separate occasions in 2011.[69]
- The FBI has created their Next Generation Identification (NGI) system with over one hundred million Americans' information stored on it.[70] It works with the Repository for Individuals of Special Concern (RISC). Officers were fingerprinting a subject based on a citizen tip that the person might be a witness or suspect in a local shopping-center murder. The subject was fingerprinted with the RISC's mobile fingerprinting device and within minutes agents found active warrants for previous charges of attempted murder, attempted robbery, and kidnapping.[71]

## NOTES

1. Yves-Alexandre de Montjoye, César A. Hidalgo, Michel Verleysen, and Vincent D. Blondel, "Unique in the Crowd: The Privacy Bounds of Human Mobility," *Scientific Reports* 3 (March 25, 2013).

2. De Montjoye et al., "Unique in the Crowd."

3. "Mobile Payments Today, Statistics," as of September 23, 2013, www.mobilepaymentstoday.com/research/312/Trends-Statistics.

4. Alex Dickinson, "Yahoo CEO Feared Jail over NSA Scandal," *New York Post*, September 12, 2013.

5. Dickinson, "Yahoo CEO Feared Jail over NSA Scandal."

6. Marcia Hoffman, Rainey Reitman, and Cindy Cohn, "2012: When the Government Comes Knocking, Who Has Your Back?" The Electronic Frontier Foundations' 2nd annual report, May 31, 2012, EFF.org.

7. Google's Transparency Report 2012, www.google.com/transparencyreport/.

8. GigaOm's Structure: Data 2013 live coverage, March 20, 2013, gigaom.com/2013/03/20/structuredata-2013-live-coverage/ and gigaom.com/2013/03/20/even-the-cia-is-struggling-to-deal-with-the-volume-of-real-time-social-data/.

9. Jason Howerton, "CIA Tech Boss on Your Data," *The Blaze*, March 20, 2013.

10. "History of the Federal Judiciary, Foreign Intelligence Surveillance Court," Federal Judicial Center, July 19, 2013, www.fjc.gov/history/home.nsf/page/courts_special_fisc.html.

11. Peter Finn and Ellen Nakashima, "Obama Defends Sweeping Surveillance Efforts," *Washington Post*, June 7, 2013.

12. Jill Reilly and *Daily Mail* reporter, "Whistleblower Edward Snowden Smuggled Out Secrets with an Everyday Thumb Drive Banned from NSA Offices," *Daily Mail*, June 13, 2013.

13. US Government Printing Office, "Fourth Amendment," www.gpo.gov/fdsys/pkg/GPO-CONAN-1992/pdf/GPO-CONAN-1992-10-5.pdf.

14. Steven J. Vaughan-Nichols, "Raytheon Riot: Defense Spying Is Coming to Social Networks," *Networking*, ZDNet, February 12, 2013, www.zdnet.com/raytheon-riot-defense-spying-is-coming-to-social-networks-7000011191/.

15. Ryan Gallagher, "Software That Tracks People on Social Media Created by Defence Firm," February 10, 2013.

16. C-Span Video Library, "FBI Oversight," March 30, 2011, www.c-spanvideo.org/program/298757-1.

17. General Keith Alexander, NSA Director, July 9, 2012 at an AEI event.

18. James Bamford, "The NSA Is Building the Country's Biggest Spy Center (Watch What You Say)," *Wired*, March 15, 2012, www.wired.com/threatlevel/2012/03/ff_nsadatacenter/all/1.

19. Reporters without Borders, "The Enemies of the Internet," special edition, surveillance.rsf.org/en/.

20. Renesys, Internet Events Bulletin, November 29, 2012, www.renesys.com/eventsbulletin/2012/11/SY-1354184790.html.

21. Google Transparency Report, Sorted by Country: Syria for Year 2013, www.google.com/transparencyreport/traffic/disruptions/#expand=Y2013.

22. Damien Gayle, "UK Government Plans to Track ALL Web Use: MI5 to Install 'Black Box' Spy Devices to Monitor British Internet Traffic," *Daily Mail*, February 16, 2013, www.dailymail.co.uk/sciencetech/article-2274388/MI5-install-black-box-spy-devices-monitor-UK-internet-traffic.html#ixzz2ZPPiRqNC.

23. Press Association, "MI5 and Industry Join Forces to Fight Cybercrime," *Guardian*, March 27, 2013.

24. China Business Climate Survey Report, AmCham China, 2013, web.resource.amchamchina.org/cmsfile/2013/03/29/0640e5a7e0c8f86ff4a380150357bbef.pdf.

25. James McGregor, "Don't Bring Your Cell Phone to Meetings in China, You Might Get Hacked," *Quartz*, September 28, 2012, qz.com/9003/9003/.

26. Frank Langfitt, "In China, Beware": A Camera May Be Watching You," NPR, January 29, 2013.

27. Langfitt, "In China, Beware."

28. Jennifer Valentino-Devries, "People's Locations Could Be Tracked," *Wall Street Journal*, June 7, 2013.

29. Research provided by Privacy International on Afghanistan. From the Court of Afghanistan, January 4, 2004.

30. Robert Verkaik, "EU Super Spies to Get Right to Snoop on Your Emails, Website Visits, Medical Data and Police Records," *Daily Mail*, February 9, 2013.

31. "Top 10 Countries That Censor The Internet," List Verse, October 2, 2010, listverse.com/2010/10/02/top-10-countries-that-censor-the-internet/.

32. David Silito, "Libraries to Store All UK Web Content," BBC Europe, April 5, 2013.

33. Jay Alabaster, "Library of Congress Saves 500 Million Tweets Per Day in Archives," *Computerworld*, January 8, 2013.

34. Silito, "Libraries to Store All UK Web Content."

35. EPIC, "EPIC v. Department of Homeland Security: Media Monitoring," February 23, 2012, epic.org/foia/epic-v-dhs-media-monitoring/default.html.

36. *Russia Today* interview with William Binney, the former head of NSA's global digital data-gathering program, December 4, 2012, rt.com/usa/surveillance-spying-e-mail-citizens-178/.

37. Ian Drury, "Catch These Men! 16 of Europe's Most Wanted Criminals Are on the Run in the UK," *Daily Mail*, February 3, 2013, www.dailymail.co.uk/news/article-2272977/Europes-wanted-16-criminals-list-run-UK.html.

38. Shaun Waterman, "Terror Watch List Grows to 75,000," *Washington Times*, May 3, 2013.

39. Binney interview.

40. Case of M.M. v. The United Kingdom (Application no. 24029/07), European Court of Human Rights, hudoc.echr.coe.int/sites/fra/pages/search.aspx?i=001-114517#.

41. Douglas, J., Opinion of the Court, Supreme Court of the United States, 357 U.S. 116, Kent v. Dulles, Certiorari to the United States Court of Appeals for the District of Columbia Circuit, No. 481 Argued: April 10, 1958 — Decided: June 16, 1958.

42. DHS Electronic Advance Passenger Information System, https://ea-pis.cbp.dhs.gov.

43. BBC News Europe, "MEPs Back Deal to Give Air Passenger Data to US," April 19, 2012.

44. Jennifer Valentino-DeVries, "Judges Questioned Use of Cellphone Tracking Devices," *Wall Street Journal*, March 27, 2013.

45. Wyn Hornbucklet, "Hacker Indicted in Massive Tax, Mail, and Wire Fraud Scheme," Public Affairs, FBI, April 8, 2010. www.justice.gov/criminal/cybercrime/press-releases/2010/rigmaidenIndict.pdf.

46. "New NCTC Guidelines," EPIC.org, https://epic.org/privacy/profiling/2012-NCTC-Guidelines.pdf.

47. Raphael Satter, "Sarkozy: Jail Those Who Browse Terror Websites," AP/*Bloomberg Businessweek*, March 22, 2012, quoting Nicolas Sarkozy during a campaign rally in Strasbourg, France.

48. Karen DeYoung, "Terror Database Has Quadrupled in Four Years," *Washington Post*, March 25, 2007.

49. Eric Schmitt and Michael S. Schmidt, "2 U.S. Agencies Added Boston Bomb Suspect to Watch Lists," *New York Times*, April 24, 2013, www.nytimes.com/2013/04/25/us/tamerlan-tsarnaev-bomb-suspect-was-on-watch-lists.html?_r=0.

50. Luis Martinez, "Boston Bombing Suspect's Name Was in US Terrorism Databases," ABC News, April 25, 2013, abcnews.go.com/US/boston-bombing-suspects-us-terrorism-databases/story?id=19037892.

51. Luchina Fisher, "Stars Tweet on Election Night," ABC News, November 7, 2012.

52. US Department of Defense site on social media,.

53. See Google.org Flu Trends at www.google.org/flutrends/us/.

54. Aliya Sternstein, "DHS Tries Monitoring Social Media for Signs of Biological Attacks," NextGov, November 9, 2012, www.nextgov.com/defense/2012/11/dhs-tries-monitoring-social-media-signs-biological-attacks/59406/.

55. "Social Media in Strategic Communication," DARPA, www.darpa.mil/Our_Work/I2O/Programs/Social_Media_in_Strategic_Communication_(SMISC).aspx.

56. Emily Gogolak, "Inside the Weird World of Tracking Gangs on Social Media," *The Atlantic*, July 27, 2012.

57. Neal Ungerleider, "The Federal Reserve Plans to Monitor Facebook, Twitter, Google News," Fast Company, October 11, 2011, www.fastcompany.com/1786730/federal-reserve-plans-monitor-facebook-twitter-google-news.

58. Walter Hamilton, "New York Fed to Monitor Facebook and Twitter," *Los Angeles Times*, September 29, 2011.

59. Steven Erlanger, "France, Too, Is Sweeping Up Data, Newspaper Reveals," *New York Times*, July 4, 2013.

60. Erlanger, "France, Too, Is Sweeping Up Data, Newspaper Reveals."

61. Pranesh Prakash, "How Surveillance Works in India," *New York Times*, July 10, 2013.

62. Ryan Grenoble, "'Harlem Shake' FAA Investigation: Colorado College Students' Dance in Plane Triggers Federal Inquiry," *Huffington Post*, March 1, 2013, www.huffingtonpost.com/2013/02/28/harlem-shake-faa-plane-colorado-college_n_2783065.html.

63. Justine Sharrock, "To Pin a Criminal," BuzzFeed FWD, January 11, 2013.

64. United States District Court, Southern District of New York, United States of America against Joshua Meregildo et al., defendants, William H. Pauley III District Judge, August 10, 2012.

65. James Bamford, "The NSA Is Building the Country's Biggest Spy Center (Watch What You Say)," *Wired*, March 15, 2012.

66. Lee Child, *A Wanted Man* (New York: Delacorte Press, 2012), 245.

67. *The National Biometrics Challenge*, National Science and Technology Council Subcommittee on Biometrics and Identity Management, September 2011.

68. *The National Biometrics Challenge*.

69. *The National Biometrics Challenge*

70. Christina DesMarais, "How the Feds Are Tracking Us," *PC World*, September 8, 2012.

71. *The National Biometrics Challenge*.

# FOUR

## Chased Online by Criminals and Snoops

If you ever come home to discover your door kicked in and valuables taken, you realize two things right away: that you are a victim, and that your home is a crime scene. After the initial shock, you might leave the scene without touching anything, to avoid interfering with evidence that could help investigators find your stolen items and the criminals. You call 911, then wait for local law officers to arrive so that you can walk through everything together. Your neighbors might even recall details of possible suspects in the area that day.

> **I am not sure who owns cybercrime at the local level. And that is a problem.**
> —Chuck Wexler, executive director of the Police Executive Research
> Forum[1]

In contrast, the digital world makes it difficult to determine what constitutes a victim, a crime scene, and a criminal. For example, if your credit card company is hacked into and your identity stolen, both you and the company are victims. However, your local police department is not staffed and probably not trained to deal with these crimes. When the computer breach is realized, those responsible for the technology systems often need to shut the breach down immediately to keep others from being impacted, which destroys valuable forensic evidence. There are typically no eyewitnesses to the crime.

For those reasons and others, it is important to understand where your data is online, how criminals and cybersnoops go after it, and what you can do to minimize the damage when a breach occurs. Privacy is crucial to stopping online criminals. The more they know or can figure out about your online activity—your bank accounts, your tax filings, your electronic medical records, your children's activities—the easier it will be for a criminal to take what he wants from you. Protecting your privacy is the first line of defense against the bad guys.

## IN THE CLOUD WHETHER YOU WANT TO BE OR NOT

Since the start of the twenty-first century, a new great migration has been happening: our data is moving off our personal computers and onto the cloud. In many respects, this move occurs because we like what the cloud has to offer.[2]

Whether you want to be in the cloud or not, you are already there. Do you use online movie services such as Hulu, Amazon, or Netflix? Those movies are in the cloud. Do you use AOL, Yahoo!, Google, Hotmail, or other email services? Almost all of the versions supported now are cloud based. If you use photo-sharing sites such as Shutterfly, Snapfish, Smug-Mug, Photobucket, Flickr, or Instagram, your pictures are in the cloud. When you access map services, social networks, music, and video, almost all of these apps are managed in the cloud.

### What Is the Cloud, and How Can It Help Me?

The cloud is a vast system of interrelated computer resources located remotely and accessible over a network. One way to think of the cloud is to visualize the post office boxes in your local post office. You may have mail circulating all around the globe in various stages, sometimes landing in a post office box at another city to move to the next destination, but eventually, your mail is delivered to your own personal post office box. That is just one part of how the cloud works.

By storing your information in the cloud, you can synchronize and access it across all of your devices, so that any device can be your post office box at any moment. If you store cute pet photos in the cloud, you can show any of your photos to a friend or coworker at any time on your smartphone, tablet, or any other Internet-connected device.

### Easy Access and Offsite Storage

Convenient access to your information is not the only advantage the cloud offers. Cloud providers also offer cost-effective (often free) and easy ways to store your information offsite. Over time, our phones, tablets, and computers turn into scrapbooks of our lives. Messages from loved ones, important projects, pictures, and videos become irreplaceable records of real-life moments. If all that is stored locally, you have to remember to back up your information to an external drive or flash drive. But what if you forget to back up those wedding photos that your friends took, and suddenly your device crashes? Cloud providers promise to wipe away those disasters if you just trust them with your data.

However, before you move everything to the cloud, it is important to understand the risks involved and your security and privacy options.

---

TOOLBOX

**Are you interested in storing your data in the cloud for convenience and to guard against losing important files to crashed hard drives or stolen devices? Do your research before choosing a data-storage provider. Here are a few popular options that you may want to sample to see if they are right for you.**

- **Apple Cloud: www.apple.com/icloud/**
- **Google Drive: https://drive.google.com/start#home**
- **Dropbox: www.dropbox.com/**
- **Microsoft SkyDrive: https://skydrive.live.com**
- **Amazon Cloud Drive: www.amazon.com/clouddrive/learn-more**

---

## HOW DATA STORED IN THE CLOUD IS AT RISK

**Did you know the volume of information in the world is doubling every two years and less than 1 percent of the world's data is analyzed, and less than 20 percent of it is protected?**
—Arthur Coviello Jr., executive chairman, RSA[3]

Arthur Coviello Jr., the executive chairman at the security company RSA, opened up the RSA security conference in 2013 with some staggering facts. He said that the world stored a "pettabyte of data in the cloud, which would be the equivalent of 4.9 quadrillion books, yet less than 20 percent of that pettabyte of information was protected." He posed the question to the group—"Is your data in that 20 percent?"[4]

The Cloud Security Alliance issued a report for the top threats to data stored in the cloud for 2013. Ranking in the top three are data breaches, data loss, and account hijacking.[5]

- **Data breaches** occur when cybercriminals access the cloud services provider's system and steal information. The key target during a data breach is often intellectual property such as programming code or end-user account information, which might include name, address, email address, account ID and password, and possibly credit card information.
- **Data loss** is either accidental or intentional loss of your data. The data loss could be due to natural disasters such as hurricanes or earthquakes; manmade disasters such as poor maintenance prac-

tices or a disgruntled employee; or due to cybercriminals breaching the system and running off with the data, leaving destruction behind them.

- **Account hijacking** is when cybercriminals trick you into clicking on a link or opening an attachment so they can sit and watch your keystrokes and take over your account when they see a website or set of commands that interests them. As demand for cloud services grow, cybercriminals will be less interested in accessing your hard drive and more interested in stealing your account credentials so they can take over your life in the cloud.

The points of entry are increasingly sophisticated. Some cybercriminals use sophisticated spear phishing, a focused email scam, to target a specific person or entity. Others hijack press releases of legitimate companies and convince you to click or download information.

Yet another set of cybercriminals are particularly expert at poisoning search-engine results. Google reported that 1.3 percent of their search results are infected, which means that if you get one hundred potential hits for your search request, one of them could be a trap. These cybercriminals are fond of using current news events to set their malicious software trap. Any hot news topic presents perfect opportunities to poison search results.

## The Hazards of "Free" Services

When you store your data in the cloud, your data is no longer on your personal device storage. This requires a level of trust and confidence that the service provider will keep your information private, not sell your information to others for their own financial gain, make your information available to you every minute of every day, and protect you from cybercriminals.

These implied promises may be logical assumptions on your part, but that does mean they are actually spelled out in the service-level agreements, security statements, or privacy agreements that you must choose to "accept" before you can finish signing in to access the service. This is especially true when the service is free.

- **Software Glitches and Security Breaches**. Unfortunately, some cloud consumers have found out the hard way how hard it is for the cloud services provider to live up to all of the assumptions and promises made. For example, at one point in 2011 the free storage service Dropbox had a software glitch that allowed people to log into any account without a password for roughly four hours before it was fixed. In March 2013, the popular free idea- and note-storing service called Evernote had a security breach the resulted in fifty million users having their user names, passwords, and email addresses compromised. Since many consumers use the same email address across services, this can create a major risk.

- **Whose Data Is It?** When you sign up for a free cloud service, it is important to ask up front, "Whose data is it?" There are several reasons why you need a definitive answer to what seems like a simple question. You probably answered, "I created it, the data is mine." But the privacy statements of many free services say that the information you provide and post belongs to them. For example, on Facebook, the privacy policy implies that your "gender," which you can change at any time, belongs to them.[6] Facebook may sell your profile data to a marketing company, including your gender, because it belongs to them.[7] That is why it is important that you understand the privacy and security agreement between you and the service provider. Make sure you know up front what the service level agreement is to get "your" data back in case the company goes bankrupt and the service goes offline.
- **Is My Data Always Available to Me?** Availability is also key. Data on your computer's hard drive or your smartphone is always available to you unless the device crashes or is physically someplace else. Your free cloud services (and even the cloud services you pay a subscription for) may not be. For example, the sites for Amazon's Prime and Netflix had a major service disruption on Christmas Eve 2012 when the Amazon cloud had service problems.[8] Cloud service disruptions are common, and free services rarely offer anyone that you can talk with to find out the status. This growing problem has opened the door to services that track cloud service outages, such as DownRightNow.com. If "your" data is currently unavailable to you because the cloud service is not working, you can check DownRightNow.com to see if it is just you and your data that are separated, or if the rest of the world is experiencing the same separation anxiety.

## If Colin Powell Can Be Hacked, So Can You

If the Bush family, Colin Powell, Hillary Clinton, and Burger King aren't safe from hackers, are you?

- The Bush family had a hacker break in and steal their personal emails and pictures. The same hackers went after Colin Powell's Facebook account and posted some of the photographs they stole from the Bush family onto Colin Powell's Facebook page. The hackers posted messages such as "YOU WILL BURN IN HE--, BUSH" and "KILL THE ILLUMINATI!" Powell sent out a public apology to his followers, saying "I'm sorry you have to see all the stupid, obscene posts that are popping up."[9]

- Vice President Biden and First Lady Michele Obama were hacked and had their credit profiles posted online.[10]
- Burger King's Twitter account was hacked in February 2013 for roughly an hour. While the hackers had control, they announced that Burger King had sold themselves to McDonalds. They sent out fifty-five tweets, some of which included some obscene messages and threats, before Burger King contacted Twitter to suspend the tweets.[11] On April 23, 2013, the Twitter account of the Associated Press was hacked. Before the AP could stop the hackers, they sent out thousands of tweets. One tweet made the stock market plunge temporarily. The tweet in question was, "Breaking: Two Explosions in the White House and Barack Obama is injured."[12]
- Your university email account is not safe either. In a recent example of how hard it is to protect email accounts, California State University–San Marcos had an incident of voter fraud during their Student Council election, and the mastermind was sentenced to a one-year jail sentence.[13] The computer team that runs the university network noticed odd digital traffic, dug into the traffic, and found a number of election votes were coming from one computer. They watched that same computer log into a university official's account to read a few emails. Using keyloggers that he installed, the twenty-two-year-old student created an account takeover of roughly 745 university user IDs and passwords.[14] The student used the stolen credentials to vote for himself and his friends. Police searched his computer and found search terms such as "rig," "keylogger," and even "jail time for keylogger." He further compounded the issue by creating fake Facebook pages using real students' names, posted fake posts, and tried to make it look as if he was being framed. After hearing the case, Judge Larry Burns said, "That's the phenomenal misjudgment I can't get around. He's on fire for this crime, and then he pours gasoline on it to try to cover it up."[15]

## PROTECTING YOURSELF IN THE CLOUD

The best protection in the cloud is similar to the best protection on the street: don't trust strangers with your keys, and don't look or act like a victim. You can minimize risk while online by taking reasonable precautions and presenting yourself with consistency and confidence.

### Keeping the Bad Guys at Bay

Though nothing gives a 100 percent guarantee that you can keep all hackers out, here are some good steps to take:

- Use a different password and strong passwords for every cloud account.
- Have more than one email address that you use to separate your social media accounts from your home email and from your online purchases.
- Wherever available, implement second-factor authentication, which means you only access the service from a trusted computer or by typing in a code sent to your mobile phone.
- Think twice before linking accounts to each other. For example, if you set up LinkedIn so that one post on LinkedIn updates Facebook and Twitter at the same time, a hacker that takes over your account on LinkedIn now controls your social media life.
- Click with care so you don't infect your computer or get your account taken over.
- Never click on links in emails that tell you to change your social-media network's password.

## Building an Identity on the Internet

> The possibility that one's personal content will be published and become known one day—either by mistake or through criminal interference—will always exist. People will be held responsible for their virtual associations, past and present, which raises the risk for nearly everyone since people's online networks tend to be larger and more diffuse than their physical ones.
> —Eric Schmidt and Jared Cohen, *The New Digital Age: Reshaping the Future of People, Nations and Business*[16]

Like it or not, you will be researched on the web. If you have digital footprint at all or a very small one, the person doing the search may be left wondering what you are hiding. Unless you are completely out of the job market, whether for paid positions or volunteer positions, it is wise to proactively build and manage your identity on the Internet. If you do not, you run the risk of being perceived negatively or having an Internet troll pretend they are you.

Many people start by searching for their name on their favorite search engine and end there. They find that they do not have the time or the interest in going much further. If you stop there you might be missing some essential strategies for establishing your identity while actively managing your brand, your security, and your privacy.

Here are three easy steps you can take to establish your online identity, manage your brand, and protect your privacy and security:

- Define your brand. If you want the world to see a multifaceted you online—a single, hip professional, who loves to hike, works hard, is a leader in community service, provides mentoring to others, and is a thought leader in your field—then see every online account you hold and post you make as an *opportunity* to let that brand shine. You do not want to repeat the mistake of a Delta Gamma sorority woman at the University of Maryland. She wrote a letter to her sorority sisters voicing her displeasure at how they were conducting themselves at social events. Rather than taking a sweet or professional tone, her email was laced with the "F-bomb" and other unmentionable crude references.[17] She will have some work to do online to regain her reputation and polish her brand.

- Establish your good name on key social-networking accounts such as Twitter, Facebook, LinkedIn, and About.me. You may find that other social networking sites such as Instagram and Pinterest add a visual dimension to your brand. If you have videos that complement your brand, whether they feature you or other thought leaders, you can set up a YouTube channel and post those videos. Do not pick too many platforms, or you run the risk of not keeping them up to date. When setting up your account, lock down those privacy and security settings and think carefully before you begin mixing your weekend pals with your weekday work associates.

- Stay in touch. Create and post thoughtful musings, find articles that you like and share them, and post topical videos or graphics. Then ask a trusted friend or family member to critique you on a regular basis. Ask them to help you with your online brand, starting with these questions: Are your posts interesting? Do they enhance or conflict with your personal brand? Are any of your posts too revealing? Is there a possibility that the posts may put your privacy or security at risk?

---

**TOOLBOX**

**Vizify (www.vizify.com) is a cloud tool created in 2011 that helps you create a graphical profile online. Think of it as a visual, digital "bio" that pulls in images and text from your social media and professional accounts such as Instagram, Twitter, LinkedIn, Foursquare, and Facebook.**

**The goal is a visual profile of both your professional and personal side. Vizify provides you with a quick snapshot of how you portray your identity online, helping you manage your online identity and share it with potential employers, potential or current mates, coworkers, neighbors, or anyone that you plan on meeting or interacting with online or in person.**

**In addition to the visual profile, you can also create vizcards, which are pithy sound bites about you shown in a graphical way.**

## SNOOPS AND WHAT YOU CAN DO ABOUT THEM

The digital devices you use and the information stored about you at lightning speed in the cloud make you vulnerable to snoops. Digital surveillance technology has improved vastly, and now most anyone can afford to play James Bond. Many people don't realize just how pervasive digital devices are in our lives and how they are recording everything we say and do. So make sure you live the Golden Rule at all times because you might end up on YouTube!

*How Snoops Set Up Their Tradecraft*

Typically, snooping starts when the snoops insert a program onto your phone, laptop, or tablet using infected links or attachments in emails or websites. They then have the control over your device that they need to spy using simple apps that record pictures, videos, and audio—all silently and hard to detect. If your digital devices are acting strangely by powering down and on without warning, performing overly slow, or apps are crashing, you might be under surveillance.

Some cybercriminals, or even snoops like a soon-to-be-ex or a neighbor, conduct their crimes with their own gadgets. They can buy what looks like a toy airplane or helicopter and launch it like a personal drone, recording hours of video and audio. A quick search on popular Internet stores show everyday items such as stuffed animals, plug outlets in a wall, thumb drives, clocks, calculators, pens, and glasses can now be equipped with chips that can record images, text, photos, and videos. (By the way, this technology is not only for snoops and cybercriminals. It can be helpful as a way to double check on things at home while you are away and to even provide a little assurance if you are worried about children or the elderly.)

*Protecting Yourself from Snoops*

As described in chapter 2, to protect yourself from snoops and cybercriminals, you can disable video cameras on phones and tablets when not actively in use and turn off video and voice mode when you are not using your social networking or messaging platforms. Pay attention to devices at work and at home. Red or green blinking lights may indicate a wireless connection or that they are recording.

Technologies are also available to help you uncover a snoop or a cybercriminal who has implanted a device in your home or office. For example, radio frequency (RF) bug detectors can scan a room looking for the frequencies that a video camera would emit. They may also pick up a Wi-Fi network, so before you point the finger at someone, be sure that you verify what the RF bug detector found. Spy camera detectors can find cameras that might not transmit a frequency by looking for the small glass viewfinder of a camera and alerting you.

Remember that if you want to digitally snoop on someone else, you should be aware of legal lines that you might cross. Claiming ignorance of the law does not keep you out of jail. Before becoming a "spy," remember to check state and federal laws. Often you must notify that an area is under surveillance or ask permission for recordings.

---

TOOLBOX

**The following is a short list of tools you may want to sample on your computers and/or mobile devices. They offer easy ways to encrypt software, anonymize traffic (somewhat), and force messages to expire. These apps may not be right for you,and remember, no system is foolproof. However, these apps create extra work for a snoop to scoop your digital data.**

- **Silent Circle: Encrypts messages, phone calls, and texts**
- **HushMail: Allows you to send encrypted and private emails**
- **10 minute mail: provides disposable emails**
- **"Off the record" features: Many chat platforms have "off the record" features that disable logging**
- **TOR: An online anonymity router developed by the Naval Observatory to help prevent traffic-flow surveillance[18]**
- **SnapChat: Send a photo or text and it will be deleted within ten seconds**

---

## FINANCIAL VULNERABILITIES IN THE CLOUD

Cyberattacks on banks seem to hit the headlines at least a few times a month, but what exactly do these attacks mean? Prior to online banking, financial companies faced a series of threats—armed bank robberies, forged checks, fraudulent account openings, unauthorized access to accounts, insider threats from stealing from the vault, and selling customer information. The banks still face those threats, but they have added to their list of worries with online transactions.

Ironically, the surge in cybercrime has had an unexpected benefit: bank robberies are down.[19] Robbing a bank is considered old school in crime circles with very high risk and low payouts. In 2010, criminals robbing banks made about $29.5 million, while cybercriminals leveraged the Internet to steal roughly $1.8 billion from accounts, committing debit and credit card fraud, and leveraging ATM and point-of-sale skimming devices in 2012.

*How Safe Is Online Banking?*

When discussing banking transactions, safety is a relative term. If you physically go to a branch, you run the risk of a car or pedestrian accident, or bumping into check fraud thieves, or even a bank robbery. When you bank online those issues melt into the background, but you expose yourself to different attacks. If your device is infected you may become a victim of "account takeover." If the site you are visiting is compromised, your data and identity might be stolen. If you get an email that tells you that you need to follow their helpful links, you could become the victim of a scam.

The good news for US consumer accounts is that you have financial Regulation E concerning electronic transfers of money to back you up. Regulation E states that any unauthorized activity on your online consumer account that is reported by you within sixty days must be reimbursed to you by your bank. (Note that business accounts do not have this level of protection. If you are worried about protecting your business accounts, talk to your relationship manager at the bank.)

So for consumers, banking online is relatively safe, but there is a word of caution from the FBI director. Back in 2009, FBI Director Robert Mueller and his wife had a "teachable moment"; as a result, they no longer bank online. The teachable moment arrived in the form of a convincing email sent to Director Mueller's email account. "It looked pretty legitimate . . . ," said Director Mueller. "They had mimicked the e-mails that the bank would ordinarily send out to its customers; they'd mimicked them very well."[20] Thankfully, Director Mueller did not fall for the scam and showed the fake email to his wife. His wife decided at that moment that the scammers were too close for comfort, and she announced that they would no longer bank online.

*Is It Safe to File Taxes Online?*

Online tax filings are on the rise, but so are cybercriminals that attempt to intercept your data or get in between you and your refund. Identity thefts from tax cases, committed through offline and online means, increased 62 percent in 2013. The IRS stated that nearly 80 percent of taxpayers filed online for 2012, which means that cybercriminals are inventing new tools to try to get in between you and your refunds or to steal your identity.

If you decide to file your taxes online in the United States, here are some tips that help reduce the risks:

- **Background check your filing service.** If you are using a service to do the filing for you, do a background check first. The IRS maintains a page on its .gov site that lists authorized IRS e-file providers.

Search the IRS site for "Authorized IRS e-file Providers for Individuals." It offers you a listing based upon your zip code.

- **Be link savvy.** The IRS will never send you an email asking you to click on a link and provide them with personal information. They will also not send you attachments that you "need to open" without contacting you first. If you receive an email and you are not sure if it is legitimate, call the IRS directly.
- **Download forms with caution.** Only download tax forms from IRS.gov and not any other "helpful" sites, because they might be scam tax sites.
- **Know your computer.** If you are filling out information or filing online, do not use a public computer. Make sure you know the computer and are relatively sure that the operating system, browser, and antivirus software are up to date.
- **Store your return securely.** Although it is tempting to keep your return on your hard drive, it is best to save it in offline storage such as a thumb drive. Keep that offline storage locked up so it does not accidentally walk away with your identity.

For those filing taxes online in the UK, you can find information on filing online at the official website of HM Revenue and Customs.

### Tax Collectors Watch from the Clouds

Around the globe, tax collectors are going online to catch tax cheats and filers that made mistakes. It is best to be online with your tax collector so you know what you are dealing with.

For example, the tax authority in Lithuania uses Google Maps Street View to check on taxpayers. Using the technology, Lithuania claims to have found one hundred property owners and thirty construction companies that either filed incorrectly or they were trying to cheat the system.

In the United States, the IRS has already cross-referenced tax rolls with Facebook and Twitter. Greece uses satellite maps from various sources to find swimming pools, which carry their own taxes.

## RISKS TO ONLINE MEDICAL RECORDS

When medical records move online, both patients and providers can reap the benefits of data storage and quick access that the cloud provides. If you need care and cannot get to your primary doctor, another provider can access your records online. The convenience of doctor conferences across experts is also expedited when they can share a patient's profile electronically. Some hospitals even provide an app to their patients so they can see their records online. An online app that shows your health record could potentially alert you to medical identity theft and fraud, similar to the way online banking lets you see your statement every day or even by the hour and transaction.

Some experts say that health care systems that move to the cloud have better security and reliability. However, does the information about you, at the individual level, get afforded the protections it needs so your records are not wide open to health care fraud, identity theft, or worse?

The problem for health care systems is less about whether or not the systems are in the cloud, but how they capture information about you during your patient visit and who watches that data as it moves through your life. Some of the systems are time-consuming and clunky, leaving doctors and nurses to complain they see fewer patients each day and spend more time in front of the computer. Electronic records have become hard to manage, and when nobody's watching that particular record, fraudulent billing and transactions have occurred.

A search of the Privacyrights.org database for the full year of 2012 and the first quarter of 2013 revealed 266 breaches of medical records reported during the fifteen-month time span. And those are the breaches we know about. The range of records impacted during each incident ranged from one thousand to one hundred thousand per breach. In the United States, the new health care laws under the Affordable Care Act require each state to use a process to determine a person's health care insurance eligibility. Each state can use its own system or the system built by the US government. They will aggregate, in one place, data from your personal life that is located across seven federal and state agencies, including agencies such as the Social Security Administration, the Department of Homeland Security, and the Veterans Administration.[21]

Your best protection is to be informed. Take the time to ask your doctor where your patient records are stored and how they are treated. Consider using a specific email address for all of your health care interactions that you do not use for your online banking, social media, or other online interactions.

## CHILDREN AT RISK ON THE INTERNET

**I'm absolutely convinced that parents will have to have the "online privacy" talk with their children before "the sex talk.". . . It might be when they're eight years old, you'll be saying "'on't put that online! It'll come back to bite you!" and then have to explain why.**
**—Eric Schmidt, CEO of Google**[22]

Children are one of the fastest-growing age demographics to be hit by cybercriminals. To protect our children, we need to stay aware of their online behavior and experiences. Unfortunately, that is easier said than done.

*Hiding from the Good Guys*

Unfortunately, when a teenager thinks about protecting privacy, the teen usually is concerned about protecting certain information from dis- covery by his or her parents. Children do not naturally think of chatting with strangers online as dangerous, and they must be taught by their parents or the other caring adults in their lives. At a relatively young age, most children know how to set up security and privacy settings. The problem is that children typically set up their privacy and security set- tings to keep their parents out, and unbeknownst to them, they let the bad guys in.

In a recent McAfee study, 70 percent of teens admitted they hide their online behavior very well from their parents.[23] If you are thinking, "Not my teen," just remember that number: seven out of ten teens are going around the rules online.

What do parents have to say about their teens' online behavior? Ac- cording to the same McAfee study, 73.5 percent of parents say they trust that their teens stay away from inappropriate content, and another 22.8 percent of parents say they are so overwhelmed they just hope for the best.

Those trusting or overwhelmed parents might be surprised to see the survey results that 43 percent of teens look at online violence every day. And what else are teens doing online? Fifteen percent admitted they have hacked into someone else's social-media account. Thirty-two percent ad- mitted they have purposely accessed porn online.

According to a Pew Internet study, almost one in five teens has used their cell phone to send sexually suggestive images of themselves.[24] Old- er teens are much more likely than younger teens to send and receive "sexts," or sexually based text messages.

Here are the top three ways teens keep parents from following their tracks:

1. Clearing the browser history when they are done surfing.
2. Closing what they look at when the parent enters the room.
3. Hiding and deleting instant messages and videos.

*Children Are Vulnerable to Identity Theft*

Even if you and your kids are in perfect sync regarding their online security, they are still at risk for identity theft.

Roughly half a million children are victims of identity theft each year, and roughly half of those are under the age of six.[25] Studies by the Iden- tity Theft Assistance Center (ITAC) indicate that the top compromised piece of ID for a child ID-theft victim is their social security number, and that that one in forty households with children will have a minor with their identity stolen.

The best way to protect your children from identity theft is to call the credit-reporting companies and ask that their credit file be frozen. You can also request a free credit report annually to check their credit background.

In addition, it is critical that you teach your children never to use their names online or to provide any personal information such as address, phone number, or date of birth without consulting with you first.

### Sexual Predators Target Kids Online

> **Many of the child exploitation cases under Operation Orion began with a child or teen chatting with someone he or she met online.**
> —ICE Director John Morton, after busting a child pornography ring and rescuing eighteen victims [26]

Recent studies [27] show that although sexual predators still hang out near schools, malls, and other places where kids will be, the Internet has become the predators' preferred tool to target youths and pull them into a relationship online so the child trusts them. Predators look for indicators that a child may be vulnerable by looking for kids who post suggestive photos, make posts late at night, and make posts that are sad or angry.

Sexual cybercrimes against kids may involve sex tourism, child pornography, or online enticement/luring. When the cyberpredators solicit children online for racy photos or inappropriate conversations, in those cases where there is inappropriate online contact, one in twenty-five of those youths received an offer to meet in person. [28]

According to the Internet Watch Foundation in the United Kingdom, there has been a 1,500 percent increase in the number of child pornography images since 1997. [29] Sex tourism or sex trafficking supported by the cloud has grown so dramatically in the United States that President Obama declared January to be National Slavery and Human Trafficking Prevention Month.

These criminals use cloud services to recruit their next victim and future customers of their slave services. The pimps target children in the cloud, plan their moves on cloud services, and even use the cloud to market the children in public and online. In sting operations, criminals in the child porn or child sex-trafficking trade have used Facebook, Twitter, Myspace, cloud-storage sites, and even online classified ads such as Craigslist to run their operations. [30]

Favorite places in the cloud for these cybercriminals include:

- **Auctions.** Sites such as Craigslist that have auctions are considered a magnet for international sex trade of children via the adult services section.

- **Photo-Sharing Sites.** Allows the pornography or trafficking operations to bypass printing photos and to disseminate photos online for viewing by prospective buyers.
- **Social Media**. Chatrooms and social sites such as Facebook and Myspace are used to recruit or trick kids into joining the cybercriminal's trafficking scheme. They use these sites and blogs to connect to other cybercreeps to barter, trade, and sell their victims.

Take the case of Xavier Orlando Crespo, who met girls via Facebook and would message them to send him racy photos.[31] Police filed charges against the twenty-one-year-old Bethlehem man after he allegedly asked a thirteen-year-old girl to text him naked pictures of herself. The girl's father had found the racy photos his daughter sent via her phone and called the police.

Police said Xavier Orlando Crespo contacted the teenager on Facebook under the name FlyBoii. Crespo told the girl he was two years older than she and even adjusted his age as the girl did. The girl finally said she was fourteen, and Crespo changed his age to sixteen.[32] Since the police were involved, the offline meeting with Crespo and the young girl turned out to be a surprise to Crespo when he met face to face with the police force. This case has a good ending.

The tragic case of seventeen-year-old Ashleigh Hall did not end as well. Although Peter Chapman had previously been sentenced for a sex offense and was a registered sex offender, he slipped through the cracks and created an identity online, saying he was a teenager. He befriended Ashleigh Hall on Facebook. Ashleigh thought he was a teen and eventually agreed to meet him. Ashleigh told her mom that she would be sleeping at her friend's house and instead went to meet Peter Chapman. He drove her to a motel, raped her, and killed her. He then dumped her body in a field.[33]

Kids unknowingly supply pornographers with new material when they take suggestive or inappropriate photos of themselves and post them on Facebook and other sites. In most cases the children believe only their friends can see these posts. Unfortunately, that is not the case.

As the number of photos on Facebook and other social media sites increases, so do the number of Internet trolls looking for photos. The Internet Watch Foundation (IWF) developed a study in which it visited sites known for trafficking in child pornography and also sexually suggestive photos and videos of children. They traced the origin of the photos and videos and estimated that 88 percent of the photos and videos on these reprehensible sites were cut and pasted from legitimate social media sites or were taken from lost or stolen digital devices. The IWF team spent forty-eight hours combing the web, finding sixty-eight sites with over twelve thousand sexually inappropriate images.[34]

Sarah Smith, IWF technical researcher, said, "During the course of our work we encounter large quantities of self-generated sexual content which has been copied from its original location and then uploaded elsewhere to form collections, but this is the first time we've been able to demonstrate the extent to which this occurs."[35]

The issues are global and growing. The Child Exploitation Tracking System is a tool developed to assist in worldwide investigations and is in use in Australia, Brazil, Canada, Chile, Italy, Romania, Spain, and the UK. In addition, researchers in Spain built the Negobot.[36] This Internet robot simulates a fourteen-year-old girl with the purpose of befriending child predators so that law enforcement can track them in online chatrooms. The goal of Negobot is to lure in the predators before they harm children.

Here are some of the warning signs that a child is a victim of trafficking, or is being recruited:

- Has unexplained absences.
- Runs away or discusses running away from home.
- Exhibits bruises, suddenly withdraws from social gatherings, or displays depression.
- Demonstrates a sudden change in attire.
- Develops erratic behavior and severe mood swings.
- Suddenly has material possessions given to him or her by a "friend."
- Hides emails, text messages, or other online posts.
- Shows an extreme change in online behavior—suddenly online all the time or suddenly not interested.

*How to Protect Our Children from Online Sexual Predators*

These key rules for parents foster an environment that helps protect children from sexual predators online:

- **Talk, Talk, Talk.** The number-one best rule is to talk to your kids. Remind them that digital can be forever and that they should not text inappropriate messages or photos under any circumstances.
- **No Digital Zone.** Be where your kids are online. Have your teens turn in their devices before they head to bed. They are more likely to get wrapped up in a texting session if they are alone in their room.
- **Cell Phone Review.** Occasionally have your kids show you their phone. Ask them to log into apps that are unfamiliar to you.
- **Find Out What You Can Find Out.** Look into features from your mobile-phone company for usage and tracking options.
- **Set Parental Controls.** Talk to your cell phone services provider about the features they offer. Many offer the ability to limit the time

of day that text messages and phone calls can be received or sent, with the exception of 911 or preset numbers. Some cell phone or software providers can help you monitor and prevent the use of the camera, block certain phone numbers from sending calls or texts, set strict time of day or usage limits for Internet access, and even prevent or delay the installation of downloaded apps until you approve.

- **Maintain Access.** Do not spy or snoop. Be open about having and maintaining access. Obtain your children's email and social network passwords.

By opening lines of communication between you and your loved ones, you can help them stay safe while in the cloud. Teaching children how to protect their own privacy may be the best safety lesson. Kids who understand the lines between chatting and oversharing are safer online.

## NOTES

1. Associated Press, "Local Police Grapple with Response to Cybercrimes," *USA Today*, April 13, 2013, www.usatoday.com/story/news/nation/2013/04/13/local-police-response-cybercrimes/2079693/.
2. Rachel King, "Consumers Actually Really Like Cloud Storage, Report Says," *Between the Lines*, ZDNet.com, October 15, 2012, www.zdnet.com/consumers-actually-really-like-cloud-storage-report-says-7000005784/.
3. Arthur Coviello, "RSA Executive's Speech: Big Data Transforms Security," speech given at RSA Conference, Singapore, June 5, 2013, www.rsaconference.com/videos/76/big-data-transforms-security.
4. Arthur Coviello, "RSA Executive's Speech: Keynote Speech," speech given at RSA Conference, San Francisco, February 26, 2013; notes taken by coauthor Theresa Payton.
5. Cloud Security Alliance, *The Notorious Nine: Cloud Computing Top Threats in 2013*, February 25, 2013.
6. "Facebook Privacy," EPIC.org, December 13, 2012.
7. Claire Davenport, "Europe Wants to Limit Google and Facebook's Ability to Sell Your Personal Data," *Business Insider*, January 9, 2013, accessed July 18, 2013, www.businessinsider.com/europe-wants-to-limit-google-and-facebooks-ability-to-sell-your-personal-data-2013-1.
8. Brian X. Chen, "'The Cloud' Challenges Amazon," *New York Times*, December 26, 2012.
9. Kristen A. Lee, "Hacked! Colin Powell's Facebook Page Gets Hijacked by Prankster," *NY Daily News*, March 11, 2013, www.nydailynews.com/news/politics/colin-powell-facebook-page-hacked-article-1.1285231.
10. Nancy Dillon and Thomas Tracy, "Michelle Obama, Beyoncé, Jay-Z, Hillary Clinton, VP Joe Biden, FBI Boss among Big Shots Whose Financial Details Lifted by Hacker Read More," NY Daily News, March 11, 2013, www.nydailynews.com/entertainment/gossip/hacker-takes-info-jay-z-hil-clinton-article-1.1285605.
11. Annie Colber, "Burger King Twitter Account Hacked," Mashable, February 18, 2013, mashable.com/2013/02/18/burger-king-twitter-account-hacked/.
12. "U.S. Stocks Tank Briefly in Wake of Associated Press Twitter Acount Hack, *Wall Street Journal*, Mike Isacc, April 23, 2013.

13. Associated Press, "Calif. Man Gets 1 Year in Jail for Rigging College Election," July 16, 2013, www.foxnews.com/us/2013/07/16/calif-college-student-gets-1-year-in-jail-for-rigging-student-body-president/.

14. Associated Press, "Calif. Man Gets 1 Year in Jail for Rigging College Election."

15. Michael Walsh, "College Student Faces One-Year Prison Sentence for Stealing Computer Passwords to Rig Student Council Election," *NY Daily News*, July 16, 2013, www.nydailynews.com/news/crime/college-student-faces-one-year-prison-sentence-stealing-computer-passwords-rig-student-council-election-article-1.1400125.

16. Eric Schmidt, *The New Digital Age: Reshaping the Future of People, Nations and Business* (New York: Knopf, 2013), 55.

17. Caty Weaver, "The Most Deranged Sorority Girl Email You Will Ever Read," *Gawker*, n.d., accessed April 18, 2013.

18. https://www.torproject.org.

19. Jack Nicas, "Crime That No Longer Pays: Bank Robberies on the Decline as Criminals See Greater Rewards in Online Theft," *Wall Street Journal*, February 4, 2013.

20. Robert McMillan, "Citing Cybercrime, FBI Director Doesn't Bank Online," *Computerworld*, October 7, 2009.

21. The Federal Register, 78th volume of the Federal Register, pages 8538–42.

22. Charles Arthur, "Google's Eric Schmidt: Drone Wars, Virtual Kidnaps and Privacy for Kids," *Guardian*, January 29, 2013, www.guardian.co.uk/technology/2013/jan/29/google-eric-schmidt-drone-wars-privacy.

23. Jamie Leigh Lee, "70% of Teens Hide Their Online Behavior from Their Parents, McAfee Reveals What U.S. Teens Are Really Doing Online, and How Little Their Parents Actually Know," mcafee.com, June 25, 2012, www.mcafee.com/us/about/news/2012/q2/20120625-01.aspx.

24. Pew Research Center's Internet and American Life Project, *Trend Data (Teens)*, July 2011, www.pewinternet.org/Static-Pages/Trend-Data-(Teens).aspx.

25. "Child Identity Theft a Growing Problem—Children Are Increasingly Targeted by Identity Thieves, Don't Discover Theft until Years Later," ITAC, March 6, 2013.

26. Brad Lendon, "18 Rescued in Child Pornography Raids, Feds Say," CNN, June 8, 2012, news.blogs.cnn.com/2012/06/08/18-rescued-in-child-pornography-raids-feds-say/.

27. *Crimes against Children Research Center*, University of New Hampshire, www.unh.edu/ccrc/internet-crimes/papers.html.

28. J. Wolak, D. Finkelhor, K. Mitchell, and M. Ybarra, "Online 'Predators' and Their Victims: Myths, Realities, and Implications for Prevention and Treatment," *American Psychologist* 63, no. 2 (February–March 2008): 111–28.

29. "Global Campaign against Child Pornography," Internet Centre for Missing and Exploited Children, www.icmec.org/missingkids/servlet/PageServlet?LanguageCountry=en_X1andPageId=1742.

30. Ron Dicker, "Craigslist Human Trafficking—Girl Tries to Sell 12-Year-Old Brother on Craigslist," *Huffington Post*, October 29, 2012, www.huffingtonpost.com/tag/craigslist-human-trafficking.

31. Sarah Cassi, "Bethlehem Man Faces Two Years in Prison for Sexting with Minors," *The Express-Times-Lehigh Valley Live*, September 16, 2011, www.lehighvalleylive.com/bethlehem/index.ssf/2011/09/bethlehem_man_faces_two_years_1.html.

32. Sarah Cassi, "Bethlehem Man Admits Meeting Girls on Facebook, Sexting Two of Them," *The Express-Times-Lehigh Valley Live*, June 9, 2011, www.lehighvalleylive.com/bethlehem/index.ssf/2011/06/bethlehem_man_admits_meeting_g.html.

33. Paul Sims, James Tozer, and Liz Hull, "Ashleigh Hall: 'We've Learned a Terrible Lesson,' Says Mother of Girl Killed After Going to See 'Boy' She Met on Facebook," *Daily Mail*, March 12, 2010, www.dailymail.co.uk/news/article-1223709/Ashleigh-Hall-Weve-learned-terrible-lesson-says-mother-girl-killed-going-boy-met-Facebook.html.

34.  Internet Watch Foundation 2012 study.

35.  Internet Watch Foundation 2012 study.

36. Jillian Scharr, "Controversial 'Lolita' Chatbot Catches Online Predators," NBCNews.com, *TechNewsDaily*, July 13, 2013, www.nbcnews.com/technology/contro-versial-lolita-chatbot-catches-online-predators-6C10622694.

# FIVE

## Just Hanging Out Online . . .

You may not realize it, but you are connected to the Internet all day, and the cyberazzi are with you every digital step of the way. *Cyberazzi* are data companies that follow you around and store your habits and behaviors so they can sell that information to those who hope to profit from knowing all about you.

> **A host of invisible cyberazzi—cookies and other data catchers—follow us as we browse, reporting our every stop and action to marketing firms that, in turn, collect an astonishingly complete profile of our online behavior. Whenever we click, so do they.**
> **—Federal Trade Commission chairman Jon Leibowitz**[1]

When you drive with the GPS turned on, you are connected to the Internet, and your speed, direction, and where you go are recorded. If you are on the smart grid, more than just you and your family dog know you are home when you enter your house and turn up the thermostat. The energy company and anyone they provide that data to also knows. If you stopped on your way home to pick up a prescription and used a debit or credit card to pay for it, the prescription history was transmitted via the Internet to your insurance company. That information also eventually makes its way into a database, so it can be fed to data-mining companies, research labs, and pharma companies. Did you use a loyalty card that gives you miles or dollars back? Then your purchase, location, time and date of purchase, and retail location were all tracked. At a later date, this data will be transmitted via databases to marketing firms, the retailer, and perhaps even law enforcement.

In fact, the only way you can go offline would be to stop doing your daily activities and hide away in a remote location. Just do not use GPS to get there, do not buy anything with debit or credit cards, and absolutely no talking on your cell phone.

## TRACKED AT EVERY CLICK

**Consumers are very pragmatic people. They want free content. They understand there's a value exchange. And they're OK with it.**
**—Lou Mastria, managing director of the Digital Advertising Alliance[2]**

Except not everyone is "OK with it." The Digital Advertising Alliance's opt-out site provides consumers a way to opt out of behavioral tracking for participating advertisers. Guess what? A million people have taken advantage of the opt-out service.[3]

It is late fall and you want to get a jump-start on your holiday shopping. You begin surfing your favorite shopping sites on your computer. You do comparison shopping across sites, post a few questions on the sites asking other users if they have bought an item, and rate reviews that you read on shopping sites. You make some purchases, check your social-media account, and then check the online news sites. Every click, move to another page, search, and purchase creates an ID trail and lots of cookies. (A *cookie* is a small piece of data that a website you visit installs on your browser, so they can "recognize" you when you return to their site.) Web crawlers and trackers have perked up, and they are all hanging out with you while you hang out on the web.

Everyone else in your house is asleep, so you feel as if only you know about all the treasures you are purchasing online for loved ones. But everyone on the web is awake. Websites that you visited begin collecting a profile on you and checking you against their massive databases. They love to look at your keyword searches, filing away that you asked for "automatic corkscrew" and not "electric corkscrew," and then actually clicked on a wine-of-the-month-club ad below the corkscrews displayed.

When did the trackers wake up and know you were online? The first website you went to, or a landing page, started it all. A session was started as you clicked on and off that site. The session grabbed your current Internet protocol (IP) address (your exact physical location on the Internet at that moment), whatever unique ID that has been assigned to your digital device of choice, your browser choice, the version of the operating system, your Internet provider, and their best guess at either your geographic location or your home address.

You might even be presented with a higher price based on the website's best guess at what you might be willing to pay and whether or not their competitors are near your house. The *Wall Street Journal* researched this new pricing scheme and found that the Staples Inc. website would take a guess at where you lived based on what your computer's browser told them, and then would display prices that were different, by location. The *Wall Street Journal* also noted that Staples Inc. also seemed to know whether their competitors were within driving distance of your house and would discount an item based on the competition.[4]

When you visit a site, have you ever clicked on the social media icons to quickly share what you see on the site to your social media sites, such as Facebook or Twitter? Most people love these features. But if you click on the icons, a series of scripts run behind the scenes. The scripts not only help you repost that item on your favorite social media site but also snoop on you and take whatever data they can about you from your browser to share with that social media site. Think of it as a little welcome party that sees you, walks you over to the site, and then says to that site, "Hi! My friend here wants to repost something on this site but first let me tell you that my friend uses a Safari browser on a Mac and I think my friend is a woman that lives in Annapolis, Maryland."

### Tracking Your Search Terms

Behavioral advertisers use information about what people are thinking and doing to target their ad campaigns more effectively. They love to know about your search queries, because your search queries can often tell more about you than you would share in a phone conversation or in writing to another person. Your most personal and sensitive thoughts and secrets may be wrapped up in search terms.

For example, suppose you are wondering if you have a deadly disease, but you do not want to worry your family until you know for sure. When behavioral advertisers snoop in on your searches, they take in your search terms, the links followed, and even what you clicked on. Unless they tell you otherwise, all the search engines collect this information. Once the search-engine companies collect your data, they bundle it for marketing firms. If requested, they also provide it to law enforcement.

**Opting Out.** Search engines such as Google, Yahoo!, and Bing have privacy policies you can read and settings that give you some control over how they store and share your search information. Other search engines are designed to give extra privacy. DuckDuckGo, for example, tells you up front they will not collect or sell your searches to anyone. Another option that you may want to consider is using the search engine Ask.com with the AskEraser option turned on. It creates one cookie that makes sure that no other cookies or storage of your search terms are kept on file unless otherwise directed or necessary.[5]

### Just Browsing . . . and Being Tracked

Behavioral advertisers also love to collect, analyze, and review your web-browsing data: your cookies, the pages you visit, the browser you use, and more. By combining your browsing data with your search queries and social networks, they try to learn enough about you to anticipate what you might want to buy next. When you visit a website, the site begins collecting data in the nanosecond it took to load your page. The service may ask your computer to send it the browser you are using, your device ID, and even your email address. Do you use any media players to watch videos or listen to music? Often these handy media players store lots of information about you and pass that information along to third-party marketing firms. They then take any data they gathered about you during your web-browsing habits and collate that against marketing databases to build a more robust profile of you, online and offline. This is passed along to companies and can be passed along to law enforcement.

**Opting Out.** Internet browsers such as Safari, Chrome, Firefox, and Microsoft offer features to block cookies and tracking. They regularly update those features to respond to the changing marketplace. Look for Privacy and Security in your browser's Help system, then review the privacy policy and select the settings you want.

Unfortunately, as more people learn how to manage cookies, some firms have moved from cookies to web bugs. Web bugs are tiny graphical objects that track you under the radar, so you do not know they are there. Many web bugs collect detailed information about you, such as the device ID, IP addresses, dates and times you are online, and perhaps even where you visited.

### Tracking Your Email

Most people on the planet today can send and receive email. Many have several accounts, some active and some forgotten. But not everyone realizes that all email providers can and will access their emails. Your email provider looks at your message headers, which usually include the date and timestamp, the email address, where the email originated using the IP address, and where the email was sent. The content of your messages may also be scanned by intelligent search engines that look for key words to send you targeted ads. Your own government might have other search engines in place that may trigger a flag for law enforcement to read your email messages at a detailed level.

**Opting Out.** Tired of the snooping and want to take matters into your own hands? A variety of products on the market promise to help you with more private messaging. No system is 100 percent safe from bad guys and the service still might be subject to a subpoena from law enforcement, so read those privacy statements carefully. You could start by using a system that helps protect your identity from bad guys—fraudsters as well as marketers. One example is a tool called Tor, which stands for "The Onion Router." [6] Tor was developed by the Naval Observatory and is used by journalists that need to report egregious government behavior within a repressive regime. They have also used Tor to keep their communication lines open even when a country's government may take their own government or another government offline. Tor basically hides you by traveling across random paths and layers of the Internet, hence the name "onion" for layers of an onion.

Once you use Tor, you can investigate using an email service that promises not to snoop on you or to sell your data, such as Hushmail, Anonymouse, and Hide My Ass!. You might also want to consider using a tool called DeadDrop. You might have heard that the *New Yorker* magazine is using a service called Strongbox for people to send them news leads.[7] Strongbox uses DeadDrop technology. DeadDrop works just like it sounds. You drop off your information for another person to pick up, like in the old spy movies where you left a packet of information in a secret hiding place. You can use Tor and DeadDrop together to cover your tracks.

If you want a simple way to use email without worrying about snooping, just give up and assume that all of your emails will be snooped on.

### The Ads You View Are Looking Back at You

The cyberazzi may also follow you through adware, those annoying banners and pop ups that get in your way while you browse online. Some are so pervasive they wiggle around your pop-up-blocker settings. Adware can even be installed on your computer through an app you download, though you may not remember authorizing the installation. Adware is not necessarily evil, but it could be snooping on your digital life and passing that information along to marketing and advertising firms.

**Opting Out.** For protection against adware, review the features of your antivirus program. They may provide settings to block adware altogether, or at least block adware from snooping and telling others.

### Disclosure Standards Are Coming

The behavioral advertising industry in the United States would rather offer proactive options to allow consumers to opt out of tracking than be forced into it by regulation, so they are designing disclosure standards. Once these are in place, newly downloaded apps and games will most likely tell you in plain terms what data they will be sharing, such as location, your address book, and sites you visit.

---

**TOOLBOX**
**To fight back against the trackers, you might want to check out the product Disconnect, designed to help you track and pull back some of your privacy in your browsing history.**

---

Built by former Google engineer Brian Kennish, Disconnect becomes an extension on your browser. When launched, the product blocked roughly two thousand tracking companies with plans to block more.[8]

Other tools that you may want to consider are Abine and Ghostery.

You can also set up "Do Not Track" preferences on your web browser. Sites that can read this flag will honor your wishes.

## SOCIAL MEDIA IS WATCHING YOU

It takes 20 years to build a reputation and only five minutes to ruin it. If you think about that, you will do things differently.
—Warren Buffett[9]

Over half the people in the world now have some type of social network account on sites such as Myspace and Facebook or platforms such as Twitter, YouTube, Pinterest, Instagram, and Reddit.[10] The challenge with social networks is not only are you social, but your identity and your personal information are also social, and the way they are used can affect your life offline.

Social networking sites are theoretically opposed to privacy, and they collect and may pass along to others your name, your connections to friends, personal information in your profile, and any other websites you visited while you were logged into your account. Many employers use this information to check on prospective hires or existing employees. Law enforcement has been using social networking sites for years to find criminals, look for clues in crimes, and to work within their local communities to foster a relationship of sharing and to extend the neighborhood watch programs.

Some tips you can use to avoid the snoops are to always check your privacy settings on your social-networking accounts. Wherever possible, select privacy settings by post versus just defaulting to one setting. Also, do not forget your family and friends. Ask them to limit what they share about you, including posts, locations, photos, and videos.

In criminal cases, almost all evidence (posted on the Internet) is discoverable and police can obtain the evidence. It's just a matter of what hoops they have to jump through.
—Bradley Shear, Washington-area lawyer specializing in social media law[11]

In one case, a man posted what could be considered a parody. A short video shows a man driving and opening a bottle of what appears to be beer and taking a sip. The man behind the wheel then says, "We all know drinking and driving is against the law. You're not supposed to do that. But they didn't say anything about driving and then drinking."[12]

Then one day, law enforcement showed up at his personal residence in Hawaii to arrest him. The charge? Drinking alcohol while driving a car. He maintains that he is innocent, the bottle did not contain beer, and that he was just joking around.

In a more high-profile case, the motivations of the Boston Marathon Bombers were examined through their postings on social media. Less than six months before the bombings, the oldest of the two suspects, Tamerlan Tsarnaev, created his own personal YouTube channel, naming it Terrorists. He then posted his favorite hits, including as a video by Amir Abu Dudzhan that quotes Dudzhan saying, "Jihad is the duty of every able-bodied Muslim."[13] Tsarnaev also posted among his favorite videos footage that features one of the leaders of the 1990s Chechen resistance, Timur Mutsuraev, which asks believers to follow the call to jihad.

---

TOOLBOX

**The wrong person can find out a lot about you, using tools that are free and easy to use. When demonstrating these tools for people, we found information about them that surprised even the most cautious social networking user.**

- **Spokeo.com will show what you look like on the Internet across public records and social media sites.**
- **Facebook Search, called "Graph Search," allows people to look across Facebook based on key search terms. Why search person-by-person when you can do a mass search of everyone with key terms? CEO Mark Zuckerberg predicts that Graph Search could evolve into a "dating service" of sorts, but not to worry because this new feature was built to be "privacy aware." If you are not sure how this tool would reveal you to strangers, there is a blog site set up to illustrate it. The blog site takes random terms and shows you what Facebook sends back. As of this writing, the blog is called actualfacebookgraphsearches.tumblr.com/.**
- **Other tools that may be used to search social media networks to find out more about you include ZabaSearch, Pipl, and 123people.**

---

## FEATURE: INTERVIEW ON TRACKING IN A DIVORCE CASE

We talked to Cammie, a thirty-something mom living in the Southwest, who had her entire Internet life flash before her eyes. OK, it didn't really flash, because someone had printed it out in binders. Yes, paper copies of more than three years of her digital life were collated, correlated, and organized into binders.

Q: Cammie, tell us why someone decided to do this for you. Were they surprising you for your birthday or was it something else?

A: I am going through a difficult divorce and my husband decided to print out my entire profile from Facebook and Twitter. I think his motive was to show how often I was on social media sites and I am sure he was hoping to find something he could use against me. As a mom blogger and cybersafety advocate, I am very active online. I have a lot of friends and colleagues that I collaborate with on a regular basis and have worked on several social media campaigns. So, my digital footprint just from Facebook and Twitter is quite extensive.

Q: Was the enormity of it shocking to you? To see how many digital footprints you had?

A: I have to admit I was very overwhelmed when I saw the large conference room table stacked with huge binders and completely shocked when I realized at least five of the huge binders were filled with every post, picture, comment, and status from Facebook and Twitter. My initial reaction was a sick, nauseated feeling in the pit of my stomach and fearful of what I would find. Thankfully, I follow a few key rules when I post anything online. First, I make sure I represent myself well and am the same person on and offline. Second, I believe it is important to encourage and support each other, especially online. I have seen it used as an avenue to bully and be mean to others. Third, I try my best to inform others about steps they can take to present a positive online image and how they can manage their online reputation.

Q: Cammie, what other words of wisdom would you share with everyone?

A: Be careful about everything you post online. Anything and everything you post could come back to haunt you one day. Your online reputation is extremely important; it is an avenue that can help provide great opportunities or hurt your chances. Think twice before you post and if you are upset and tempted to post something, sleep on it first. Think about how it will come across and if it will hurt someone or help someone. And remember to check your online reputation. Google yourself and make sure what you see is how you want to be represented. Are you wondering if online reputation/management is important? Could your Facebook posts that you write in the moment, regardless of your mood, be used for/against you? A friendly warning, it's incredibly important! I saw a printout of every Facebook post on my account. Just the Facebook account alone took about four HUGE binders. Thank goodness I am careful about my posts!

## WHAT YOU LIKE TODAY REVEALS WHAT YOU'LL LIKE TOMORROW

Your likes on Facebook say so much about you. You are searching your news feed and see a cute picture of a kitten and choose "like." Your friends post a picture of themselves on vacation, another "like." A co-worker posts a motivational quote that absolutely makes your day, "like." And so it goes, you like your way through your Facebook friends' posts.

The Proceedings of the National Academy of Sciences of the U.S.A. (PNAS), created a research study to find out just what those Facebook likes say about you.[14] In their study, they ran a computer model against the likes of fifty-eight thousand volunteers whose profiles were anonymous to the model. The researchers asked the computer model to predict key characteristics about each profile based only on "likes."[15]

The computer model accurately predicted which volunteers were Single vs. In a Relationship, Cigarettes or Alcohol User, High vs. Low IQ. It even predicted Moods/Emotions. The model hit an 88 percent accuracy rate for guessing "male" and was 95 percent accurate in guessing that someone was an African American.

How did it do it? The model looked for correlations across music, TV shows, quotes, pictures, and a variety of posts and likes. Curly fries correlated with high intelligence and people who liked the Dark Knight tended to have fewer Facebook friends," reported researcher David Stillwell.[16]

### How Facebook and Advertisers Work Together

Facebook has created a tool that will surf your friends, your likes, and your friends' likes, then match that information with third-party databases, correlating data back to you that shows the Internet sites you visit, any email lists you are currently on, and even how you spend money both on and off the Internet. All this information about you is then aggregated with information about others to define groups with similar interests. Marketing firms buy these bundles of social networking profiles to build out their product campaigns. The tool is so powerfully accurate that Pepsi shows different ads to different people based on whether they are extremely loyal Pepsi fans or just cost-conscious soda slurpers who drink the cheapest name brand at the moment.[17]

In sharing this information, Facebook promises not to include data that identifies you personally, such as your name and email address. However, by aggregating details about your behavior with other users' behavior, they can provide a very comprehensive view of who you are and what you are likely to purchase.

The *Wall Street Journal* did a study of the most popular one thousand websites and found that three-quarters of them include code from many of the popular social networks, including Twitter and Facebook, to help them match back a visitor to a socialnetworking profile. [18]

## Facebook Home—Every Minute of Every Day

> **This application erodes any idea of privacy. If you install this, then it is very likely that Facebook is going to be able to track your every move, and every little action.**
> **—Om Malik, GigaOm site, referring to Facebook Home** [19]

Facebook Home is an app that replaces your home screen on a smart-phone with a Facebook app. If you install Facebook Home, you can do your common phone tasks—text your coworker, read the news, check your appointment calendar, call your spouse, and send an email with your status report to work—all through Facebook Home.

If you are on Facebook already, this might be a convenient way to use your phone, since the interface is familiar. Just remember that with Facebook Home installed on your smartphone, Facebook is always tracking you, not simply when you are logged in and using Facebook. With Facebook Home, you may have a more integrated and easier Internet experience, but you will also let Facebook follow you through every tweet, message, location, and more.

## How Discreet Is That Dating Service?

If you are having a hard time meeting people in the physical world, there are fabulous sites in the digital world that have connected people to new friends, people with the same interests, and even a soul mate. But before you sign up and create your profile, be sure to read the privacy statements carefully, do your homework, and research which sites might be right for you.

For example, the *Wall Street Journal* found that the free online dating service OkCupid sent usernames, gender, sexual orientation, age, drug-use information, and zip codes from their users' profiles to other companies. [20,21] Their justification? "None of this information is personally identifiable," said OkCupid's CEO Sam Yagan.

Many of the subscribers of OkCupid did not recall being asked for their permission to do this. But if they had read the privacy policy closely, they might have noticed that it does not say OkCupid will *not* forward the information along.

## AT THE MARKET, AT HOME, AND ON THE ROAD

As our stores, homes, and personal devices become smarter and interconnected, more and more details about our daily lives are collected, stored, and possibly shared.

### *Data Collection at Every Swipe*

**For the majority of the country, the zip code is going to be the piece of the puzzle that is going to enable a merchant to identify you.**
**—Paul Stephens, director of policy and advocacy at the Privacy Rights Clearinghouse[22]**

When you swipe a credit card at the checkout counter at your favorite retailer and give them your zip code, the swiper may fire off a transaction that is checked against a marketing database to try to predict what you might need, or to encourage you that you might need, to buy next. For example, the marketing database company Acxiom has built one of the most coveted databases about people that tracks their education level, hobbies, socioeconomic demographics, political views, and health interests based on over-the-counter purchases of medicine and other health aids, and age. Acxiom's database contains information on 190 million individuals, and you could be one of them.[23]

Privacy laws in the United States are still evolving, but Massachusetts and California have both ruled that a zip code is considered personal information.

### *Data Collection from Your "Smart" Home*

Homes are quickly becoming more integrated with smart systems and the smart grid. Smart systems allow you to manage your home's temperature, on/off lighting, music, alarm systems, and more, all from a finger swipe on a tablet or smartphone or click of the mouse. All of these actions go across the Internet and leave digital clues about where you are or are not.

If your home has been connected to the smart grid, you have the latest and greatest Internet-connected electric meters and systems. You are a virtual treasure trove to the energy company, marketers, the government, law enforcement, and cybersnoops and cybercriminals. Homes connected to the smart grid collect electricity usage, types of appliances used, billing preferences, digital recorders in use, time of day, and day of week.

Have a gaming system, digital video recorder, or Internet-connected TV? You are a behavioral advertiser's dream. Now they can virtually step into your living room and watch you watch TV. They can study your viewing habits, choices, and previews, and use this along with other data to enrich their profile about you.

And if you ever need an alibi, keep this in mind: between your smartphone, your car GPS, purchases you made that day, and your smart-grid connected home, police have all the clues they need to place you at your alibi or to question it.

## Data Collection When You Are Out and About

Your cell phone is always transmitting information that reveals your physical location with remarkable accuracy, either through its GPS or through its constant communication with cell towers. When cell phones first became popular, stores hated them because consumers could look for price comparisons while shopping. Now store owners realize they can use your smartphone to track you while you shop. Many shops track the cell phones that enter their stores and even track the device as it moves through the store.[24] They can look at a screen and seeing little blips of light going around the store: those are your smartphones giving you away.

Your smartphone is a treasure trove of information, storing your personal, and in many cases, professional life all in one neat compartment, and the phone companies and app companies are tracking your ID everywhere you go.

Even reading a good book in the park or at home in bed is not as private as it used to be. The convenience of having a personal library that can slip into a briefcase or purse is appealing. The challenge is that e-readers also snoop on you and broadcast your information. Your e-reader account tells behavioral advertisers the books you have purchased, how many pages you have read of each book, and any parts of the book that you have highlighted or shared with others. If law enforcement requests this data, the e-reader book company will make it available.

The Federal Trade Commission (FTC) is so concerned about the abuse of trust between smartphone makers, apps, and consumers that they are publishing policies and consumer awareness information and pursuing companies that they believe are overstepping the boundaries of trust. In 2013, the FTC talked to HTC America for not securing the privacy of data on their phones. HTC and the FTC reached an agreement, and HTC agreed to update their phones to reflect greater security and privacy.[25]

The FTC has urged the smartphone vendors to institute disclosure forms in consumer language (not legalese) to help consumers understand when data is being collected, by whom, and when and why data is shared about them.

**Opting Out.** To better safeguard your ID tracks via your smartphone, read the privacy policy before you download an app, so you know what they will do with your information. Turn location settings to "off" when using most apps other than a map app. You can also leverage your smartphone privacy settings by turning off geocodes, location tracking, and app sharing. When you are not using an app, log off the app so it cannot continue to follow you around the Internet.

For more about how smartphones and other portable devices invade your privacy, see chapter 6, "The Spy in Your Pocket."

### When Digital Tracking Helps Catch the Bad Guys

The case of the Boston Marathon bombing demonstrates some advantages and disadvantages of digital tracking for law enforcement. [26] Using cell-phone-provider data and triangulation, police could identify and track cell phones that were in the vicinity of the bomb sites. Facial-recognition software helped them identify one of the suspects running away from the scene. Text messages from one of the suspects eventually led police to bring in his friends for questioning. Photos of the blast taken by the crowd and law enforcement show a complex trigger mechanism with battery power and synchronization capabilities. Matching these photos back to databases of evidence helped law enforcement understand more about the signature of the bomb maker. [27]

But what happens when the Internet crowd takes matters into their own hands with their own investigation? *Crowdsourcing* is the practice of gathering data and ideas from a large group of people, often online. In the first two days following the Boston Marathon bombing, crowdsourcing Internet users reviewed videos, photos, and every clue they could find. Theories were discussed and shared on Facebook, Twitter, and other social networking sites such as YouTube, Reddit, and 4Chan. Unfortunately, this free-form investigation resulted in an innocent person being briefly misidentified as a suspect. [28]

## TOTAL RECALL IN HUGE DATABASES

In the fight against crime, the Bureau of Alcohol, Tobacco, and Firearms (ATF) plans to build, borrow, and leverage volumes of information that not only reveal everything there is to know about you, but also all about your friends, family, and associations. [29] They want to create a huge database to reveal everything about you with a few keywords. They believe this capability is crucial to faster criminal investigations. If the ATF has their way, just part of your social security number could lead to a dossier full of data points about you, some from long ago and perhaps long forgotten by you.

That's the thing about digital records: they never forget. Visualize it as if you were seeing a personal connections web starting with you at the middle and connecting out through friends, family, coworkers, charity functions, and any other civic duties you have, reaching back into the past as well as out into the present.

Even our spoken conversations, formerly held in memory alone, can now be digitally recorded forever. The Defense Advanced Research Projects Agency (DARPA) has embarked on a project to analyze speech and record your conversations, turning each conversation into a transcript, and filing it away in a database for future reference.[30] Any conversation could be captured, stored, preserved, and indexed so it is searchable and easily recalled for listening or reading. Even though we may forget what we said yesterday, the world can remember it tomorrow.

The challenge with all this data collection is the lack of protection from misuse and breaches. You may be innocent of wrongdoing and yet dragged into the spotlight of law enforcement by association. In that case, they can examine all the data they have stored about you.

Or your data may be housed in a database that is hacked by cybercriminals. Even if your perspective is "I'm an honest person, I have nothing to hide," you still need to hide your private information from the cybercriminals that lurk out there on the web. Data breaches are commonplace at large organizations such as universities, in the cloud services where your data sits, on social networking platforms, in email systems, and more. Your information in the wrong hands could lead to identity theft, extortion, and more.

> This is an unfortunate but perfectly cautionary tale of not only how we should look more carefully at protecting data after it is collected, but also how the data is to be safeguarded before we collect it to make sure it isn't used improperly or disclosed accidentally.
> —Lee Tien, a senior staff lawyer at the digital rights group Electronic Frontier Foundation[31]

In the fall of 2012, employees at the National Aeronautics and Space Administration (NASA) learned that a laptop left in a NASA employee's car had been stolen. As a result, approximately ten thousand to forty thousand NASA employees, contractors, and other related associates, current and former, may have had their data compromised. Some of the stolen information included background checks, which contain detailed information derived from sources such as visits to elementary school teachers, chats with neighbors from ten years ago, and every address the subject ever domiciled. Having your background check stolen is like handing your biography over to a criminal and saying, "Please, take over my life and my identity."

## FEATURE: INTERVIEW ON WHEN DIGITAL TRACKING HELPS LOVED ONES STAY ALIVE

Tammy B., a forty-something mom in the northern Virginia area, has a story about digital stalking on the highway with more twists and turns than any map, but every parent with a young adult driver in their home will see themselves. And anyone that remembers learning how to drive will also see himself or herself in this case.

Tammy begins: When I found out I was pregnant with my daughter, I was ecstatic. I was overcome with joy when I held her in my arms for the first time and saw her looking into my eyes. I couldn't believe it when I heard her sing her ABCs when she was a mere two years old. We often remember all the firsts. The first time they smiled, laughed, crawled, sat up by themselves, first steps, first foods, all sorts of firsts. As they grow up, we sort of put the baby book away and get bogged down with the issues every parent faces in raising their children. The experience I am sharing with you is when I decided I had no choice but to digitally stalk my daughter.

Q: So, did you digitally stalk your daughter?

A: Yes, you bet I did, but not at first. My little girl is all grown up and has made it to the big time—driving without me in the car. We only have one car, my 2007 Toyota Camry. Her soccer team is playing indoor soccer. One Saturday afternoon, she has a game and we decide to let her drive it alone. I research the safest route for her online, print off directions for her, review them with her and off she goes.

Q: Sounds good so far. I don't hear anything that sounds like stalking . . .

A: Since I'm nervous, I tell her she must call me the minute she gets there. I wait for what feels like days but it's only forty-five minutes. I am on pins and needles. Finally, my phone rings. She made it, I thought. Relief starts to flood through me. I answer the phone excited to hear the details of how the drive went. Then my daughter says, "MOM!!!! YOU DIDN"T TELL ME THERE WERE TOLLS ON THE ROAD! I DIDN"T HAVE ANY MONEY SO I HAD TO RUN IT." *There are no tolls on the route I chose for her,* I thought. My mind was reeling. Are you at the park? "YES, I need to go, I am late," she yells.

Q: So then what did you decide to do?

A: She hangs up and I am in a daze. I get out my map book and look at it. Hmmm, I think. She must have missed a turn and took a different route. But how will she get back? I only have one car. If she gets lost this will be my motherhood's largest EPIC FAILURE. Suddenly a light bulb went on. Sprint has a GPS tracker service. Maybe I can sign up for it real quick and at least have an idea where she is at when she calls me saying she is lost. I went straight to the computer and fumbled my way to the Sprint site. I was in luck! Both of our phones could be tracked using their GPS positioning service. I signed up for it and was relieved that I now had instant access to where she was.

Q: So now you can digitally stalk your daughter's whereabouts, did it help?

A: Well, eventually yes. She begins driving home with me stalking her on the computer hitting refresh every thirty seconds so I could see her location. About five minutes went by. HMMMMM . . . that's interesting. She seems to be on the Dulles toll road. Wonder where she will get off at? I kept watching . . . and watching . . . and watching . . . She did not get off the parkway until she got to 495!!!! Are you serious? Is this kid really going to drive on 495? Yup, there she goes, she's following the beltway . . . OMGOSH! I look again and she is on 95 south. OMGOSH! My kid is gonna die! She's too young to be driving on the interstate! The interstate in DC is CRAZY. . . . Then she gets off at exit 160. Ugh. I can relax. She will make it home.

Q: So, now you can relax until she pulls into the driveway?

A: Well, I was going to relax and then the phone rings, "MOM WHY ARE YOU TRACKING ME?" Sprint was kind enough to send her a text message letting her know she was being tracked. I tried to explain it to her. Then my daughter states the obvious—"MOM, DUH, I AM USING THE GPS ON MY PHONE. I have always used it to go places I have never been. I type in the address and it takes me right there. Doesn't everyone use GPS?"

Q: So what would you tell others that may want to resort to digital surveillance?

A: First of all, tell the person you are digitally tracking them. No matter how helpful you think you are trying to be, you should tell them so they don't think that you don't trust them. Realize that when you work with the younger generation, they may have more tools at their disposal then you realize, just ask! I grew up with maps, and directions, and knowing what roads went were. She grew up knowing that her GPS would get her there.

Digital tracking was a comfort to Tammy, and her daughter was noti-fied about the surveillance. Note that private information of all types is available online for our loved ones to use, but it is more likely used by businesses to track our actions and influence and predict our next actions.

## NOTES

1.  Sheila Shayon, "FTC Chairman Calls out Online Tracking 'Cyberazzi,'" Brand Channel, October 13, 2011.
2. Associated Press, "Online Privacy Is Evolving. Does It Matter to You?," FOX News Network, April 24, 2013, www.foxnews.com/politics/2013/04/24/online-privacy-is-evolving-does-it-matter-to/.
3.  Associated Press, "Online Privacy Is Evolving."
4.  Jennifer Valentino-Devries, Jeremy Singer-Vine, and Ashkan Soltani, "Websites Vary Prices, Deals Based on Users' Information," *Wall Street Journal*, December 24, 2012.
5.  "Ask.com AskEraser," Ask.com.
6.  www.torproject.org
7.  Amy Davidson, "Introducing Strongbox," *The New Yorker*, May 15, 2013, www.newyorker.com/online/blogs/closeread/2013/05/introducing-strongbox-anony-mous-document-sharing-tool.html.
8.  Somini Sengupta, "Start Up Lets Users Track Who Tracks Them," *New York Times*, April 16, 2013.
9.  www.quotedb.com/quotes/2180
10.  Frank Berkman, "How the World Consumes Social Media," Mashable.com, January 17, 2013, mashable.com/2013/01/17/social-media-global/.
11.  Lauren Russell, "When Oversharing Online Can Get You Arrested," CNN.com, April 24, 2013, www.cnn.com/2013/04/18/tech/social-media/online-oversharing-ar-rests.
12.  Russell, "When Oversharing Online Can Get You Arrested."
13.  Simon Shuster, "The Brothers Tsarnaev: Clues to the Motives of the Alleged Boston Bombers," *Time*, April 19, 2013.
14.  Michal Kosinski, David Stillwell, and Thore Graepel, "Private Traits and Attrib-utes Are Predictable from Digital Records of Human Behavior," Proceedings of the National Academy of the United States of America 2013, pnas.org, www.pnas.org/content/early/2013/03/06/1218772110.full.pdf+html.
15.  "Facebook 'Likes' Predict Personality," *BBC News*, bbc.co.uk, March 11, 2013, www.bbc.co.uk/news/technology-21699305.
16.  "Facebook 'Likes' Predict Personality."
17.  Evelyn M. Rusli, "Buy Signal: Facebook Widens Data Targeting," *Wall Street Journal*, April 9, 2013.
18.  Jennifer Valentino-Devries and Jeremy Singer-Vine, "They Know What You're Shopping For," *Wall Street Journal*, December 7, 2012.
19.  Heather Kelly, "Facebook Home, Privacy and You," *Our Mobile Society*, CNN.com, April 24, 2013, www.cnn.com/2013/04/05/tech/social-media/facebook-home-privacy.
20.  Julia Angwin, "Privacy Study: Top U.S. Websites Share Visitor Personal Data," *Wall Street Journal*, October 11, 2011.
21.  Jeremy Singer-Vine, "OkCupid App Bug Exposed Email Addresses and Birth Dates," *Wall Street Journal*, January 15, 2013.
22.  Melanie Hicken, "What Your Zip Code Reveals about You," *CNN Money*, CNN.com, April 18, 2013, money.cnn.com/2013/04/18/pf/data-privacy/index.html.

23. Natasha Singer, "Mapping, and Sharing, the Consumer Genome," *New York Times*, June 16, 2012, www.nytimes.com/2012/06/17/technology/acxiom-the-quiet-giant-of-consumer-database-marketing.html?pagewanted=all&_r=0.

24. "How Stores Spy on You. Many Retailers Are Snooping More Than Ever," *ShopSmart*, ConsumerReports.org, March 2013, www.consumerreports.org/cro/2013/03/how-stores-spy-on-you/index.htm.

25. Caroline Mayer, "Don't be Dumb about Smartphone Privacy," *Forbes*, March 5, 2013.

26. Rachel Quigley, Lydia Warren, Annette Witheridge, and James Nye, "FBI Gives Its Agents Images of TWO Boston Bombing 'Suspects': Hunt for Men Seen Wearing Back-Packs Near the Marathon Finish Line before Terror Attack," *Daily Mail*, April 17, 2013, www.dailymail.co.uk/news/article-2310596/Boston-bombings-latest-FBI-use-phone-records-identify-suspect.html.

27. Spencer Ackerman, "Things You Shouldn't Text When You're Accused of Bombing Boston: 'LOL,'" *Wired*, May 1, 2013.

28. Dave Lee, "Boston Bombing: How Internet Detectives Got It Very Wrong," *BBC News Technology*, bbc.co.uk, April 19, 2013, www.bbc.co.uk/news/technology-22214511.

29. Robert Beckhusen, "The ATF Wants 'Massive' Online Database to Find Out Who Your Friends Are," *Wired*, April 5, 2013.

30. Robert Beckhusen, "Darpa Wants You to Transcribe, and Instantly Recall, All of Your Conversations," *Wired*, March 4, 2013.

31. Natasha Singer, "If You're Collecting Our Data, You Ought to Protect It," *New York Times*, February 16, 2013.

# SIX

# The Spy in Your Pocket

The power, convenience, and plain fun of our smartphones and tablets turn them into constant companions. And that means, whether you know it or not, that you just might just have a spy in your pocket. There is no question that the miniature computers we carry around with us enhance our lives in many ways. However, indiscriminate and careless use of the technology can ruin your privacy, as criminals, corporations, police, and even hostile governments fill their files about you with intimate information about where you go and what you do.

By understanding what data is being captured by your mobile devices and who is using that information, you can better control how your life is monitored and what others know about you.

## JOHN MCAFEE AND THE SECRET LOCATION

John McAfee is a pioneer in Internet security and a Silicon Valley legend. A highly sophisticated programmer and businessman, McAfee created the antivirus program and company that still bear his name. He sold his remaining stake in this company in the 1990s, two years after it went public. But McAfee is known as much for peculiar behavior as business and technology acumen. A former cocaine dealer who later took out newspaper ads discouraging drug use,[1] he has taught yoga and published yoga books, collected guns and ammunition, and lived with eight women at a time.

By 2009, McAfee had sold off nearly all his major holdings, including estates in Hawaii, Texas, New Mexico, and Colorado. He moved into the jungle in Belize, a small country located on the northeastern coast of Central America. There McAfee started a new venture called QuoremEx, which was founded to produce commercial antibiotics. Living in the jungle brought McAfee closer to the wild in more ways than one. He wrote to friends, "My fragile connection with the world of polite society has, without a doubt, been severed. My attire would rank me among the worst-dressed Tijuana panhandlers. My hygiene is no better."[2]

McAfee argued with his neighbor, Greg Faull, about McAfee's eleven dogs and the noise they made. Faull filed police reports and threatened to shoot the dogs. On November 9, 2012, McAfee's dogs were poisoned and died. Two days later, Greg Faull was found lying in a pool of blood, shot execution style. When the Belizean police arrive at McAfee's house to question him about the murder, McAfee dug a shallow trench and buried himself for hours.[3] Then he disappeared.

Wanted in Belize for questioning in the murder of Greg Faull, McAfee went into hiding. He claimed to be innocent of the murder; however, from previous experience in a Belizean jail, he also feared for his life in the hands of the police. The international press speculated for weeks on the whereabouts of the eccentric software tycoon. Authorities were stymied. Then all the speculation came to an end thanks to data captured by a cell phone.

McAfee agreed to meet with journalists at a secret location. During the meeting, one of the journalists took McAfee's picture with his smartphone camera. He posted the image on the Internet with the caption, "We are with John McAfee right now, suckers."[4]

Apparently, neither the journalist nor McAfee realized that nearly all smartphone pictures include metadata—information about the picture itself—contained in the same file as the photograph. The journalist's cell phone captured data relating to the time the picture was taken and the exact global coordinates where it was taken. When a cell phone picture is posted on the Internet, its metadata can be examined by anyone who has the right tools. In the case of John McAfee, a hacker called Simple Nomad examined the metadata and promptly published his finding that "McAfee's image emanated from an iPhone 4S at the following location: 'Latitude/longitude: 15 39' 29.4 north, 88 59' 31.8 west' at 12:26pm Monday.'"[5] McAfee was quickly traced to a Guatemalan villa.

On December 5, 2012, Guatemalan police arrested John McAfee for illegally entering the country. A week later, he was deported to the United States.[6] If a paranoid programming master like John McAfee, while hiding from the police and in fear of his life, can lose his valuable privacy because of the extensive data capture and reporting from smartphones, what chance of privacy do the rest of us have? We carry this spy in our pockets that sends out a steady stream of information about us. The only way to stop the cell phone's reporting is to remove its battery, but many models make battery removal impossible. The smartphone may be the most significant threat to the private information that matters the most to you.

## WHAT INFORMATION DO MODERN SMARTPHONES CAPTURE?

Your authors are old enough to remember when beepers were the most effective mobile-communication device available to the general public. Although beepers could only send and receive a short text message, they became the pocketknife of the 1980s, providing a single-function tool that easily fit in your pocket or purse. In comparison, today's smartphones are the ultimate Swiss-army knife of electronics, providing an array of diverse tools in pocket-friendly form. Smartphones are full computers, capable of managing an entire office, accessing documents and video online, and acting as a mail server and text message machine. Your smartphone can replace your camera, watch, and compass while providing maps and directions for travel. It has full browser capability with hundreds of thousands of mobile apps that help you find a taxi, provide a flashlight in the dark, or fling colorful angry birds at elaborately constructed pig shelters. Oh yes, and it makes telephone calls from nearly everywhere.

But this amazing power comes at a significant cost. While the price of a two-year cell and data plan is expensive enough, the cost to your privacy is astronomical. To understand why, we look at the flexible toolset contained in a modern smartphone to see what information it is capturing around you. In the process, we discover that it's the way two or more of these data-capture tools *work together* that helps not only you in your mobile life but also marketers, thieves, law enforcement, and anyone else who wants access to detailed information about you. Remember, John McAfee could be betrayed by a posted picture first because the journalist's device was capable of taking a digital picture, and then because the device noted the time and exact global location that the picture was taken.

The same handheld technology was used to help identify the bombing suspects at the 2013 Boston Marathon,[7] as dozens of crowd participants at Copley Square uploaded time-stamped and location-stamped photographs to the FBI's website. Combining the smartphone's camera with a clock and Global Positioning System (GPS) sensors provided useful, detailed information that would likely hold up in court.

### A Variety of Location Sensors

Let's start with the location functions of a smartphone. As you would suspect, your smartphone's location at any given time can be tracked using its GPS locator. This highly accurate location device taps into the satellite-based global positioning system that was opened to nonmilitary uses during the Clinton administration, enabling your cell phone to talk to satellites to determine its location. This information is likely recorded by many applications of your phone, as well as by law enforcement or your phone's software or hardware makers if they are interested.

Though most smartphones permit you to turn the GPS feature on and off, the GPS feature is not necessarily the only locator on your phone. For example, some smartphones come preloaded with weather applications that continually ping the satellites, a process that also provides information about the phone's location.

Your phone is also talking to cell towers. Even before the introduction of GPS sensors, a cell phone's location could be determined by triangulation among cell towers. A cell phone access provider can pinpoint the location of your call by bouncing the signal off the closest three cell towers and determining your position between them. By comparing the relative strength of your phone's signal to multiple antennae towers, a tracker can determine a rough location for the device. Using your phone on the move makes this calculation easier because it provides a stream of data points as you move into the range of one cell tower and out of the range of another. In the United States, phone providers receive thousands of requests each day from law enforcement for cell-tower-triangulation data. This method of tracking is popular in part because, though many smartphone users can turn off the GPS-signaling device on the smartphone, they are unable to stop the phone from continuing to ping cell towers. Your phone is still reporting its location as long as the batteries are powering the device.

If your smartphone seeks out *Wi-Fi* networks, then it also can be tracked by which Wi-Fi networks it picks up. Wi-Fi is a term for wireless local area network using a common standard for interoperability. Wi-Fi networks are everywhere: they are business networks, home wireless routers, and even some are government-sponsored, free wireless connectivity. So as you pass a Starbucks, your phone may ping its network, telling the phone carrier that you are in that location at a certain time. Bluetooth signals can make your phone vulnerable to tracking, but only to those within close proximity.

Some hybrid methods of smartphone tracking combine these methods of locating a phone to pinpoint location. For example, Apple uses messages on the iPhone encouraging its iPhone users to turn on Wi-Fi-locating signals to help refine mapping functions. The more of these functions you keep on and available, the tighter the circle your phone company and location app providers can use to pinpoint your location.

In addition to the built-in trackers, you could allow everyone to track your location by signing up for a mobile application that facilitates tracking and broadcasts your location. Google Latitudes allows friends or relatives to connect online and see each other's smartphone location as they travel. Foursquare is a game application that uses your location in the real world to earn points, badges, and status in the game, allowing you to become "Mayor" of your local deli if you visit enough times. There are even dating applications that show you the number of interested people in your vicinity who share or complement your dating preferences, so you can find each other right away. The tradeoff is that people using the application can see when they are close to you and can read your interests as they watch you from across the room.

## Touch, Voice, and Image Sensors

In addition to GPS, Wi-Fi, and cell tower signaling/sensing devices, the current smartphone is packed with sensory equipment for detecting touch, sound, and images. Its primary input sensors are the touch screen and the microphone. Early smartphones used only touch screens to choose which apps you wish to run and which emails you want to read; today, many smartphones are also responsive to your voice and some to the wave of your hand.

On October 4, 2011, Apple introduced the Siri voice-activated personal-assistant system to its phones, and applications such as Dragon Dictation and Google Voice provide vocal interfaces into performing smartphone tasks. Smartphone manufacturers are poised to build more functionality with a voice interface as the technology becomes easier to use. Touch screens and microphones on smartphones could be used to test our health by reading pressure exerted by our fingers or the strength and inflections of our voice. Microphones can serve as biometric identifiers to authenticate your identity and authorize transactions, recording your voice and comparing it to earlier samples. The microphone can listen in and record conversations, not just over the telephone lines, but any conversation within the sensitivity range of our smartphones.

Smartphones also sense and collect images. Most smartphones sold today have two cameras, one in the back for taking pictures and video of your surroundings, and one on the front to allow you to Skype, Snapchat, or videoconference with other people, so that you can see each other's faces as you interact. Phone-front cameras could one day allow screen scrolling by watching eye movement or air gestures you make with your hands or head. Cell phone cameras are changing the face of photography, news reporting, law enforcement, and society, since many of the witnesses to unusual scenes can document on video what used to be simply described in firsthand accounts.

However, when you have a computer connected to the Internet, it is possible for someone you don't know to turn on your computer's camera or its microphone to sense where you are and what you are doing at any time. Though it takes sophisticated malicious software to do this in a sneaky fashion, it certainly is possible for law enforcement, a foreign government, or a prospective thief to listen into your life even if you thought your smartphone was inactive. This is what happens when you carry a remotely driven camera and microphone with you all the time.

*Utility Sensors*

Your handheld computer may also contain an accelerometer, magne-tometer (compass), barometer, proximity sensor, light sensor, and a gyro-scope. Any of these device-based sensors can be accessed by applications that you download or which come preloaded on your device. They can be used to sense how fast and which direction your device is moving at a given time (which often translates into how fast and where you are mov-ing), what the weather many be in the vicinity of your smartphone, and whether the phone is in your purse or out in the sun.

As more applications are built to take advantage of these sensors, they can gather more information to tell more about your activities, habits, and locations. Fordham University has established a Wireless Sensor Data Mining Lab, concerned with collecting the sensor data from mobile devices and analyzing the data recovered for useful knowledge. The Lab has already determined how to biometrically identify a user from accele-rometer data, and it has used the smartphone accelerometer to determine if its user is sitting, standing, lying down, walking, or running.

You never know how these apparently benign sensors can be used to mine information about you. For example, the accelerometer measures movement of a cell phone in space, and it is generally used to control video race cars and other game movements. However, Dr. Adam Aviv, working at Swarthmore College, was able to use the phone's accelerome-ter to determine where the phone's user was tapping on a screen to unlock the device with a passphrase. Simply by reading the internal ac-celerometer and measuring the phone's movements, Dr. Aviv's software for attacking smartphones was able to identify the correct PIN entered by a smartphone user 43 percent of the time and patterns entered by a user close to 73 percent of the time.[8] This system of attack was hindered when passwords or patterns were entered on the move. So use of the less well-known sensors, alone or in conjunction with others, may lead to informa-tion that can intrude deeply on your privacy—including learning your passwords.

In the future we can also expect an expanded set of sensors in our mobile technology. For example, adding altimeters will mean that apps can determine elevation changes for fitness measurements and could de-termine what floor the user is standing on inside a building, making for more useful indoor maps of museums and sports arenas. This could also help fire or police responders trying to find a person in need of medical attention who signaled for help. Apple has filed for various patents that may signal what device sensors are likely to be in use over the next few years, including a "smart garment" patent that involves clothing that can transmit location and body data wirelessly to an external data-processing device such as an iPhone or iPad.[9] Apple has received patents for an activity monitor for tracking acceleration, and an earbud that measures a user's blood oxygen level, body temperature, and heart rate. These Apple sensors suggest that the future of mobile technology will include tying your current device into your clothing and other wearable items to give detailed health data through your smartphone.

## Business Data Capture

Each transaction you conduct on your mobile device sends extensive data out to many businesses. Each of these companies takes your data and may save it to combine it with more data later in order to build a more accurate picture of your preferences and buying habits. The businesses that are interested in your location can make detailed maps of where you travel, how long you stay at each location, and what you do there. They can combine web-surfing data like any other Internet company, with geolocation data and data from any or all of the other sensors contained on your mobile device. This allows businesses taking your information to add entirely new layers to their knowledge base about you and your behavior.

Each transaction you undertake on your mobile device provides a set of information to a group of businesses that each claim ownership of your data. If you use a mobile sales app to buy shoes from Zappos or another online clothing store, then of course the shoe store gathers and keeps your information. They may try to capture where you were when you made your purchase, but you would have to include your name, address, and payment information to complete the transaction, and probably also include an email address. The shoe company will keep all of this information.

But your telephone company may also register that you made a purchase from your mobile phone. Some telephone companies even offer to allow certain online purchases to be credited to your telephone bill, giving them more information. It is likely that the company who operates the smartphone software ecosystem for your device will also take information regarding your use of the retail app and your purchase. So will the app provider if it is different from the retail store. It is likely that the app will use a separate payment processor, which will also hold some of your data, as will your bank, and the merchant bank for the company that made the sale. Some of these companies can take data directly from your phone during the purchase and others can't, but they all know more about you after your mobile purchase than they knew before.

## MOBILE DEVICES AND EMPLOYMENT

If your company allows or encourages you to access work documents on your personal phone, or to tend to personal business on your work-issued phone or tablet, you should be aware that the company may gain rights to the personal correspondence, pictures, and other data kept on your device. For that reason, using your smartphone for work and granting employer access can severely limit your privacy.

Many of us use our smartphones or tablet computers for work, reading email, revising documents, texting coworkers, attending meetings by videoconference and otherwise operating our entire business lives within the device. In some cases, an employer may provide mobile technology for its sales team or all employees. In others, you are expected to bring your own device to work. In either circumstance, the company may have rights over the data in the smartphone or tablet simply due to its dual use as a personal and business tool. Many businesses will install software on their worker's mobile devices that allows the business to access information from the device, and some companies use software that can wipe all data from the device when it is believed to be lost or stolen.

More employers are starting to adopt "Bring Your Own Device" (BYOD) policies and procedures. You should ask your employer how your personal data will be treated on the mobile device, and ask to see any formal policies affecting your mobile data. Many employers who adopt BYOD policies also provide information technology service assistance to employees, helping with problems, but also allowing the tech professionals from the office to see what personal apps and information you keep on your phone. The closer you tie your private mobile phone to your work, the more likely that your privacy will be lost to coworkers, bosses, and the company's information technology professionals.

In addition, your privacy can disappear quickly when you carry a machine that is relevant to a business court case. If you maintain work-related text messages or email on your smartphone or tablet, or if you keep work-related notes and documents on these devices, then those devices could be tagged as important evidence in a court case against your employer. In that case, the device could be taken and held in a safe place until it was examined for relevant data by a team of lawyers. Or, its significant data stores could be mirrored on another hard drive and reviewed by the court. Either way, groups of people related to the court case would have access to the information on your device, probably including at least some of your personal information. Furthermore, data from your device could become part of the litigation, read aloud in court, or otherwise exposed in a public forum, such as court or a legislative or administrative hearing. Keeping your personal device completely separate from your business life may be the only way to assure you can avoid this fate.

## "MY PHONE HAS BEEN HACKED!"

Given all of the personal information on your smartphone or tablet, the device can be a target for hackers. Anyone watching the news in 2012 heard about the efforts of certain British tabloids to hack into the telephone voice mail of citizens that reporters believed to be newsworthy, and the arrests of reporters and editors that followed the original news stories. One of the oldest British tabloids, *News of the World*, closed itself down due to the ensuing scandal. The privacy of both celebrities and average British citizens was compromised, as reporters were authorized by leaders of News Corporation to hack into the voice mail of deceased British soldiers, victims of the London bombings, and even murdered schoolgirl Milly Dowler. A public outcry and police investigation made it clear that the British citizenry valued its privacy and found such phone-hacking tactics to be unacceptable.[10]

### Criminal Hackers

Smartphones and tablets are targets for more than the tabloid press. As more valuable information is stored on or accessed from mobile computers, hackers develop more sophisticated tools to pry into these mobile devices. Juniper Networks noted in its 2011 *Mobile Security Report* that 2011 saw an unprecedented 155 percent increase in mobile malware attacks across all platforms.[11] Juniper also noted "a new level of sophistication of many attacks. Malware writers used new and novel ways to exploit vulnerabilities," such as DroidKungFu using encrypted payloads to avoid detection and DroidDream disguising itself as a legitimate application. As Google's Android phones grew to become the most popular platform in the world, hackers followed, writing more attacks for the phones operating on Android. Reports have been released showing that Apple phones also have dozens of features vulnerable to hackers.[12]

One of the most destructive hacking tools used against smartphones is a virus called NotCompatible, which allows hackers to take full control of a smartphone. A data security company called Lookout claims that ten thousand customers per day were being tricked into loading the virus on their phones. The virus uses spam to propagate itself, using a contact list method so the messages appear as if they came from someone you know.[13] Once hackers have control of your phone, they can shut down its functionality, take your information, or use the phone for their own purposes. For example, a hacker could force your phone to send out more spam to other phones, just to increase the number of devices under the hacker's control. Or a hacker can make money by forcing your phone to go to pay sites that bill your phone and pay the hacker for each visit. Of course, with information gathered from your smartphone, a hacker could drain your bank account or use your credit/debit card for purchases.

*Bluetooth Signals*

A smartphone will likely contain a Bluetooth signaler/sensor so that it can communicate with nearby Bluetooth-enabled devices, such as speakers for your music, printers for your documents, and hands-free automobile cockpits for your conversations while driving. The Bluetooth technology was developed to encourage security and interoperability between devices, but it has been shown to be vulnerable to both malicious attacks and to government intrusion. Bluetooth ranges are usually about thirty feet between devices to remain connected. For that reason, Bluetooth hacking is not practical on a large scale because the hacker needs to remain in close proximity to the victim during the attack.

Some of the most annoying Bluetooth vulnerability involves "Bluejacking," or sending messages, including text, video, and audio, to other devices using the Bluetooth connection. Most of the Bluejacking is currently aimed at sending spam-like marketing messages or pranks, although it could be used to transmit more malicious signals such as Trojan viruses.

"Bluesnarfing" is more dangerous and is defined as theft of information from a device through a Bluetooth connection. Bluesnarfing can target calendar information, texts, email, contact lists, and even pictures stored on your smartphone. Some brands of smartphone are known to be especially vulnerable to being hacked in a Bluesnarfing attack, so you may want to investigate this issue before you buy.

"Bluebugging," which can affect both smartphones and Bluetooth headsets, allows a skilled hacker to take control of certain aspects of a smartphone, and even to eavesdrop on a caller's conversations.

But the bad guys are not the only ones exploiting Bluetooth sensors on your phone. The US Transportation Safety Board (TSB) has announced and tested a plan called Automated Wait Time monitoring, which works by "detecting signals broadcast to the public by individual devices and calculating a wait time as the signal passes sensors positioned to cover the area in which passengers may wait in line."[14] So the TSB was capturing the Bluetooth signals emitted by cell phones to monitor passengers' time waiting in security lines.

You can shut off Bluetooth signals by setting your Bluetooth signal to "nondiscoverable." You should never pair your Bluetooth connection with unknown devices.

*Government Intrusion*

Governments are also believed to hack into smartphones. In May 2013, the Dutch government presented a bill in its legislature to grant permission to law enforcement to hack into computer systems, allowing the Dutch police to block access to child pornography, read the emails of criminals, and track suspects through the GPS signals on their cell phones.[15] But the Dutch government is an open democracy, so it must publically announce how it chooses to address hacking into mobile computing.

In contrast, the Russian and Chinese governments have no such commitments to openness. A recent *Forbes* article proposes that the Chinese government has created a virus specifically targeted at Android phones, and that the virus uses cell-tower triangulation to report the phone's location.[16] The article cites, among other sources, a Canadian human interest group from the University of Toronto who demonstrated that Tibetan activists are being targeted with sophisticated malware designed to infect Android phones, stealing the phone user's contacts and messages and tracking the phone user's location. "We don't have a smoking gun that this is the Chinese government. But let's face it," says [the group's director Ron] Deibert. "When you add it all up, there's really only one kind of organization for whom this information is useful. And we know that the Chinese have a very strong interest in tracking Tibetans, so it's a strong set of circumstantial evidence."[17]

This report is just one of many implicating the Chinese government of sponsoring hacking attacks, but it is one of the first to identify smartphones as the specific target of the Chinese government.

Not only Tibetans and Chinese political dissidents need to be concerned with government malware. The Chinese government is apparently also interested in the mobile computers of North American businesspeople and government officials. According to Joel F. Brenner, formerly the top counterintelligence official in the office of the director of national intelligence: "If a company has significant intellectual property that the Chinese and Russians are interested in, and you go over there with mobile devices, your devices will get penetrated."[18]

While both Russia and China demand that no one can enter their countries with encrypted mobile devices without government permission to use that encryption, business and government travelers are generally warned that their devices will be hacked upon entering China or Russia. In recent testimony before Congress, James Clapper, the United States' director of national intelligence, stated that the governments of Russia and China were responsible for illicit intrusions into US computer networks and theft of US intellectual property.[19] Computer experts throughout Europe and North America believe that this hacking extends to any Western mobile computer brought within their jurisdiction. Some American companies prohibit their employees from bringing company computers to China, and they demand to inspect the smartphones of anyone who visited China with their devices.[20] When the government is a coercive police state, expect that it will take steps to examine all information from visitors, including the information on your smartphone or tablet.

Governments also intrude on the privacy of other governments through their technology. The US government has been expanding resources to protect its own computers from hacks by foreign powers. In April of 2013, President Obama proposed his second large increase in a row for building a team of cyberdefenders at the Pentagon. This is in conjunction with increases in funds marked for cyber defense in other cabinet-level organizations such as the Justice Department and the Energy Department. This follows the Department of Homeland Security's announcement that it was looking to hire at least six hundred hackers to improve the department's cyberattack and defense capabilities. Since mobile computers are crucial to government and business, and also highly vulnerable to attack, we can assume some of these resources will be allotted to both protecting and attacking mobile devices.

Law enforcement within the United States is also an increasingly heavy user of information taken from private mobile devices. In July 2012, Congress asked cell phone carriers to report on law-enforcement requests for information on mobile phone customers. The carriers reported receiving 1.3 million law-enforcement demands for subscriber information in the previous year.[21] These requests included text messages and caller locations. Some of the requests included "cell tower dumps" in which the police request the names and numbers of everyone who has been in the vicinity of certain cell towers on a specific day, which could involve thousands of user names. In this report to Congress, AT & T claimed that law-enforcement demands for cell phone information tripled between 2007 and 2011, when AT & T responded to nearly seven hundred requests a day. Because it was unclear in many jurisdictions whether or not law enforcement needed a warrant or court order to receive this personal data, the phone carriers asked Congress to set clearer standards for the police's right to receive GPS or other location information from citizens.

In June 2013, a scandal erupted in the United States when federal contractor Edward Snowden released the text of a court order allowing the FBI to download and record all call detail records created by Verizon for mobile-phone communications within the United States and between the United States and abroad. The data the FBI could capture included the phone numbers involved in the call, calling card numbers, and time and duration of the call. The data collection was allowed for three months, and it addressed not only people suspected of a crime but also all calls made during the period. The order contained no limit on how long the FBI could keep this information or what it could do with the data. Many people were surprised at the sweeping collection of mobile information and the many ways that the FBI could use this data to impinge on the privacy of any Verizon customer.

The US Supreme Court decided a case in January 2012 in which it required law enforcement to hold a warrant before placing a surveillance tracking device on a suspect's car and tracking his location every ten seconds for nearly a month.[22] The majority in this case found that the act of placing the tracking device on a car trespassed on the property rights of the car owner, and therefore required a warrant. This ruling is narrowly limited to circumstances in which the police place a tracking device on a suspect's property. However, the remaining four members of the court, with agreement on some positions by Justice Sotomayor, found that the cumulative act of monitoring movements electronically for several weeks was beyond what people would expect, and therefore it would have demanded a warrant simply based on the extent of the surveillance.

Since all members of the court felt that a warrant was needed for the surveillance of the suspect, how does their difference in reasons matter?

Because the majority's opinion relies on the concept of physical trespass by police on the property of the suspect, it does not help US courts faced with a question of whether law enforcement needs a warrant to pull smartphone location records based GPS or cell-tower triangulation. When police pull cell records, they are never trespassing on the suspect's property, only examining data, either current or historical, already being tracked by a suspect's telephone. In contrast, if the concurring opinion were law, it would give direction in these cases, and would likely mean that police would need a warrant to track a suspect over a long period of time using the tracking software included in mobile devices.

For now, lower US courts are left to wonder whether a warrant is necessary in tracking suspects through their phone records. No legislation or high court decision clarifies this point in the United States, so depending on where you live in the United States, the police may be able to track your movements by following your phone, even without probable cause to believe that you committed a crime.

## PROTECTING DATA ON YOUR MOBILE DEVICE

Now that you understand what data is being captured by your mobile devices and who might want that information, you can take steps to control access and protect your privacy.

### Protecting Your Data While Traveling

When you travel to countries such as China and Russia that are known to hack travelers' devices, take special precautions. Venerable computer publication *Infoworld* recommends that people visiting China leave their mobile computers at home, take only a loaner computer and/ or a disposable phone, and have your work email forwarded to an outside email account that you can check periodically.[23]

Of course, you could go completely tech-naked, with no computing device at all, which, like abstinence, is the only way to positively avoid certain results. However, if you have to take your device overseas to one of the dangerous countries, do not let the device leave your presence. Sleep with it under the pillow and carry it with you everywhere. Also, turn it on only when needed, and do not allow Wi-Fi or Bluetooth connections to reach your phone.

*Protecting Your Data at Home*

Even when safe at home, you can take steps to protect the data on your mobile smartphone or tablet. First, take advantage of the protections provided by the phone itself. This is one place where security should outweigh convenience. Set a hardware encryption password, so that you not only slide your phone to open it, but you must enter a personal identification number or pattern as well. Android phones allow a secret gesture that you draw with your finger to unlock the screen.

You can also encrypt your data within the phone. Newer iPhones have encryption included in both the software and the hardware, making it very difficult for a stranger to crack. Certain Android phones such as the Samsung Galaxy S III also offer a password lock that encrypts and decrypts data on the phone. If the operating system does not offer this feature, you can find apps that will do it for you, such as Good Technology for either of the largest platforms, or SecureMemo for Android.

You can also find apps that will help you locate lost phones, so that if the device is turned on, you can ping the device and show its location on a map. Apple offers a free tool called Find My iPhone, and it searches for your phone from your iCloud account. An analogous app for Android is called Where's My Droid.

## WEARABLE DEVICES THAT CAN TRACK AND CAPTURE YOUR INFORMATION

While the main discussion of this mobility chapter has been smartphones and tablets, certain wearable devices can track you as well. For example, Google Glass is a computer gadget mounted on a frame that you wear like glasses. It provides an Internet overlay onto your vision of the real world that will undoubtedly include sensors that can track your location and capture information from your web-surfing habits to the applications you use most often. Other wearable computers, including wristwatch computers that Apple is developing,[24] will collect data about their wearers and have similar tracking capabilities as current smartphones.

In the spring of 2013, Disney introduced a vacation management system called MyMagic+ that includes computerized wristbands that keep track of your activities at Disney theme parks, providing your family with a more customized park experience. Imagine approaching a Sleeping Beauty character that automatically knows your daughter's name and knows that her birthday is coming soon. The MagicBand functions as a room key, park ticket, FastPass for parking, and credit card at the parks. It allows other customization as well, such as the option to receive special offers, preselect three FastPasses before you leave home to reduce waiting time on rides, or choose whether to share your children's names with park employees. In exchange for greater convenience and a personalized park experience for the whole family, you are allowing the park to track all your transactions and rides.

Great Wolf Resorts, owner of eleven water parks in North America, has been using radio-frequency wristbands since 2006 to track visitors to its parks. Great Wolf Resorts uses the wristband system to pay for food and beverages on account. The bands have been well received because they free guests from the need to carry money or keys on the waterslides. But the bands also allow the resort company to track you and your family through the park for the full length of your visit and tie all activities and purchases to your name.

In the mobility space, privacy and personal information is traded for convenience, and the theme park wristband system is one of the best examples of this trade-off. Choosing more convenience allows the companies owning the park to mine a universe of data about you, your family, and the transactions you conduct.

## NOTES

1. Joshua Davis, "Dangerous: An In-depth Investigation into the Life of John McAfee," *Wired*, March 2, 2013.

2. Davis, "Dangerous."

3. Davis, "Dangerous."

4. *Vice* staff, "We Are With John McAfee Right Now, Suckers," with photo by Robert King, *Vice*, December 3, 2012; Jeff Wise, "In Pursuit of McAfee, Media Are Part of Story," *New York Times*, December 9, 2012.

5. Craig Timberg, "Hacker Finds McAfee through Phone Trail," *The Sydney Morning Herald*, December 6, 2012; Mat Honan, "Did *Vice* Just Give Away John McAfee's Location With Photo Metadata?," *Wired*, December 3, 2012.

6. Amanda Holpuch, "John McAfee Deported to US after Week Spent in Guatemalan Detention," *Guardian*, December 12, 2012.

7. Matt Hamblen, "Consumer Tech Key in Boston Marathon Bombing Probe," *Computerworld*, April 22, 2013.

8. Mark Ward, "Smartphone Sensors Reveal Security Secrets," *BBC News*, January 28, 2013.

9. Dan Graziano, "Apple Granted 22 New Patents, Including One for 'Smart' Clothing," *BRG*, January 18, 2012.

10. James Robinson, "*News of the World* to Close as Rupert Murdoch Acts to Limit Fallout," *Guardian*, July 7, 2011; Jeffrey Kofman, "*News of the World* Is No More," *ABC World News*, July 9, 2011; Richard Allen Greene, Murdoch's Scandal-hit *News of the World* to Shut Down, *CNN*, July 7, 2011.

11. Daniel Hoffman, *Juniper Mobile Security Report 2011—Unprecedented Mobile Threat Growth*, Juniper Networks, February 14, 2012.

12. See SourceFire report by Yves Younan, *25 Years of Vulnerabilities: 1988–2012*, March 2013, labs.snort.org/blogfiles/Sourcefire-25-Years-of-Vulnerabilities-Research-Report.pdf, charting the critical vulnerabilities and exposures of various software and mobile devices.

13. Bob Sullivan, "Smartphone Hacking Comes of Age, Hitting US Victims," *NBC News*, March 13, 2013.

14. Scott MacFarlan, "TSA Internal Document Cited by Records Show TSA Tracked Bluetooths to Observe Wait Times," wsbtv.com, March 20, 2013, www.wsbtv.com/news/news/local/documents-show-tsa-tracked-bluetooth-devices-monit/nWyb3/.

15. Loek Essers, "Dutch Bill Seeks to Give Law Enforcement Hacking Powers, by *PC World*, May 2, 2013.

16. Andy Greenberg, "Evidence Mounts That Chinese Government Hackers Spread Android Malware," *Forbes*, April 1, 2013.

17. Greenberg, "Evidence Mounts That Chinese Government Hackers Spread Android Malware."

18. Nicole Perlroth, "Traveling Light in a Time of Digital Thievery," *New York Times*, February 10, 2012.

19. Unclassified statement for the record on the worldwide threat assessment of the US Intelligence Community for the Senate Select Committee on Intelligence by James R. Clapper, director of national intelligence, January 31, 2012.

20. "Traveling Light," *New York Times*, supra.

21. Eric Lichtblau, "More Demands on Cell Carriers in Surveillance," *New York Times*, July 8, 2012.

22. *Jones v. U.S.*, 132 S.Ct. 945 (2012)

23. Bob Violino, "When in China, Don't Leave Your Laptop Alone," *Infoworld*, December 12, 2012.

24. Peter Burrows and Adam Satariano, "Apple Said to Have Team Developing Wristwatch Computer," Bloomberg.com, February 13, 2013, www.bloomberg.com/news/2013-02-12/apple-said-to-have-team-developing-wristwatch-computer.html.

*Technology Section II*

# Risks in the Streets

Privacy risks abound outside your computer as well. As cities, shops, and businesses install cameras everywhere, store the information they capture, and apply software to examining the video for interesting items, we are being watched. Drones equipped with cameras are becoming more common, and nearly every street and intersection in every major city follows you with their own electronic eyes. Even your car is becoming an Internet-connected computer that sends your information far afield. The toll booths are watching you, even when you are not paying tolls, and they are recording your movements.

Increasingly, traits of your body are being used to identify you and track your movements. From banks to theme parks to the US Customs and Immigration Service, your body measurements are becoming an important way to authenticate you and know where you go. Facial recognition can be used to follow your tracks, and your voice is being used to sense your frustration level on service calls. Finally, your DNA, the core building block of your body, has become a valuable commodity for research and for law enforcement. As you move about in the world, your privacy is betrayed by your workplace, your car, and even your body. Read on to see how vulnerable we have become.

# SEVEN

## Cameras Everywhere

Whether you know it or not, you could be photographed many times today. If you run a red light or drive over the speed limit, your car's license plate might be on film. When you visit a bank or an ATM, you will be caught on video or camera still shots. If you go shopping, smile, because you are on camera. Catching a professional sports event this weekend? There may be as many cameras in the stadium watching you as recording the game. Your chances of being photographed are highest in concentrated urban areas. London, Chicago, New York, and Boston are some of the most photo- and video-grabbing cities on the planet.

Every day more cameras appear on our streets, in our shops, and even hovering in the air above our heads. Many of the cameras installed in public places help to keep us safe. All carry the potential of invading our privacy.

### SECURE AT WHAT PRICE?

London may contain more surveillance cameras than any other city in the world. The British government has roughly five hundred thousand cameras, and their system is often called the "ring of steel."[1] Local law enforcement uses camera footage to help reduce and solve crimes. For example, when suicide bombers attacked the mass transit systems on July 7, 2005, London police turned to their surveillance cameras and were able to identity suspects within days. Tips from the public helped them narrow in on the suspects and bring them in for questioning.

New York City has followed London's lead. The Lower Manhattan Security Initiative is installing cameras across the city to be monitored twenty-four hours a day by the New York Police Department (NYPD). Roughly four thousand private and public security cameras and license plate readers feed into the NYPD for review.[2] The cameras review cars, the passengers in the cars, people walking, and even inanimate objects. Sophisticated face- and object-detection software powering the cameras can look for unattended parcels, cars driving erratically, and radiation. If needed, the cameras can alert the traffic roadblock systems to insert a roadblock.

In the District of Columbia, cameras are posted on New York Avenue to help improve the overall safety of the street from people running red lights and disobeying speed limits. A series of only nine New York Avenue cameras covering roughly three miles brought in revenues of over $11 million dollars in 2012 from ticket collections.[3] Talk about the price of added security!

The security from added surveillance comes at a price beyond your wallet. Around-the-clock surveillance cameras watch innocent citizens as well as criminals, and many of the cameras send data offsite to be stored indefinitely. In most democracies, citizens are assumed innocent until proven guilty, so why watch them all day? Privacy and civil liberty experts worry about the potential abuse of power that could turn every videotape into a legal record of your behavior. For example, you might decide to run a red light or stop sign at 2 a.m., with nobody around. Technically you are breaking the law. Should you have to pay a fine?

> **Tracking and recording people's movements raises serious privacy concerns. Where we go can reveal a great deal about us, including visits to doctor's offices, political meetings, and friends. Without probable cause, that's none of the government's business.**
> **—ACLU of Texas executive director Terri Burke[4]**

Citizens around the globe struggle with how intrusive government should be in our lives to protect us. When privacy dies at the hands of security, security becomes a questionable term. Security from what?

In the weeks following the Boston Marathon bombing, two different polls illustrate how divided we feel on these issues.

- Rasmussen ran a poll in the month after the Boston Marathon bombing to ask Americans how they felt about surveillance cameras being installed and used by the government to improve security. Of those polled, 70 percent were in favor of camera surveillance in public places. In the same poll, only 23 percent thought that existing cameras in use today have violated their privacy.[5]
- A separate poll conducted by CNN/Time/ORC[6] after the Boston Marathon bombings found that Americans worry that the government may overreach and overreact, instituting increasingly invasive camera surveillance policies. Sixty-one percent of Americans in that poll said they were more concerned about the government enacting new security policies to combat terrorism that would restrict their civil liberties. In comparison, only 31 percent were con-

cerned that the government would not act to create new policies against terrorism. When asked if they would sacrifice civil liberties in the name of combating terrorism, 49 percent of the survey respondents said no, they would not be willing to do that.

New surveillance technologies to thwart terrorists and crime are coming fast. Law-enforcement agencies in the UK have purchased and deployed drones with sophisticated technology that goes beyond thermal imaging, the technique of searching for living persons or animals. Richard Tynan, who works at Privacy International, expresses concerns not only for privacy, but for what could happen if the drone technology or data is intercepted by criminals. "[Drones] can be equipped with things called IMSI-catchers that will work out the mobile phone numbers of any people in a certain area," Tynan says. "If police deploy these things for crowd control there's no issue with them figuring out every single person who's in there—and their mobile phone numbers. They can also intercept calls and send out false messages. It's not just the police either. Cyber-criminals can use these, or even business opponents. This technology already exists."[7]

Many of us do not think of our faces as private, but they are. You can walk around anywhere in the world and just be you, without your name and everything about you being highlighted in public. In Europe, laws say that a company that takes a picture of your face and applies facial recognition has to get your permission first. The United States does not require this, nor do many other countries as of this writing.

Before we can best decide how to balance security and privacy in our homes, communities, and countries, we need to understand who owns the cameras and how they are being used.

## WHO IS BEHIND THAT CAMERA, AND WHY?

Governments, law enforcement agencies, shop owners, advertisers, and even our bosses want to know what we are up to when we think they are not looking. Thanks to quiet cameras on the streets and in the corners of rooms, they can watch us almost all the time.

### Governments and Law Enforcement

Security experts and law enforcement make a strong case that cameras can both deter and help solve crimes. The US Department of Justice conducted a study within the Office of Community Oriented Policing Services to look at the effectiveness of surveillance cameras.[8] They found that if the surveillance camera teams were trained on how to spot, follow up, and forward leads, then the combination of the cameras and trained teams did reduce crime proactively. The study cited a drop of 23 percent for violent crimes after surveillance cameras were installed in Baltimore. Chicago saw crime fall 38 percent.[9, 10]

By installing even more surveillance, it will be possible to use facial-recognition technology in real time, capturing faces and leveraging behavior-based analysis to send real-time alerts to security guards that a situation could lead to a threat. However, adding cameras does have a downside. More cameras may give a better shot of catching a criminal on video, but they also produce an ever-growing number of images to review. The technology is improving. In the case of the Boston Marathon bombings, it took the FBI only three days to analyze a large number of images and release photos of the suspects to the public.

Private camera networks also provide images that help law enforcement. Some of the best surveillance footage that helped investigators identify the Boston Marathon bombing suspects came from private camera networks.

Around the world, each country has its own set of rules regarding how government can access private camera networks to suit their purposes. India's parliament in 2008 passed a law known as the Information Technology Act, which gives the government of India the ability to tap all communications, private and public, without a warrant or a court order. In Ivory Coast, the government asked the UN to consider using unmanned drones to protect the people, but also protect endangered species from poachers when peacekeeping forces are reduced later this year.[11]

Law enforcement in the UK and the United States use cameras to read license plates on the road. While sitting in a patrol car, a law-enforcement officer can tap into a vast database to look for a match against reported crimes. Police say the technology helps them recover stolen cars, find people wanted for an arrest, and even assists in tracking down missing people.

*You Are the Star at the Mall*

Modern shopping centers contain a mesh of security designed to stop shoplifting and robberies, from store employees to hidden cameras. But those same cameras installed for security can also help shop owners and advertisers track your every move to know you better so they can convince you to shop more. Many of us spot a camera now and again, and we don't mind. Occasionally we wave at the cameras, being good sports about it all. But what happens when those cameras cross the line and become creepy snoops sending data back to headquarters so they can manipulate us into spending more money?

Video cameras pulling high-quality photos and audio can track your every move. Many use facial-recognition software to either identify you or at least make a guess at your age, ethnic background, and gender. Cameras can also be designed to capture car license plates in the parking lot. These cameras watch for suspicious behavior, but savvy retailers could also collate the parking lot images with their internal camera. If you connect to the store's free Wi-Fi, they can track your unique device ID number as you shop in each department. You might decide to try their convenient smartphone app to look for a coupon, and now they can tie your customer information to your location. Add to that the spying mannequin and you have no place to hide. Using facial recognition and other information, they could cyberstalk you in the physical store.

Many retailers have hidden, tiny cameras that focus on you from behind small pin holes in the walls, shelves, and other fixtures. Cameras called gaze trackers actually watch your gaze while you shop. The gaze trackers know what you look at, what you touch, and if you checked the price. They categorize the items you looked at, and then they try to determine your demographics by looking at your face.

The sharply dressed mannequin that seems to be staring at you? It just might be. A new mannequin model built in Italy and called the EyeSee[12] has a camera inside. The camera looks through the mannequin's eye and takes your photo, matching it up against facial-recognition software databases. It will log what it believes to be your age, gender, and race.[13]

Retailers point to the benefits surveillance brings to the consumer. Monitoring the store can help the owner serve you better. It can help them align staff to be available when you are looking for an item, wanting to get something gift wrapped, or ready to check out. However, these benefits come at the cost of your privacy. Pam Dixon, executive director at the World Privacy Forum, expressed her concerns about the shopping experience turning into a digital surveillance sting. "While most consumers understand a need for security cameras," says Dixon, "few expect that the in-store video advertising monitor they're watching . . . is watching them."[14] Retailers have also started WiFi tracking of customer movements by monitoring where smartphones go within the store, so they know which displys interest you and when to send cashiers to the floor.

## The Boss Is Watching

Your boss is also interested in your behavior, especially during the times you are being paid to work. Employers are turning to cameras matched with sensor technology to monitor their employees' whereabouts and productivity. Cameras and tracking devices gather real-time information on how teams work together and their productivity. Companies on the leading edge of this trend report that the most productive teams are close knit and speak frequently — in person.

One large company wanted to see if in-person, face-to-face time versus working at home mattered, so they had their employees wear badges that had tiny sensors installed. The sensors recorded not only employees' movements but also the tone of their conversations. The company also derived information from workplace cameras to help round out their surveillance picture. They said the study proved to them that employees were more productive in the office than working at home. Productivity improved by 10 percent, and the workers were happier when they were at the office (according to the sensors).[15]

In response to these and other findings, some companies have changed the way they do business. In 2013, Yahoo! and BestBuy announced an end to flexible at-home work hours and said that employees must come back to the office.

Data on employee productivity collected at the workplace could be beneficial, but is that data safe? And what about your privacy? Or should you assume that you have no privacy in the workplace?

## DRONES—WHEN CAMERAS FLY OVERHEAD

Most of us have times when we decide to be offline. We may blast our favorite song and dance like nobody's watching. Unfortunately, someone might be watching after all through a hovering drone. Whether private or for law enforcement, drones carry cameras that now have incredible sound and audio quality and can spy on you through your windows and skylights. Anyone can buy a drone, or even create a simple homemade drone by connecting a smartphone or tablet to a model airplane. They can then fly while they spy, using simple apps that record pictures, videos, and audio, all silent and hard to detect. The legal system has not caught up with the technology. Law enforcement is still trying to understand how to govern drone flights and whether data acquired by them can be made public or used in criminal cases as evidence. Think of nonmilitary drones as flying computers, with every feature and functionality that you can imagine. Just like computers, drones can also be hacked, so it is vital there is a discussion about how data collected by drones is protected.

> **What altitude can they fly? What kind of facial recognition are they capable of at various activities? Can they take pictures of individuals through windows of their home? Drones are hard to spot for the untrained eye, so your ability to protect yourself is not great.**
> —US Senator Dianne Feinstein (D-California)[16]

While the fly time and audio and video quality of drones improve, the price is going down. This leads to concerns that need to be discussed in communities, both for legal proceedings and just as a general set of etiquette for good manners.

Citizens around the globe are asking whether or not the price of their privacy in the name of security is worth it. Just an hour's drive outside of Denver, Colorado, in the town of Deer Trail, there is such grave concern over drones that the town's leaders created a draft bill for hunting licenses to shoot drones for twenty-five dollars.[17] The draft said they would also offer a bounty of one hundred dollars for any unmanned drone shot down by its citizens. The draft bill is considered symbolic and a warning to government and nongovernment drone owners not to fly over Deer Trail. The Federal Aviation Administration, which has jurisdiction over airspace, has warned towns not to consider shooting down drones.[18]

> **Like it or not, unmanned systems are the future. Unfortunately we're not ready for them—everything from our policy to our laws to the deep, deep ethical questions.**
> **—Peter Singer, senior fellow at Brookings Institute**[19,20]

Here are some of the concerns ripe for community discussion:

- What is the effect of drones on citizen privacy?
- Airspace: What happens when drones interfere with commercial and private aircraft?
- What is the danger of drones in the wrong hands? A drone is a flying computer with video/audio and sometimes a gun. What happens when the bad guys overtake a good-guy drone? What happens when the bad guys steal, build, or buy their own?

The tool is not the problem, and it's not going away. Now is the time to openly discuss and anticipate how the bad guys would abuse drones and then come up with the right scenarios to counter those tactics. Drones are flying supercomputers. Think of your smartphone on steroids. With that in mind, what should the rules be?

## Drones around the World

In certain parts of the world, drones are almost ubiquitous. Drones for military and government usage are quickly becoming a favorite tool in countries' arsenals for surveillance and, in some cases, fire power to shoot at targets. It is currently estimated that more than seventy-five countries employ drones and that more than fifty nations are building drones.[21]

In the UK, several police forces are experimenting with drones to see if they can use them for creative purposes such as looking for a person in a large crowd. Instead of using facial-recognition technology alone, drones might also look for the signal emitted from the person's mobile phone.

Germans are tired of graffiti on their railway systems. Germany announced a plan to combat graffiti with miniature helicopter drones outfitted with thermal imaging cameras. The drones will fly around the most popular spots for graffiti, which include cities such as Berlin and Hamburg. At only a meter across in wingspan, the drones will be an extra set of eyes looking for offenders and then alerting authorities so they can apprehend the graffiti artists in the act.[22]

In Canada, the Royal Canadian Mounted Police (RCMP) from the province of Saskatchewan used a drone to rescue a man. A man called their emergency service when his car crashed. His car flipped over, and he was in a remote part of the province. After police could not find him with a traditional helicopter, they deployed a drone with an infrared camera and sent it to the last known coordinates that his cell phone provided when he made the emergency call. The drone found a heat signature that belonged to the man, and the RCMP was able to deploy a rescue team. "To our knowledge, this is the first time that a life may have been saved with the use of a sUAS (small Unmanned Aerial System) helicopter," said Zenon Dragan, president and founder of the drone-making company Draganfly.[23]

## Drones in the United States

Before 2030, a huge milestone will be hit in the United States. More than twenty thousand additional drones will be buzzing about like busy bees in a flower garden over the United States.[24]

These drones will be owned by the military, law enforcement, public-health agencies, private companies, and possibly your neighbors. American citizens did not get to vote on flying video cameras trailing their every move in the name of security; it was decided for them. The ACLU and other privacy groups know that with drones already flying overhead, they need to fight for our civil liberties to be protected as the data is collected and collated.

US law-enforcement agencies own Predator drones that have been outfitted overseas with missiles that can take out a person, a home, a car, or inflict incredible damage on large buildings.

The drone industry is aggressive and mobilized to provide equipment that can be used to secure a country and its citizens. AeroVironment, Inc. (AV) has publicly said in their SEC filings that they want to expand their product base to other markets. In their 2011 filing, AV's report says, "Initial likely non-military users of small UAS include public safety organizations such as law enforcement agencies."[25] But what happens if the drone, which is a flying computer, is hacked and control of the drone or its data falls in the wrong hands? How would we know, mitigate the threat, and recover without creating loss of life?

We can't always see or hear these drones. Many drones are small enough to fit in a duffel bag or satchel. Some have been designed to look like birds sitting on a wire or fence. Others have been designed to look like dragonflies.

The ACLU recently wrote that "US law enforcement is greatly expanding its use of domestic drones for surveillance." Colorado law enforcement has used drones for search and rescue. The US government's Department of Homeland Security uses drones for border patrol. Police showed the effectiveness of drones using thermal imaging when they were looking for the Boston Marathon bombers.

A drone has even been used to help arrest a US citizen. In the small town of Lakota, North Dakota, rancher Rodney Brossart was holding on to six cows that had trespassed on his property but belonged to another farm.[26] The police department deployed a drone to the scene to assist them in making the arrest.

Reporters are also getting in on the drone action. At the University of Missouri, journalism students learned to fly drones they call J-bots for test cases in reporting. The idea was to give them an eyewitness account in a location they could not easily get to in person. One of the University of Missouri students actually noticed a creek near his house had turned red and tracked it back to a nearby meat-processing plant.[27]

*Drones to the Rescue*

Drones, when used wisely, have been deployed to protect people and animals. Police and emergency crews have used drones for rescues, to track fugitives, and to search for missing persons. Drones have dropped medicines and supplies to stranded victims. As part of a five-million-dollar grant to the World Wildlife Fund, Google has launched drones in Africa to limit poaching.[28]

One dad built his own drone so he could safely send his son to the bus stop each morning. Like any parent, the dad may have wanted to give his son more freedom to get to the bus stop while keeping him safe. The dad went online and searched for do-it-yourself kits and settled on a quad-copter and a GPS device that would go in his son's backpack.[29] He made a few modifications to help the quadcopter with landings and tracking his son via the backpack. Soon he had eyes in the sky on his son. He did note that weather conditions can impact this DIY drone. On those days where the weather prevents the drone from flying well, he walks his son to the bus stop.

Someday perhaps government mail services around the globe will use drones to improve service delivery while cutting expenses. We recommend they start first by testing out newspaper delivery and review any lessons learned before moving on to more critical postal items.

*Drones in the Wrong Hands*

Drones have already been used by bad people for bad deeds. For example, in Latin America FARC (Fuerzas Armadas Revolucionarias de Colombia, also known as the Revolutionary Armed Forces of Colombia) worked with the narcocartels to create remote-controlled drug-smuggling submarines.[30] Rezwan Ferdaus, an al-Qaeda affiliate, plotted an attack on the Pentagon and Capitol buildings using a remote-controlled drone aircraft armed with bomblike explosives.[31] Thankfully, the FBI intercepted the plot. In Brazil, criminals who were not currently in jail sent a drone care package into a prison to deliver cell phones to prisoners there.[32] In the UK a few years ago, criminals tried to send drugs into a prison via a drone.[33]

Military drones are essentially flying computers with extensive surveillance capabilities and sometimes gun power. In a recent drone hack, Iraqi Shi'ite insurgents hacked into real-time video feeds of US drones as they flew over Iraq. The insurgents were able to see what our US military saw, monitor the feeds, and potentially compromise US military operations. In another drone hack, a keylogger virus was injected into US predator and reaper drones, allowing insurgents to log every key stroke of drone pilots as they flew in Afghanistan and the surrounding regions.[34]

## GOING INCOGNITO

Maintaining a sense of privacy and security is important to everyone. It is unsettling to think that cameras you see and don't see are taking your picture all day long. In some regard, you expect it. The cameras are part of a complex web of security systems, often privately owned by residences and businesses. Other cameras may be in place for law enforcement and the government to keep a watchful eye out for suspicious activity. So, even if unsettling, you might think the cameras are not following you, and that it's not like they can shoot you. But drones can be equipped to shoot an object or a person as well as snap photos, take video, and capture audio. The technology is way ahead of our ability to protect and defend ourselves against what it can do.

So how can you just blend into the crowd?

### Fooling Facial-Recognition Software

According to a 2013 story on *60 Minutes*, facial-recognition technology has vastly improved in the previous decade. Facial-recognition programs on computers can identify faces one hundred times better and a million times faster than ten years ago.[35] Still, facial recognition has not attained the level of accuracy of some other forms of biometric identification. Although cameras played a key role in identifying the Boston marathon suspects, it was their fingerprints that correctly identified them.[36]

Facial-recognition software has evolved from being the stuff of James Bond movies and secretive intelligence agencies to being everywhere you are. It is on your smartphone every time you take and categorize a picture. It is on Facebook. It is used in surveillance cameras by law enforcement. Some camera surveillance systems claim they can match a face and identity it within seconds after checking a database with over thirty-five million faces.

Most of us like to be recognized by friends, but that does not mean we want to be identified from a photograph any time and any place. Protestors sometimes wear face masks to block detection, especially in the event that they are caught on the evening news being arrested. Others have taken to wearing hoodies and sunglasses. Experiments are underway to use different types of makeup applications and combinations of clothing or eyewear to make it more difficult for facial-recognition software to identify you.

Blocking facial-recognition software is especially important for anyone under the age of eighteen with a picture on Facebook. Predators search Facebook for underage victims to "friend," and web crawlers can work beyond the confines of Facebook to identify you by face. For those reasons, it is vital to opt children's faces and names out of the Facebook facial-recognition system. One option for confusing data-recognition software with your online pictures is to pixelate them. Make them a lower resolution or blur the eyes. Google+ will ask you if you want to opt into facial recognition.

### Wearing Protective Gear Against Drones

Concerns about being taped from roving drones are pervasive enough that a new cottage industry has started, offering antidrone devices, blockers, and even clothing. The UK newspaper the *Daily Mail* found a secret Pakistani report via the Al Jazeera news network that revealed the fact that Osama bin Laden sported a cowboy hat during his years hiding in Pakistan to avoid being detected by a drone.[37]

Are you part of what entrepreneur Adam Harvey refers to as the "fashionably paranoid market"? If so, Harvey makes antidrone fashions, including hoodies, for you.[38] The material he uses will supposedly block the thermal imaging systems on drones. The hoodies are an expansion in Harvey's line of stealth clothing that began with a handbag to fight back the paparazzi or even the cyberazzis. If held in the person's hand while flash photography is used, the handbag lets off a counter flash that ruins the picture by fuzzing out the person in the picture with light.[39]

Harvey was inspired by the use of military technology applied to civilians.[40] When asked by *Slate* magazine about how to live with drones flying around the United States, he said, "Military technology is coming home from the war . . . These pieces are designed to live with it (drones), to cope with it—to live in a world where surveillance is happening all the time."[41] In his interview with the *Air Force Times*, Harvey talks about how he not only helps you grab your privacy and security back, but also hopes to foster a broader conversation about the legitimacy of drones off the traditional battlefield. "While I implemented this on a fashionable level, I think this is a good way to change people's sentiments about [drones and surveillance] and why we need to consider it before it becomes a greater problem," says Harvey.[42] And it's not just privacy-seeking civilians who are interested in his new clothing line. In a conversation with the *Daily Beast*, Harvey reported that his company has been inundated with requests from companies that make military equipment. He has also received requests for pieces to be custom made for operations in the Middle East. "People see it as technology they can use in their own way."[43]

## NOTES

1. Sylvia Hui, "Bloomberg Reviews London's 'Ring of Steel,'" *NBC News*, May 11, 2010, www.nbcnews.com/id/37087582/ns/world_news-europe/t/bloomberg-reviews-londons-ring-steel/.

2. Ti-Hua Chang, "Lower Manhattan Security Initiative: A Look Inside," *Fox 5 News*, April 30, 2013, www.myfoxny.com/story/22059421/lower-manhattan-security-initiative-a-look-inside#ixzz2ZXOCmySU.

3. Ashley Halsey III, "Three Golden Miles Net D.C. $28 Million," *Washington Post*, May 27, 2013.

4. Gordon Dickson, "Police Using Car-Top Cameras to Photograph License Plates," *Star Telegram*, August 17, 2012.

5. Rasmussen Reports, "70% Favor Use of Surveillance Cameras in Public Places," rasmussenreports.com, April 24, 2013, www.rasmussenreports.com/public_content/politics/general_politics/april_2013/70_favor_use_of_surveillance_cameras_in_public_places.

6. CNN/Time/ORC poll, 606 adult Americans, sampling error four points (+/-) conducted by ORC International, April 30, 2013, i2.cdn.turner.com/cnn/2013/images/05/01/top5.pdf.

7. Tom Meltzer, "The Anti-drone Hoodie that Helps You Beat Big Brother's Spy in the Sky," *Guardian*, March 31, 2013.

8. Nancy G. La Vignet, Samantha S. Lowry, Joshua A. Markman, and Allison M. Dwyer, "Evaluating the Use of Public Surveillance Cameras for Crime Control and Prevention," Urban Institute Justice Policy Center, 2011, www.cops.usdoj.gov/Publications/e071112381_EvalPublicSurveillance.pdf.

9. Hilton Collins, "Video Camera Networks Link Real-Time Partners in Crime-Solving," *Government Technology*, February 1, 2012.

10. Vignet et al., "Evaluating the Use of Public Surveillance Cameras for Crime Control and Prevention."

11. Afua Hirsch, "Drones Could Replace Peacekeepers in Ivory Coast," *Guardian*, April 17, 2013.

12. EyeSee Mannequin, site current as of July 20, 2013, www.almax-italy.com/en-US/ProgettiSpeciali/EyeSeeMannequin.aspx.

13. Andrew Roberts, "Bionic Mannequins Spy on Shoppers to Boost Luxury Sales," *Bloomberg News*, November 20, 2012.

14. "How Stores Spy on You: Many Retailers Are Snooping More Than Ever," *ShopSmart*, ConsumerReports.org, March 2013, www.consumerreports.org/cro/2013/03/how-stores-spy-on-you/index.htm.

15. Rachel Emma Silverman, "Tracking Sensors Invade the Workplace," *Wall Street Journal*, March 7, 2013.

16. "Congress Struggling to Come Up with Rules at the Dawn of the Drone Age," *Russian Times*, March 20, 2013, rt.com/usa/surveillance-drone-hearing-552/.

17. Keith Coffman, "Colorado Town Mulls Issuing Licenses to Shoot Down Drones," Reuters, July 17, 2013, www.reuters.com/article/2013/07/18/us-usa-colorado-drones-idUSBRE96H02120130718.

18. Associated Press, "FAA Warns Public against Shooting Guns at Drones," July 19, 2013, www.foxnews.com/us/2013/07/19/faa-warns-public-against-shooting-guns-at-drones/.

19. Statement of Peter Warren Singer, PhD, senior fellow and director, 21st Century Defense Initiative, The Brookings Institution, The United States House of Representatives, Committee on Oversight and Government Reform, Subcommittee on National Security and Foreign Affairs, March 23, 2010.

20. Mark Corcoran, "Rise of the Machines," *ABC News*, April 9, 2012.

21. Kristin Roberts, "When the Whole World Has Drones," *National Security*, NationalJournal.com, March 22, 2013, www.nationaljournal.com/magazine/when-the-whole-world-has-drones-20130321.

22. Jeevan Vasagar, "German Railways Deploys Surveillance Drones," *Telegraph*, May 27, 2013.

23. Carl Franzen, "Canadian Mounties Claim First Person's Life Saved by a Police Drone," *The Verge*, May 10, 2013.

24. Meltzer, "The Anti-drone Hoodie That Helps You Beat Big Brother's Spy in the Sky."

25. Glenn Greenwald, "Domestic Drones and Their Unique Dangers," *Guardian*, March 29, 2013.

26. "Rodney Brossart, American Arrested Using Predator Drone, Had Rights Violated, Lawyer Says," *Huff Post Tech*, huffingtonpost.com, May 4, 2012, www.huffingtonpost.com/2012/05/04/rodney-brossart-american-arrested-using-predator-drone_n_1477549.html.

27. "Journalism Schools Start Teaching Students to Fly Drones," *Russian Times*, March 22, 2013.

28. Neal Ungerleider, "Google Drones Launch in Africa," *Fast Company*, December 6, 2012, www.fastcompany.com/3003766/google-drones-launch-africa.

29. Paul Wallich, "The DIY Kid tracking Drone," IEEE Spectrum, December 2013.

30. Marc Goodman, "Criminals and Terrorists Can Fly Drones Too, Remote-controlled Aircraft and Robot Technology Can Be Used for Bad Just as Easily as for Good," *Ideas*, Time.com, January 31, 2013, ideas.time.com/2013/01/31/criminals-and-terrorists-can-fly-drones-too/#ixzz2ZXibBWz6http://ideas.time.com/2013/01/31/criminals-and-terrorists-can-fly-drones-too/.

31. "The Jihadist Drummer: Muslim Musician Held Over Plot to Attack Pentagon with Remote-controlled Toy Plane Packed with Explosives," *Daily Mail*, September, 29, 2011, www.dailymail.co.uk/news/article-2043017/FBI-foils-Rezwan-Ferdauss-plot-attack-Pentagon-toy-plane-packed-explosives.html.

32. Goodman, "Criminals and Terrorists Can Fly Drones Too."

33. Goodman, "Criminals and Terrorists Can Fly Drones Too."

34. Siobhan Gorman, Yochi J. Dreazen, and August Cole, "Insurgents Hack U.S. Drones," *Wall Street Journal*, December 17, 2009.

35. Lesley Stahl and Shachar Bar-On, "A Face in the Crowd," *60 Minutes*, May 19, 2013.

36. Mariano Castillo and Greg Botelho, "Timeline: How the Boston Marathon Bombing Suspects Were Hunted Down," CNN.com, April 20, 2013.

37. David Martosko and Amanda Williams, "Osama Bin Laden Wore a COWBOY HAT to Avoid Detection from U.S. Drones, Reveals Secret Report into His Life on the Run," *Daily Mail*, July 8, 2013, www.dailymail.co.uk/news/article-2358402/Pakistani-report-Osama-bin-Laden-wore-COWBOY-HAT-house-avoid-detection-youngest-wife-thought-kill-raids-noises-just-rainstorm.html.

38. Meltzer, "The Anti-drone Hoodie That Helps You Beat Big Brother's Spy in the Sky."

39. "AH Projects, Camoflash," patent application US 2012/0056546 A1, ahprojects.com/projects.

40. Oriana Pawlyk, "'Stealth Wear' Deflects Drone Detection," *Army Times*, April 7, 2013, www.armytimes.com/article/20130407/NEWS/304070007/-8216-Stealth-Wear-8217-deflects-drone-detection.

41. Ryan Gallagher, "The Anti-surveillance Clothing Line That Promises to Thwart Cell Tracking and Drones," *Slate*, January 11, 2013.

42. Pawlyk, "'Stealth Wear' Deflects Drone Detection."

43. Claire Stern, "Adam Harvey Launches Stealth Wear, an Anti-drone Clothing Line," *Daily Beast*, March 5, 2013.

# EIGHT

# When Your Car Is Just Another Computer

The coolest car in the 1960s was owned by George, patriarch of the Jetson family in the popular animated television show *The Jetsons*. The Jetson family lived in a futuristic world where everyday challenges of working and raising a family were met with the help of an endless array of utopian technology. George was always running late for work and was never sure where he was going, but this was not a problem because the family "aerocar" came to the rescue. The aerocar could fly, weave its way through traffic on its own, respond easily to being in an accident, and even had online video conferencing. Half a century later, our real-life cars are finally catching up to the Jetsons' (except for the flying part).

A new car today is more like a computer with wheels than a car with a computer. Brakes not working quite right? The mechanic may upgrade your car's software to fix the brake problem. Car not cooling down quickly enough? Might be a dead bug in the air conditioner, or a coding bug in the software.

The computerization of cars has led to many safety features and fuel economy advances while improving the overall comfort of the ride. However, consumer laws designed to protect your privacy have not kept up with the data your own car generates about you.

## YOUR SMART CAR HAS A MIND OF ITS OWN

Today's new cars arrive equipped with software and smart devices designed to improve your driving experience and help the car run right. Some built-in devices also record what happens while your car is running. But who really controls the software and devices in your car? And who owns the data they record?

*How Car Makers Stay in Touch*

In 2012, some 250,000 Ford and Lincoln car owners opened their mail at home to find an interesting package from Ford Motor Company. The package held a thumb drive that contained software updates for the My-Ford Touch and MyLincoln Touch dashboards. To get the update, the owners were told to plug the thumb drive into their car's USB port.

To upgrade software on their Mercedes Benz 2013 SL roadster, Mercedes now downloads updates wirelessly while the car is running. The same basic process you use to update your smartphone can now update your car.

Google wants to take us one step closer to George Jetson's world by developing a car that drives itself. You might have seen one of their test fleet of self-driving cars on the road, typically a Toyota Prius outfitted with a radar or satellite hat on top so Google engineers can navigate the car remotely. They use a laser to watch the car and send it directions. The car is programmed to be a polite driver that stops for pedestrians and always follows the road rules—no more rolling stops at stop signs.

Not to be outdone by Google, Audi is testing features for a car that parks itself. In a sneak preview, Audi demonstrated a test car that could receive instructions sent to it from a smartphone. Following the commands sent from the smartphone, the car could park itself, then leave its parking space and drive over to you. Imagine having that feature on those awful weather days. Now all the car needs is a cup of hot coffee waiting for you in the cup holder.

Buyers of a new Chevrolet Volt are likely to sign an agreement in the closing paperwork that gives GM permission to tap into their car to check its performance. Nissan Leaf owners can download a smartphone app that helps them monitor many of their car's features, at the same time allowing Nissan to collect GPS information, speed, and driving habits of those who use the car. Nissan says that all of this information is stored by vehicle identification number, or VIN, and not tied to personal information.[1] However, VINs are unique and registered with the car owner. Unless you bought your Nissan Leaf under another name, it is easy to tie all that information directly to you.

*A Black Box Takes Notes While You Drive*

Every commercial plane carries a black box that records information that can be used to discover what happened during a crash, from hardware malfunctions to cockpit conversations. If you bought your car after

1996, you might be surprised to learn that a black box is hidden some-place in your car as well.

Today, more than 90 percent of new cars come with the standard black box.[2] The black box in your car does not capture your cockpit conversations, but it does record your driving habits. It can be the key to saving you money on insurance. It can become the other eyewitness dur-ing a crash, or warn you that you need important maintenance. These features are helpful, and adding a black box to every car costs only about twenty US dollars.

What's the catch? The black box is not built to be secure to prevent tampering, and it was not created with your personal privacy in mind. That black box is a treasure trove for insurance companies that want to charge you more for reckless and careless moments behind the wheel. Law enforcement also uses this data for crime scenes and accident scenes. State laws do not necessarily recognize the data as your private property, which means law enforcement may be able to access it without obtaining a subpoena or a warrant.

Consider the case of Massachusetts Lieutenant Governor Timothy Murray after he was in a car accident. According to Murray's account, he was driving the speed limit and prudently wearing his seatbelt when he crashed.[3] But an eyewitness was on the scene, and it happened to be in the car with him. Inside that car was the little black box, and its electronic data recorder (EDR) told a different story.[4] The evidence on the EDR said that not only was Mr. Murray not buckled in, but he hit speeds of over ninety miles per hour. [5]

The car in Mr. Murray's accident was government owned, so he should naturally assume the government owned the data, too. But even when you own the car you drive, the government does not protect your right to that data. In fact, the National Highway Traffic Safety Adminis-tration (NHTSA) does not seem to care that your car's data might be used against you without due process. The best they could do is ask car mak-ers to mention the black box in the owner's manual.

After just a few minutes of searching to locate that black box, law enforcement can plug it in and find out your second-by-second actions before, during, and after the time of a crime or accident. They can track your braking, slow-downs, and acceleration. Some cars even have sen-sors in the seats so the car would know how many passengers were in the car (or not) during the time in question.

> **The amount of data that they record is vast. And it's not capped. And I found that to be quite problematic.**
> —**Nate Cardozo, a staff attorney with the Electronic Frontier Founda-tion, when asked to comment on the black boxes in all new cars**[6]

In the wrong hands, all that data collected about you could be used against you or manipulated to frame you in a bad light. On February 11,

2013, the Electronic Frontier Foundation (EFF) wrote a letter to the NHTSA expressing their concerns about the lack of policies covering what is collected. They specifically recommended that NHTSA prohibit the recorder from capturing location-specific information, audio or video.[7] Another key suggestion in their letter included a mandate for a locking feature so owners could lock down their data.

### Driving through the Cloud

According to ABI Research, by the year 2017 more than 60 percent of vehicles across the globe will have an active and direct Internet connection.[8] They predict the percentage to be closer to 80 percent in regions of North America and Europe. In a study about connected drivers, the technology research group Gartner found that many drivers ask for the very connectivity that can be used to track them.[9] Most drivers know that they should not be on their smartphone surfing while driving, so they want a display into their dashboard that allows them to surf smart apps by voice or touch without scrambling for the phone. Almost 40 percent want their car's overall health to be tracked, and they want proactive alerts to get things fixed before they break. Almost one-third of respondents want their car to drive itself or provide driver assistance in situations such as parking, cars weaving, or driver fatigue.[10]

## "FULLY LOADED"—THE OPTIONS THAT KEEP TRACK OF YOU

Options and third-party products for today's cars help you make hands-free phone calls, find a nearby rest stop, and even keep track of your teen driver. But who, besides yourself, has access to the personal information these products collect about you?

### What Does Your Telematics System Know and Tell?

Onboard car telematics systems such as OnStar offer a variety of services that provide security and convenience to car owners, especially in emergency situations such as accidents or violent weather conditions. A telematics system can track your car maintenance, call for help when there are safety issues, and help you locate a restaurant. Telematics systems integrate information and telecommunications. The system needs to know where you are in order to be useful to you. Some of the data it collects to respond to your queries is anonymized (stripped of personal information), but information such as speed, destination times, and driving habits is not.

**It's troubling. Any time a new service like this is introduced you have to think beyond what's described in the press release. It's im-**

portant to remember that you can provide a service that is valuable and useful and still be violating people's privacy.
                    —Parker Higgins of the Electronic Frontier Foundation[11]

OnStar even offers a family tracking service to let you keep tabs on your family. This can be useful to make sure loved ones arrived at their destination safely. However, this service presents stalking and safety concerns if a family had a domestic dispute. The police and the government can use it to track you as well.

Many telematics systems come built into new vehicles and have a free trial period, after which you pay a subscription to continue receiving the service. OnStar wanted to keep their surveillance going even after car owners shut off their service, but a consumer backlash changed the company's mind. Now the onboard device they use to track you is not enabled until you manually press it and contact their service.

## Bluetooth and Traffic Control

Bluetooth, the helpful hands-free technology that allows you to connect computers, devices, and phones without cords, has grown so popular that many new cars are now equipped with Bluetooth built in. As a result, traffic-monitoring systems that track and report traffic conditions count traffic by listening to "pings" from Bluetooth devices on cars. But the system that is supposed to help you avoid a traffic jam could put your driving patterns at risk. Unfortunately, the data collected has not always been protected as it should be, making the system vulnerable to hackers eavesdropping, disrupting traffic control, and potentially stealing your personal data.

Fortunately, researchers from the University of California at San Diego and the University of Michigan found the issue and alerted the industry so they could fix it. As of the time this book is being written, there are no confirmed hacks of this vulnerability. Even so, often it's just a matter of time, or the hackers are so skilled and stealthy we do not ever know they are there.

As discussed in chapter 6, "Bluesnarfing" is when criminals eavesdrop on Bluetooth-broadcasted messages. If Bluetooth is built into your car, ask your car manufacturer how they protect your Bluetooth traffic.

---

TOOLBOX

**Tiwi is a tracking tool that can be used to track loved ones or even employees. Tiwi is passionate about stopping teens from distracted or dangerous driving. According to Tiwi's website (www.tiwi.com), "Every 55 seconds, a teen is injured or killed in a car crash."[12] Plugged into your car's system, Tiwi's onboard computer tracks speeding, aggressive turns, lack of seat-belt use, hard**

braking, or unsafe acceleration. If your teen driver is practicing unsafe driving, a computer voice tells the driver what is wrong and how to change it. Tiwi will even provide a report card on your teen's driving.

Tiwi is like a little brother or little sister who tells all: it sends an alert for any metric you request. You may want to know if your daughter has broken the nasty habit of forgetting to put on her seat belt. You may want to know if your son has lived up to his promise to stop following cars too closely. You can also set up geographic boundaries and be notified when your car with your teen driver leaves those boundaries. Think of it as an electric dog-gie fence for your teen. When your teen crosses that line, Tiwi will warn the driver and send you an alert.

Tiwi also has an onboard on-call unit for communications be-tween you and your teen or your teen and an emergency operator.

## YOUR INSURANCE AGENT IN THE PASSENGER SEAT

Some insurance companies offer lower rates to drivers who can prove their driving habits match certain "safe" criteria. How do they get the proof? The insurance company installs an app or device that tracks and measures your moves behind the wheel.

If you are an Aviva customer in the UK, you may have already down-loaded Aviva's RateMyDrive smartphone app in hopes of cheaper car insurance. RateMyDrive looks at your first two hundred miles and records your braking habits, how you take turns and corners, and how heavy you put the pedal to the medal. The app feeds that data into a model that scores you according to your risk. The safest drivers might see a discount as high as 20 percent by letting Aviva watch them drive.[13]

In the United States, Progressive's Snapshot takes a snapshot of your driving habits. When you agree to the Snapshot program, Progressive sends you a small device that you can plug directly into your car's diag-nostics port. Snapshot gets behind the wheel when you do and logs the time of day for each drive, the miles you drive, and when and how hard you step on the brakes. Progressive has found that if you have a heavy braking foot, you might be an aggressive driver. After six months of observation, you might get a discount on your premiums.[14] But what if other drivers in the family are heavy on the brakes when you are not around?

## A ROAD TRIP WITH BIG BROTHER

Every year, more and more new technology makes it easier for law enforcement and the government to know where your car has been and track you to your next destination. Laws and policies that protect your privacy have fallen behind in rapidly changing times, and interpretation of the law is often in a state of flux.

*License Plate Scanners*

Thanks to license plate scanners, the watchful guardians of law enforcement can now track and record the movements of your car and thousands of others as you travel or go about your daily business. Scanners on patrol cars installed all over towns tirelessly snap pictures of license plates as cars zoom by. Some of the latest license-plate scanners can grab an image of a plate at the rate of 1,800 cars per minute. The plate information is run against various databases and can help police identify missing cars, uninsured motorists, and people with outstanding subpoenas or warrants.

Located just north of San Francisco, the scenic town of Tiburon, California, attracts visitors with its quaint shops, breathtaking views, and friendly locals. But do not let the small-town ambience of Tiburon fool you. Every license plate that enters and exits the town is scanned, tracked, and checked against massive databases. When the data is pulled into the California town systems, it takes a second hop over to the Northern California Regional Intelligence Center (NCRIC) and often finds its way into the California data feed that goes to the Feds.[15]

Tiburon is not alone in having law enforcement scan the coming and going of automobiles that motor about their streets. Sugar Land, Texas, began scanning license plates from patrol cars in 2009. Three years later, the police chief proposed adding stationary scanners on routes in and out of the city.[16] The beautiful town of Piedmont, California, which is surrounded by Oakland, decided that they were tired of rising crime. The police department recommended mounting license-plate-scanning equipment around the borders of the city of Piedmont as well. It is as if these towns are building modern-day moats around their borders, only these moats are not passive—they scan every plate.

What rights do you have as a motorist to come and go as you please? In a recent study of police departments that have installed automated license-plate scanners, only a third had a written policy on when the scanners could be used and how long the records would be stored.[17] The data, sometimes stored for days, weeks, months or indefinitely, could be devastating in the wrong hands.

No matter how careful your police department is, they could be hacked or ordered to provide that data to another authority. In December

2012, a public records request was granted by a Minneapolis police department. As part of their response to the request, the department provided 2.1 million license-plate scans and GPS vehicle-location tags. After this alarmed the public, the mayor of Minneapolis asked that scanned license-plate data be considered nonpublic data.[18]

And it's not just police departments snapping images of your car or scanning your plates. Private-sector companies are scanning plates for a variety of purposes such as private investigations or tracking down deadbeat car owners who owe them money for their car lease or car loan.[19] The companies are capturing data that might include the license plate number or an image of it, and some databases may hold additional information such as photos of people getting in and out of the car, the date and time of the image, and estimated location of the vehicle.[20]

*Automatic Toll Collection*

When you use an electronic toll collection system such as E-ZPass to pay tolls on roads and bridges without stopping, you also open a door for possible government snooping.

In New Jersey, law enforcement can and will access E-ZPass records for criminal cases. They can only do so with a court order. As of this writing, New Jersey stores their toll records indefinitely.

How about when you are not at the toll booth? Transportation authorities can install readers that read the tag on your windshield anywhere and monitor your tag anytime you pass, not just when you pay for the privilege of driving on a road. In the San Francisco area, the Metropolitan Transportation Commission tracks and collects information from fast passes. If you know about the tracking and want to opt out, they provide a bag made of Mylar so you can block signals when you are not using the pass to pay a toll.

In Brooklyn, New York, white boxes hanging off traffic lights scan E-ZPass cards even though no toll booth is nearby. Instead of deducting money for a toll, the reader just captures the device information, date, and time, so most card owners are unaware they are being tracked. When the *Brooklyn Paper* contacted the city to ask for a list of all installed scanners and more information about the program, they were given a vague answer. The paper reported "Multiple spokespeople for the Department of Transportation told us that the new devices were in use to collect 'aggregate data,' and that the devices weren't being used to charge drivers with traffic violations such as speeding or running red lights."[21] *Forbes* reported that a man using the Internet handle of "Puking Monkey" decided to see just how much tracking was going on behind the scenes.[22] He hacked his E-ZPass toll card's RFID (radio-frequency identification) so he would receive an alert every time the card was accessed or scanned by a reader. Puking Monkey found the results "intrusive and unsettling"[23] as he drove around midtown Manhattan, getting alerts that his card was being scanned even though there were no E-ZPass toll booths around. *Forbes* reviewed the terms and conditions for the E-ZPass and said this type of tracking, even though E-ZPass says it is anonymized, is not included in the terms and conditions.[24]

## *Is a Warrant Required to Track You Using GPS?*

You probably recognize the ways that your car's GPS and telematics system track you for your own good. Their tracking gives you directions. It means you will be found in the event of a crash. But the convenience and safety of onboard tracking systems comes at the price of your privacy. Law enforcement and other government agencies want to use the same technology to track you. Do they need to obtain a warrant before they can track you using GPS? Court cases are confused, and this issue will probably be up for debate as the technology changes.

In 2011, the US Supreme Court ruled in *US v. Jones* that, in light of the Fourth Amendment, which protects US citizens from unlawful search and seizure, GPS tracking was to be considered an official search.[25]

> The right of the people to be secure in their persons, houses, papers, and effects, against unreasonable searches and seizures, shall not be violated, and no Warrants shall issue, but upon probable cause, supported by Oath or affirmation, and particularly describing the place to be searched, and the persons or things to be seized.
> —US Supreme Court Justice Antonin Scalia when reviewing the GPS tracking case of Antoine Jones[26]

However, the Supreme Court ruling left a gray area on whether the federal government *always* needs a warrant to "search" you using GPS tracking. The Department of Justice has gone to the appeals court in an attempt to clarify when they can use GPS tracking without a warrant.

In 2013, the Department of Justice appealed a case in which the trial judge threw out evidence from warrantless GPS tracking. The defendants were brothers suspected of a string of robberies. The FBI attached a GPS to their car, let them rob a Rite Aid, and then caught them red-handed with the stolen goods. During the court trial, the court found in favor of the defendants, saying that the GPS tracking was illegal. The Department of Justice appealed the court ruling to the Third US Circuit Court of Appeals in Philadelphia, arguing that the GPS tracking without a warrant was permissible under the "automobile exception," which allows law enforcement to search your vehicle without a warrant.[27]

NOTES

1. Chris Woodyard and Jayne O'Donnell, "Your Car May Be Invading Your Privacy," *USA Today*, March 24, 2013, www.usatoday.com/story/money/cars/2013/03/24/car-spying-edr-data-privacy/1991751/.

2. Tara Baukus Mello, "Black Boxes in Cars Likely to Become Standard, Privacy Advocates, Automakers, Insurance Companies All Have a Stake in Potential Legislation," *Autoweek*, December 18, 2012, www.autoweek.com/article/20121218/carnews/121219892.

3. Scott Coen, "Lt. Governor Tim Murray Car Crash Story Hitting the Skids, New Accident Photos," *The Republican*, masslive.com, January 5, 2012, www.masslive.com/mywideworld/index.ssf/2012/01/lt_governor_tim_murray_car_crash_story_hitting_the_skids_new_accident_photos_released.html.

4. Shaun Sutner and Thomas Caywood, "'Black Box' Speaks in Murray Crash, Computer Data Sheds New Light on Crash," telegram.com, January 4, 2012, www.telegram.com/article/20120104/NEWS/101049859/1116.

5. Dan Ring, "Lt. Gov. Timothy Murray Leaves Mixed Legacy on Beacon Hill as He Announces Resignation," *The Republican*, masslive.com, May 22, 2013, www.masslive.com/politics/index.ssf/2013/05/lt_gov_timothy_p_murray_to_res.html.

6. Martin Kaste, "Yes, Your New Car Has a 'Black Box.' Where's the Off Switch?," NPR, March 20, 2013.

7. "EFF's Comments to the NHTSA about Black Boxes in Cars," EFF, February 11, 2013.

8. ABI Research, "By 2017 60% of New Cars Shipping Globally Will Feature Connected Car Solutions," abiesearch.com, London, July 3, 2012, www.abiresearch.com/press/by-2017-60-of-new-cars-shipping-globally-will-feat.

9. Wm. L. Hah and Thilo Koslowski, "Market Trends: CSPs Climbing Onboard the Connected Car, Worldwide, 2013," *Gartner*, June 25, 2013.

10. ABI Research, "By 2017 60% of New Cars Shipping Globally Will Feature Connected Car Solutions."

11. Damon Lavrinc, "OnStar Lets You Track Your Spouse for $0.12 a Day," *Wired*, March 28, 2012.

12. Tiwi, "Say Hello to the Biggest Safety Breakthrough since the Seat Belt," 2013, Tiwi website, www.Tiwi.com.

13. Hilary Osborne, "Aviva to Trial Smartphone Car Insurance Technology," *Guardian*, August 13, 2012.

14. "How Snapshot® Works: Plug a Little Device into Your Car and Within 30 Days, You Could Save Big!," Progressive, website information active as of July 19, 2013, www.progressive.com/auto/snapshot-how-it-works/.

15. Cyrus Farivar, "Rich California Town Considers License Plate Readers for Entire City Limits," ARS Technica, March 5, 2013.

16. Robert Stanton and James Pinkerton, "Plan for Cameras Pit Safety vs. Privacy in Sugar Land," *Houston Chronicle*, November 6, 2012.

17. Shawn Musgrave, "License Plate-reading Devices Fuel Privacy Debate," *Boston Globe*, April 9, 2013.

18. Musgrave, "License Plate-reading Devices Fuel Privacy Debate."

19. Gil Aegerter, "License Plate Data Not Just for Cops: Private Companies Are Tracking Your Car," *NBC News*, July 19, 2013, investigations.nbcnews.com/_news/2013/07/19/19548772-license-plate-data-not-just-for-cops-private-companies-are-tracking-your-car?lite.

20. Aegerter, "License Plate Data Not Just for Cops."

21. Jamie Lutz, "Big Brother Has It 'E-Z': City Now Tracking Cars through Local Streets Thanks to E-ZPass," *Brooklyn Paper*, May 8, 2013.

22. Kashmir Hill, "E-ZPasses Get Read All Over New York (Not Just At Toll Booths)," *Forbes*, September 12, 2013.

23. Hill, "E-ZPasses Get Read All Over New York (Not Just At Toll Booths)."

24. Hill, "E-ZPasses Get Read All Over New York (Not Just At Toll Booths)."

25. Supreme Court of the United States, Syllabus, *United States v. Jones*, Certiorari to the United States Court of Appeals for the District of Columbia Circuit, No. 10–1259. Argued November 8, 2011—Decided January 23, 2012.

26. Supreme Court of the United States, Syllabus, *United States v. Jones*.

27. Lorenzo Franceschi-Bicchierai, "DOJ Still Arguing It Doesn't Need Warrant to Track You with GPS," Mashable.com, March 19, 2013, mashable.com/2013/03/19/doj-warrant-tracking-gps/.

# NINE
## When Your Own Body Gives You Away

We find and recognize our friends and family members with the help of biometric identifiers. We look for the lovely brunette who is only five feet in heels, or the tall redhead with the big ears and goofy smile. We recognize a family member by voice over the phone or in the pattern of footsteps from the next room. We can distinguish our spouse or child in the dark by nothing more than the touch of a hand. Humans are particularly adept at finding familiar patterns in other people.

We have now reached the age when machines can also recognize people by their looks, their voice, their footsteps, or the feel of their skin. The machines are better than we are at differentiating between tiny discrepancies in body type or vocal register. For this reason, your physical presence has become an important way for machines, as well as friends, to find and recognize you. But the machines currently using this physical information to find, catalogue, and learn about you are owned by governments and businesses, and they are not always your friends. Though tools for biometric identification have brought important benefits to society, often these same measurements compromise your privacy.

### HOW BIOMETRICS WORK TO IDENTIFY PEOPLE

Rather than searching for distinguishing characteristics among a person's many physical traits the way you do, a biometric identification machine reads a single specific trait of each person and measures it against a database.

You might identify a friend by height, weight, hair, eyes, face shape, voice, laugh, fashion sense, skin color, teeth, or dozens of other factors or special combinations of those factors. In contrast, a machine might measure only iris patterns, or hand geometry, then compare that measurement against samples previously provided by the subject, or against a large database filled with the same measurement taken from thousands of people.

Biometrics fall into two categories of measureable characteristics:

- **Physiological biometrics** measure certain physical aspects of a body, such as palm prints, DNA, or the distance between a person's eyes.
- **Behavioral biometrics** measure aspects of behavior, such as voice, gait, signature, or typing rhythm. We have used written signatures to seal bargains for as long as people knew how to write their names, but measuring typing rhythm is a new field, and very useful for identifying people who are entering deals on the Internet. Both signatures and typing rhythm are behavioral traits unique to each person and are difficult, though not impossible, to fake.

*Machines That "Read" Your Identifying Traits*

A biometric reader is not a complicated machine. To build one, you need only a data-entry device that consistently reads the image, video, sound, smell (yes, we all have unique scents, and dogs are the ultimate scent-authentication machines), or pattern recognizer.

Data-entry devices such as fingerprint readers and voice analyzers take data directly from a human. Other devices are fed secondary information derived from samples that another person takes from the subject. The pattern recognition accomplished in comparing DNA samples is a good example of this second type of reading. A person takes a blood, hair, skin, or mouth sample from the subject. The sample is broken down and the DNA is isolated, read, and then graphed. Using the graphical derivations, the biometric reading device compares a small portion of the subject's DNA against the same small sample portion of people's DNA.

*Finding a Match in a Database*

In recognizing a friend, you match what you see and hear with memories stored from previous experience of the person. Similarly, biometric authentication or matching machines use a database of comparative samples to find a match and identify the subject.

That database could be relatively small. For example, this chapter is being written on a laptop computer with biometric security that requires a fingerprint scan to deactivate hardware encryption and open the computer. My computer's fingerprint database consists of several samples of my own fingerprints. Today, my computer's security mechanism checked my fingerprint against that comparative database and found a match, allowing me to write this chapter.

Other databases used for biometric identification can be huge. The FBI's fingerprint files contain hundreds of millions of samples from tens of millions of people. A new fingerprint sample from a crime scene could be compared against some or all of that database.

Any practical biometric machine for authentication or comparison also needs software that compares the subject sample with the previously harvested samples from the database until the software identifies a match. Someone calibrates the software to determine how close the target sample must be to the database sample for the software to declare a match, and this can be the one of the most difficult parts of the process. If she makes the required match too perfect, the machine is likely to miss some clear positive equivalent findings. If she makes the required match too loose, half of the database will seem to fit. The calibrations must also take into account inefficiencies in the sample readers, such as what happens when a fingerprint reader is dirty or smudged.

## WHAT DO WE MEASURE?

Hundreds of unique measurements can be made on any human being, from toe prints to electrical patterns emitted by the brain. Here are some of the more common measurements taken today for identification purposes.

**Fingerprints.** When you want a measurement that is easy to take, fingerprints are the most practical biometric reading. Fingerprint reading is noninvasive (although possibly unsanitary), and people are accustomed to using the fingerprint as an identifying attribute. Many small scanners exist to read fingerprints. However, fingerprint scanners can be easy to fool. A researcher in Japan successfully beat fingerprint-reading machines four out of five times using only gummi candy to transfer his print.[1]

**DNA.** Every cell in your body carries your unique DNA. Though very accurate, DNA authentication is expensive, intrusive, and complicated compared to fingerprint analysis.

**Scent.** For centuries we have used dogs to pick up the scent of a criminal on the run or a lost child, and to follow that scent until the person is discovered. We still use dogs, not only to sniff out fugitives and lost children but also to smell the unique scent of cancer in a person or pick a suspect out of a line-up.

**Retinal Scan.** If it is important that your biometric reading cannot be faked into providing false positive results, then a retinal scan may be the best choice. You can use a modified camera for the reading and do not have to physically touch anyone to take a picture. Since

retinal patterns are on the back wall of a person's eye, no current
technology can provide a contact lens or other measure to fake it.
But people resist eye-scanning devices, finding them creepy, uncomfortable, and futuristic. Also, the technology must be highly
sensitive, therefore susceptible to false readings and other equipment failure. And finally, retinal-scanning technology has not been
as extensively tested as fingerprint scanners have, so we do not
necessarily know all of the technological pitfalls.

**Voice.** If you want to take a biometric reading over the telephone,
voice is the only answer. But voiceprints can be prerecorded or
faked in other ways, and your reading is only as good as the telephone equipment held by both parties. Cheap cell phones may
make a successful reading impossible.

### Issues in Choosing Which Trait to Measure

Two factors can affect the choice of which biometric trait to measure:
the method of data collection, and access to appropriate, dependable
equipment.

An important issue in data collection involves whether the human
body needs to be touched or invaded to capture a reading. For example,
some people refuse to touch a pad where others have been swiping their
fingers all day. Concerns also arise when the portion of the human body
measured is not usually exposed in daily activity. This makes it problematic to use nipple prints, belly buttons, or any measurements of women
in strict Moslem countries. Finally, practical considerations come up
when the person providing the sample must be monitored by a living
person while submitting the sample. Hair, saliva, or other standard DNA
offerings are generally collected by a separate person who can confirm
other aspects of the donor's identity.

Equipment concerns are also important. Smartphone cameras or
microphones can be useful in situations calling for scanning equipment
that is small and easily portable or widely available. It is also important
to choose readers that are dependable enough to capture usable scans in
the conditions you expect to use them. For example, scanners in the
desert are more likely to break than those attached to a wall in a sparsely
populated, air-conditioned facility.

### Biometrics Are Not Always the Right Choice

The sensitivity of a biometric reader to false positives or false negatives can drive the choice of whether to use biometrics for identification
in the first place. For example, retail stores do not currently use biometric
scans because purchase prices are generally too small to require such a
high level of security. Besides, retail shoppers have no tolerance for false

negatives in the checkout line. No one wants his purchase held up because a machine refuses to accept that the shopper's thumb is truly his thumb.

Conversely, a person who works in a nuclear plant may be willing to make several attempts to be authenticated by a biometric reader. After all, the power plant management cannot afford to let the wrong people into the control room, so no false positives can be tolerated.

Every system has errors. The owner of a biometric system must decide which side of the equation—false positive or false negative—is the greater risk.

### A Mountain of Data on the Horizon

We are only at the start of the biometric revolution. Before long, biometric collection and data will overwhelm us. Law-enforcement databases, already stocked with millions of readings, will cover everyone born in the industrialized world.

This should come as no surprise. The hospitals where we were born took our baby footprints and kept them in a file, so why wouldn't future hospitals take a small DNA sample of all babies and file the samples away in a digital database?

As reading human characteristics becomes cheaper, easier, and simpler to do from a distance, governments and businesses will use these readings to know where we go and how long we stay.

Soon, voice readings will tell the listener who we are and whether we are hostile or friendly. Some businesses already use voice readings to know if a customer is distressed or relaxed when calling the service line, so why wouldn't businesses read our voices, posture, and even brain waves to know whether their sales pitch is working and when we are ready to buy?

The government currently takes facial pictures and fingerprints for certain visa holders entering the country. How long before those measurements are used to test how nervous a traveler is about crossing the border, flagging him as a possible smuggler or terrorist?

## WHEN BIOMETRICS HELP US TO BE SAFE AND SECURE

Thinking about how we have used biometric measurements in past centuries demonstrates their value to us today, particularly as the human population explodes to cover the globe with millions more people every year. In the past, governments and businesses have relied on government-issued papers or cards to prove identity, and in some cultures important people carried a special ring or inscribed Chinese chop to prove who they were. But if portable machines can register a face or fingerprint, then no one would need to carry identification because a person's body would be her proof of identity.

Today, biometric measurements are used primarily as security features, from helping companies identify which employees are allowed in the laboratory or who is authorized to visit the eightieth floor of the headquarters building, to helping individuals secure their own personal computers and other property.

In addition to offering common security benefits, biometrics are taking on a larger role in solving crimes, identifying victims and missing persons, facilitating business contracts, and protecting the people's basic rights and benefits in society.

*Solving Crime*

Early in the twentieth century, French criminologist Dr. Edward Locard famously realized that every human contact leaves a trace—that criminals bring physical evidence to a crime scene and take physical evidence away from it.[2] We humans shed hair and skin cells wherever we go. We leave footprints, fingerprints, bite marks, and impressions in chairs and pillows. In committing a violent act, a person is likely to lose saliva, blood, or other fluids. The act itself may suggest obvious physical qualities of the suspect, such as height and strength. And parts of the victim and the crime scene, such as hairs, fibers, blood, and dust are carried away on the criminal's body.

The revolution in biometrics lies not only in understanding Locard's exchange principal but also in developing the tools to compare the fingerprints and footprints found at a crime scene to the police database of fingerprints or commercially sold shoes. Experts are needed who have the scientific and statistical knowledge to testify to the meaning of a matched print and the statistical probabilities of a thirty-point fingerprint match being wrong.

We have also extended the search from a surface look at physical specimens, such as hair and skin, to pulling DNA from these specimens and using it to obtain a much more accurate identification. For example, in May 2013, a St. Louis man pleaded guilty to a rape that occurred in 2001 after the DNA he left on his victim's pants was finally matched back to him. He was sentenced to forty-eight years in prison.[3]

At nearly the same time, federal prosecutors in Kansas City, Missouri, charged a fifty-year-old inmate with three counts of rape for an attack that took place in August of 1986. The Kansas City case was supported by DNA evidence left at the scene that had recently been tested and matched.[4]

The act of rape nearly always leaves physical evidence of the attacker at the scene. Because we can now pull biometric evidence like DNA from the scene and match it to the attacker, we can solve a much higher percentage of rapes than we could in the past.

> **In recent years, numerous individuals who confessed to and were convicted of serious felony crimes have been released from prison— some after many years of incarceration—and declared factually innocent, often as a result of DNA tests that were not possible at the time of arrest, prosecution, and conviction. DNA testing has also exonerated numerous individuals who confessed to serious crimes before their cases went to trial.**
> **—Professors Steven Drizin, Northwestern University School of Law,**
> **and Richard Leo, University of California–Irvine[5]**

According to the *New York Times*, the US military has registered biometric information on over a million Afghans, "roughly one of every six males of fighting age, ages 15 to 64."[6] When the Taliban helped 475 prisoners escape a prison in southern Afghanistan in the spring of 2011, Afghan officials used the US biometric technology to quickly round up thirty-five prisoners at internal checkpoints and border crossings. All of the prisoners had provided eye scans, fingerprints, and facial images a month before the prison break.[7] American and Afghan soldiers carried handheld digital scanners they could use to check fingerprints and eyes anyplace in the country they encountered a subject. Biometric scans are crucial in Afghanistan, where many people do not have birth certificates or other reliable government-issued identification, and people often are found with forged identity papers.

## Identifying Victims and Missing People

With the rise of identity theft, biometrics help solve or stop certain crimes by proving the identity of people who have been victimized. For example, a Columbus, Ohio, man was convicted for posing as another man while incurring more than $300,000 in medical bills at Ohio State University's Wexner Medical Center.[8] Fortunately, the medical work took long enough for the hospital to be tipped to the presence of an impostor, when the victim complained that he did not receive the treatment that led to early bills. The hospital had accepted a driver's license as identification. If it had required any type of biometric identification, from fingerprint to eye scan, then the victim would not have been charged $300,000 for medical treatment he never received.

Similarly, banks have found that requiring thumbprints on cashed checks not only helps catch criminals who commit check fraud but also greatly reduces the number of people who attempt check fraud at those locations that require the procedure. Incorporating biometric readings helps squeeze fraud out of many systems and leaves fewer people victimized.

But catching and convicting criminals is not the only important benefit of biometric identification. The advance in this science helps victims in
other ways. The fog of war has led to uncertainty for the families of
millions of missing people. Combining the losses on both sides, at the
end of World War I six million people were missing and presumed dead.
The International World History Center lists more than two thousand
American service members as missing in action in the war in Vietnam.[9]
Biometric testing can reduce the number of war missing in at least two
ways. First, the US military currently keeps biometric information, including DNA, on all service members, and this data is used to identify
the remains of those killed in battle. In addition, since DNA traits are
passed to family members, even soldiers, pilots, sailors, and marines
from earlier wars can be identified by comparing DNA from remains
with a DNA sample from the service member's parents or children. Second, if missing or stolen children are found later in life, they can now be
identified by comparing biometric indicators, from facial structure to
DNA samples. And biometric improvements in identification of discovered bodies means that many more families reach certainty about what
happened to their loved ones, rather than being left in limbo.

### Providing Security in Business Transactions

Commercial contracting depends on a level of certainty. The more
money involved in a deal, the more both sides of a transaction need to
know for certain who they are dealing with. The home is the largest
purchase most of us ever undertake, so we are not surprised when photo
identification and presence at a closing is required for the purchase.

For even larger transactions, buyers, sellers, and lenders have started
to require biometric proof beyond a signature that the parties are who
they claim to be. In 2008, the US Department of Defense announced that
certain enlistment contracts would be executed through fingerprint acceptance rather than a "wet" pen-and-ink signature.[10]

The only thing required to execute a contract is a clear manifestation
of assent to the terms of the deal. Whether a biometric reading is used as
the "manifestation of assent" itself, or whether it supplements an electronic signature or a regular "wet" signature, the advance in biometrics
removes much of the risk of misidentification and contract repudiation.

### Establishing Rights and Benefits

The nation of India has 1.2 billion residents, the vast majority of whom
live in poverty. In April 2013, nearly four hundred million Indians were
enrolled in a government-operated biometric identification program.[11]

The Indian government uses facial recognition, fingerprinting, and
iris scans for biometric measurements. Once a person's biometric identity

is established and stored, he can verify and authenticate his identity using a cell phone, smartphone, tablet, or other Internet-enabled device.[12] Each person is also assigned a randomly generated twelve-digit number.

The purpose of this ambitious and impressive system is to assure that millions of needy Indians have access to health care and welfare programs. India has been riddled with billions of dollars in fraud and waste in the welfare system, as middlemen and criminals use fake identification cards to take other people's benefits. Under the biometric identification program, a person must prove who she is and what she is entitled to before rights can be established.

In another expected benefit of this program, previously anonymous poor Indians can gain access to services such as bank accounts, mobile phones, and drivers' licenses, which have eluded them until now. Hundreds of millions of Indians will have better lives and more access to the modern world thanks to India's biometric identification system.

## WHEN BIOMETRICS GO WRONG

Biometric authentication and identification tools provide important benefits, but they can be misused, and they create inherent problems for the privacy of people whose biometric readings are taken. Widespread use of certain biometrics completely steals the privacy of individuals. When your face or body can be spotted and correctly identified from a distance everywhere you go, then nowhere is private to you. Pervasive biometric identification may lead to a world where we cannot rely on obscurity in a crowd to protect our privacy. For these and other reasons, we must tighten controls on how biometric authentication can be used in the future.

### Biometric Interpretations Can Be Wrong — With Terrible Consequences

Though biometric information appears to be the perfect solution to many of the complexities of modern investigations and identifications, its impressive results create one of its biggest problems: the evidence is so strong, it *seems* infallible. But it's not.

As explained earlier, biometric readers are calibrated to be more likely to generate false negative readings or false positive readings, depending on the priorities of those using the identifications. In other words, biometric identifications are based on statistical probability, which means they are wrong a certain percentage of the time. But when a biometric test shows that the odds are high in favor of a certain result, we humans have a tendency to perceive the test as infallible.

For example, suppose your DNA is found at the scene of a crime, and you are suspected of committing the crime. Those who suspect you might not take into account the possibility of errors — errors in sample collection and storage, in choice of samples to compare, in the comparison itself, or in reporting and interpreting the tests. Even if your DNA was truly at the scene of the crime, someone else might have placed it there, either by accident or on purpose, such as by stealing your hairbrush and then dropping it at the scene. Even though it appears that your DNA was found at the scene, maybe you were never there. The strength of DNA and other biometric tests to identify and authenticate people can lead others to accept all such results as true, then draw their own conclusions.

Oregon attorney Brandon Mayfield suffered from the illusion of biometric infallibility. In March 2004, terrorists detonated a bomb in the train station of Madrid, Spain, killing 191 people and injuring more than two thousand. Digital images of partial latent fingerprints obtained from plastic bags containing detonator caps were submitted by Spanish authorities to the FBI for analysis.[13] The FBI fed the latent prints into its fingerprint-identification system, comparing the latents to millions of known prints. Initially, the FBI found no matches for the discovered fingerprints, but a second search turned up twenty possible matches. Trained FBI fingerprint experts determined that a latent print from the short list of possible matches belonged to Brandon Mayfield, a man who had converted to Islam in 1989. In his legal practice, attorney Mayfield had once represented in a child custody case a person who had previously been convicted of conspiring to aid the Taliban and al-Qaeda.[14]

The FBI arrested Mayfield and kept him jailed for two weeks before acknowledging that the fingerprint from Madrid was not his.[15] The Inspector General's report on this case found that FBI examiners failed to adhere to the FBI's own rules for identifying latent fingerprints, and that the bureau's overconfidence in its own skills prevented it from listening to reason. In addition, the FBI's overzealousness in using "national security letters" under the USA-PATRIOT Act to evade normal judicial process and gather Mr. Mayfield's records from banks, telephone companies, and other businesses, led to a court finding parts of the USA-PATRIOT Act unconstitutional.[16]

## *Fingers Are Forever: The Permanence Problem*

Overreliance on biometric interpretations is not the only kind of mistakes made with biometric systems. For example, a doctor working for the Ferraz Vasconcelos Hospital in Sao Paulo, Brazil, was arrested after being caught using silicone "fake fingers" to punch in the clock on behalf of his coworkers, defrauding the hospital's biometric time-accounting system.[17] More advanced biometric systems include a "viability" reader that reads the pulse of the finger being offered or the veins beneath the skin. Those readers cannot be fooled with gummy bears, silicone fingers, or digits cut off the person with rightful access. However, not all readers are so advanced.

Immutability is one of the primary attributes that makes biometric identification so useful. Nearly all aspects of personal identification may change, except for certain biometric measurements that are immutable. A person can be assigned a new name or social security number and can create a new password or PIN code. Banks and doctors' offices can change your account numbers. But fingerprints are forever, and so are iris patterns, retinal scans, and the vein patterns beneath your skin. Though trauma or disease can affect a finger or eye, that would be an obvious external factor affecting the pattern, not a change in the fingerprint or iris pattern itself.

Biometric immutability helps the US and Afghan military identify and capture escaped prisoners, and it would help you prove that you are the correct person to receive the health benefits offered by your employer or the state. However, that same immutability causes significant problems if your data is lost. When your credit card is stolen, the bank can simply issue you a new card with a new account number and eliminate the old one. But when the database containing your thumbprint image is stolen, the bank can't simply issue you a new thumb. The criminals who stole the database can use that image at the same institution or in different places to steal your identity, possibly gaining access to your accounts.

For that reason, many security consultants advise institutions using biometric indicators to rely on secondary algorithms derived from your biometric data, rather than a picture of your iris or your finger. Sophisticated biometric readers can extrapolate certain data from the readings they take. The extrapolated data is still unique to you, but if it is stolen, the thief has not captured a description of one of your immutable characteristics. Instead, the thief has a worthless number that can be changed as easily as the bank changes your credit card account.

Unfortunately, this method of capture and comparison is more expensive than a simple picture comparison, so many current biometric databases risk losing data of your immutable physical characteristics that bad guys can use. The math can be changed, but fingers patterns are forever.

### The Special Problem of Facial Recognition

Of all the immutable physical characteristics captured and recorded by biometric authentication systems, the most important to you is likely your face. Your face is how your baby first recognizes you, and it is how your friends and colleagues find you. Humans are hardwired for recognizing faces. Although some aspects of a face change with age, weight, and grooming choices, we will generally recognize thirty-year-old pictures of family and friends. A face can be changed through surgery, as we have all seen with Hollywood stars, but to most of us, our face is the personalized image that we present to the world.

For this reason, we are rightfully sensitive and suspicious of facial-recognition systems that claim to keep huge databases of faces and constantly monitor them for criminal activity and even simple location tracking. Faces can be read by a camera from a distance and can be captured by each traffic cam, ATM video surveillance, and smartphone in the vicinity. Millions of face pictures are entering social media every day, making the Internet the world's largest facial-recognition database. Most of our faces are online somewhere and searchable by anyone with the right tools.

The frightening aspect of this technology lies in the democratization of search tools, combined with the enormous databases containing pictures of almost all of us. We know that governments have the tools to search for our face and discover information about us, and that maybe some businesses do as well. But it is scary to realize that anyone with access to the Internet can use a tool provided by Facebook or another social company to find us anywhere. No one can hide. People who are in witness protection must take care not to be at a gathering where pictures are taken and posted to the Internet. Women who have hidden to avoid abusive ex-boyfriends must limit their social interactions. Everybody can find anybody else, for better or for worse.

Google recognized this problem while working on a tool that would allow everyone to find anyone else. With its stated goal to make all of the world's information available to everyone, Google has created superb databases, search software, and matching tools. To help you locate and identify anyone anywhere, Google developed a tool with mobile face recognition, enabling smartphone cameras to snap a picture while the facial-recognition software found other pictures of that person on social networks and other public sites. Using this tool, a creepy guy who saw your daughter shopping could just snap her picture, and the Google application would tell him her name and lead him to her social media pages, her school, or workplace, and other sites that are important to her. Though many people would find such a tool useful, it would certainly be a stalker's dream.

After CNN reported on the new tool, Google claimed that it was not ready for release because the privacy features had not been addressed.[18] Whether or not Google ever releases a tool with that exact capability, we know that such a tool has already been created and may be offered by someone else. For example, a company called Mugr began beta testing a facial-recognition mobile search engine in 2007, but the company has disappeared from the web. Though Google has already stated that voice and face recognition will not be available to users of Google Glass, the wearable computer that projects data onto the surface of your glasses, the hardware could be hacked, with third-party companies providing facial-recognition software. A startup company called Lambda Labs has developed software that could allow Google Glass to search the names of people it sees.[19]

### Few Watching Many—Anywhere and All the Time

Most Americans were confronted with facial-recognition technology for the first time during and after Super Bowl XXXV, when we learned that face-recognition software surreptitiously scanned the people as each one passed through the turnstile. The pictures were compared to a database of known and wanted criminals. The American Civil Liberties Union (ACLU) complained that such indiscriminant use of face-finding technology violated the Fourth Amendment prohibition on unreasonable searches and seizures. They pointed out that in earlier eras, it would have taken hundreds, if not thousands, of manhours of police work to look at all of the faces from everyone that came to the Super Bowl and then compare them to even a small list of wanted outlaws. But now, through the miracle of the new technology of cameras, databases, and comparative software, only a few people can monitor the entire crowd.

This kind of surveillance was certainly never contemplated by the founders of our republic, and most people in 2001 would have been shocked to know that it was possible with such limited resources. The technology turns every public place into a perfect spot for surveillance and searching for criminals. If the government can do this at the Super Bowl, then why not at your local grocery store?

> **Cameras make a practical difference. They make it practically possible to monitor things that one just never had the manpower to monitor before. If we've reached the point where we can't go to a football game without having our photos run through a database in Washington, then we'll only have privacy when we're sitting in our living rooms.**
>
> **—Former federal prosecutor Andrew Grosso[20]**

### Should Huge Databases Be Widely Shared?

The FBI clearly sees biometric technology as the future of law enforcement. In 2012, the FBI developed a facial-recognition matching tool that it offered to local policing agencies. Using only a personal computer and access to the Internet, local agencies could use the tool to tap into the FBI mug shot database of over twelve million photographs,[21] granting local law enforcement similar access to national face databases as US federal investigators. Previously, the agency offered local law enforcement a tool for matching latent handprints, and it may offer a similar tool to match iris scans.

The FBI is in the process of creating a billion-dollar biometric system called Next Generation Identification (NGI) that will use DNA databases,

facial records, iris scans, voice samples, and other biometric measurements for identification purposes. The agency intends to share access to
NGI with local police. Though the picture gallery was started as a collection of mug shots and photos of known criminals, the FBI is uncommitted
on whether future versions will contain every driver's license photograph and passport picture, and other sources of voice and DNA data.

Concerns about police overreach and opening facial-recognition
search tools to everybody have led to a backlash against facial-recognition technology. Privacy and civil liberties groups voice their alarm. The
Electronic Privacy Information Center in the United States has sued the
FBI to learn more details about the NGI system and what biometric data
it would collect.

Technologists are addressing the issue as well. Japanese researchers at
Tokyo's National Institute of Informatics and Kogakuin University have
developed a set of glasses that, when worn, would thwart facial-recognition software.[22] The glasses, which look like thick lab goggles, include
small, circular lights that are only visible to cameras. The near-infrared
lights in the glasses block facial-recognition cameras by creating visual
"noise" across key visual areas of the face, such as the eyes and nose.
While the current models of these glasses work from a battery held in a
pocket, the researchers have received offers to develop the glasses into a
commercial product.

Do you live in North Carolina or Arizona? The FBI has been working
with these two states and several others in a project called "Face Mask."[23]
As you enter your Department of Motor Vehicles (DMV) office to get
your picture taken for your driver's license, the FBI can access and match
your mug shot against an FBI database. The facial-recognition software is
surprisingly fast to use and fairly accurate. The FBI's Facial Analysis
Comparison and Evaluation (FACE) team routinely reviews the facial
images of people in their investigations databases and compares them
against DMV requests. The FBI's FACE team can also send queries to
DMVs to ask them to look for a particular face on their systems.

According to one report, an FBI system used to track terrorist groups
was recently extended to help with domestic criminal investigations. The
database collects digital information from the web, hotels, car rental companies, department stores, and more.[24] The database has more than 1.5
billion records on foreigners and citizens. The ACLU reports on their
website that cell phones of citizens are being tracked without warrants by
federal, state, and local law enforcement groups across the United States.

## BIOMETRICS ARE HERE TO STAY

Identifying people through biometrics is becoming cheaper and easier all
the time. The software to read faces in low light or at odd angles is

improving. The sensors to read irises, retinas, and subdural vein patterns are becoming less expensive and more consistent. To encourage customers to lock their phones while providing an easy way to unlock the phone, Samsung integrated facial recognition into their Galaxy line of smartphones, and Apple's iPhone 5 uses a fingerprint scan. Given the many advantages to using biometric identifiers and authentications, business and law enforcement are likely to continue to build on current database technologies. Eventually, mobile facial-recognition technology will be made available to the general public. Cameras that currently monitor your movements on the street and in the cities will soon be able to read your face as well, and assign a name to your picture.

If the prospect of universal facial recognition or an all-encompassing DNA database concerns you, there is very little you can do to stop the inevitable progress of this technology. However, laws can be changed to be more protective of individual privacy and less protective of the rights of government and business to use your biometric measurements. You can write to your congressperson, state representative, or governor to build privacy protections into the law. Such protections for individual privacy exist in Europe, Japan, Canada, and much of Latin America, but not in the United States. This can only change if regular people stand up and tell elected officials that privacy is important.

## NOTES

1. John Leyden, "Gummi Bears Defeat Fingerprint Sensors: Sticky Problem for Biometrics Firms," *Register*, May 16, 2002.

2. W. J. Chisum and B. Turvey, "Evidence Dynamics: Locard's Exchange Principle and Crime Reconstruction," *Journal of Behavioral Profiling* 1, no. 1 (January 2000).

3. Jennifer Mann, "DNA Leads to Guilty Pleas in St. Louis County Cold Case Rape," *St. Louis Post-Dispatch*, May 17, 2013.

4. Christine Vendel, "DNA Links Inmate to 1986 Rape of Deaf Woman," *Kansas City Star*, May 17, 2013.

5. Richard Leo and Steven Drizin, "The Problem of False Confessions in a Post-DNA World," 82 N.C. L. REV. 891, March 2004.

6. Thom Shanker, "To Track Militants, U.S. Has System That Never Forgets a Face," *New York Times*, July 13, 2011.

7. Shanker, "To Track Militants, U.S. Has System That Never Forgets a Face."

8. Ryan Clark, "Police: Patient Tallied $300,000 in Medical Bills at OSU Using Another Man's Identity," *Columbus Dispatch*, April 5, 2013.

9. International World History Project, history-world.org.

10. First Enlistment Contract with Biometric Signature, US Department of Defense, Office of the Assistant Secretary of Defense for Public Affairs, Release No. 0316-08, April 17, 2008.

11. Mahesh Sharma, "India's Biometric ID Projects Near 400M People Milestone," ZDNet.com, April 24, 2013, www.zdnet.com/in/indias-biometric-id-projects-near-400m-people-milestone-7000014448/.

12. Saritha Rai, "Why India's Identity Scheme is Groundbreaking," *BBC News India*, June 5, 2012.

13. Statement on Brandon Mayfield Case, national press release, US Federal Bureau of Investigation, May 24, 2004.

14. Susan Jo Keller, "Judge Rules Provisions in Patriot Act to be Illegal," *New York Times*, September 27, 2007.

15. "FBI Error a 'Watershed' in Fingerprinting," compiled from the Tribune News Service, *Chicago Tribune*, March 12, 2006.

16. *Mayfield v. United States*, 504 F.Supp.2d 1023 (D.Or. 2007).

17. "Brazilian Doctor Caught Using Fake Fingers in Biometrics Scam," *The Province*, March 13, 2013.

18. Jared Newman, "Google Won't Release Awesome Facial Recognition App," *PCWorld*, April 1, 2011.

19. Dan Nosowitz, "Will Google (and the US Government) Permit Google Glass to Recognize Faces on Site?," *Popular Science*, May 24, 2013.

20. Declan McCullagh, "Call It Super Bowl Face Scan I," *Wired*, February 2, 2001.

21. Aliya Sternstein, "FBI Gives Police Free Tool to Convert Photos for Facial Recognition," NextGov.com, August 16, 2012, www.nextgov.com/emerging-tech/2012/08/fbi-gives-police-free-tool-convert-photos-facial-recognition/57463/.

22. Ryan Gallagher, "These Goofy-Looking Glasses Could Make You Invisible to Facial Recognition Technology," *Slate*, January 18, 2013.

23. US Department of Justice, Office of Legislative Affairs, letter to the Honorable Patrick J. Leahy, chairman, by Judith C. Appelbaum, acting assistant attorney general, October 31, 2012, and "Questions for the Record" by Jerome Pender, deputy assistant director of Criminal Justice Information Services Division, FBI on July 18, 2012.

24. Ryan Single, "Newly Declassified Files Detail Massive FBI Data Mining Project," *Wired*, September 23, 2009.

# TEN

## DNA and Your Health Records

While biometric identification such as fingerprinting and face recognition poses a significant threat to your privacy, an even greater threat lurks in your basic health information. Biometrics focus primarily on locating and identifying specific people through comparisons in vast databases. In contrast, if your health information becomes public, it can reveal deep secrets about who you are and what you are likely to become.

The more we know about proteins, DNA, and the other basic building blocks of life, the more we can learn about you from a dropped hair or a flake of your skin. And because genetic material and markers are held in common by blood relatives, the revelation that gives away your health secrets may not even be made by you, but could come from a cousin or uncle.

Advances in the technology of genetic testing and analysis also put your privacy at risk. Scientists can now work backward and divine the donor's name from an anonymous DNA sample. DNA trophy hunters can learn the health secrets of the stars. Someday, targeted viruses could be created that seek out only your family's genetic makeup.

### WHAT YOUR DNA CAN TELL YOU

In May of 2013, actress Angelina Jolie announced that she had chosen to undergo a double mastectomy rather than live with an 87 percent chance of developing breast cancer. By taking a DNA test, Ms. Jolie discovered that her genetic makeup favored the development of breast cancer. As if to confirm this fact, her aunt died of breast cancer days after the initial announcement and news coverage of Ms. Jolie's surgery.[1]

We are at the very early stages of our understanding of human genetics. We may have "mapped" certain portions of the human genome, but

155

despite news reports to the contrary, we are miles from finding all the useful information that a full understanding of the genome can give us. That said, we, like Angelina Jolie, may still learn useful information about ourselves and our families from analysis of our DNA. As tens of thousands of researchers perform tests in this area, the discoveries compound. The list of things we can learn from DNA analysis will likely grow rapidly every year for the next several years.

## Personal Genetic Testing Has Arrived

If you have health issues that call for the genetic information, your doctor can order any number of genetic tests for you. But you do not need to wait for a solid health-related reason to run your own genetic review. Several companies exist to analyze DNA and provide results that can speak to ancestry, racial makeup, and genetic influence on disease, biological aging, or paternity.

Genetic analysis company 23andMe calls itself the leading health and ancestry DNA service. The 23 refers to the twenty-three pairs of chromosomes in the human genome. The company scans about one million points on the genome that are known to vary among humans. At this writing, they charge just under three hundred dollars for the test. For this fee, the company processes a saliva sample that you take of yourself with the kit 23andMe sends you. It then shares hundreds of health reports available for different conditions, from benign traits such as male pattern baldness and eye color to risks for diseases such as breast cancer and Alzheimer's disease. As new genetic research is published and new genetic markers or susceptibilities are catalogued, the company adds more reports.

The company also provides videos that offer more detailed information about some of the diseases that could be highlighted in their testing. They work with a genetic-counseling service that can help you understand what the numbers mean. The company offers two different sets of information for one price: ancestry and health data. All of the results are posted to a secure website. In November of 2013, the FDA forced 23andMe to stop marketing its test in the United States until the company established the science behind its claims. A class action lawsuit has been filed based on the FDA accusations.

As expertise in DNA testing and interest in the results grows, dozens more DNA testing companies spring up in response. Some provide broad genetic analysis as described above; others focus on more specific tests such as testing for paternity in children. Some DNA testing companies are offshoots of medical labs and primarily perform health care testing prescribed by doctors to address clinical issues.

The following pages provide an overview of results you can obtain from the basic genetic screen test offered by companies such as 23andMe.

Genetic sequencing, a more complicated technique, reviews about three billion points, covering nearly all of a person's genetic code. The current cost for genetic sequencing is substantially higher than basic screening, and it starts around $4,000.[2] These tests reveal vast amounts of information, much of which we cannot yet interpret in a meaningful way. We still don't know everything about the way that human genes affect illness, body type, aging, or behavior, though we learn more each day.

## What DNA Tests Reveal About Your Ancestors

The ancestry information provided by 23andMe can tell you if you are connected to one or more of several lineages that include well-known people throughout history. For example, the DNA of Genghis Khan has been found in people from China to Scotland, so a DNA test may link the contributor to this famous lineage.

The company uses maps to trace maternal ancestry and to show concentrations and movements of a contributor's family over centuries. The tests tell which fraction of the donor's ancestors were European, African, Native American, or Asian, and can pinpoint populations with the most similar DNA.

## What DNA Tests Reveal About Your Health

While ancestry information is interesting and entertaining, the health analysis from a DNA test provides you immediate value.

One in twenty-nine Caucasians carry the genes that cause cystic fibrosis, and the 23andMe test shows whether the donor is a carrier of this deadly disease. If both parents are carriers, their child has a 25 percent chance of being born with the disease. The company also tests for inherited diseases passed on recessive genes such as sickle cell anemia, Taye-Sachs disease, and Bloom's syndrome. These diseases can be passed to children even though the parent carrier shows no symptoms.[3]

The test shows a variety of disease risks, including risks for several types of cancer, bipolar disorder, endometriosis, gallstones, gout, Tourette's Syndrome, diabetes, stroke, obesity, migraines, and alcohol dependency. With this information, the subject may be able to mitigate known risks by changing behaviors, undergoing more frequent testing, or even taking more extreme measures such as preventative surgery.

Similarly, each submitted sample is tested for responses and sensitivities to a wide variety of drugs, including sensitivity to Warfarin (sold to millions as Coumadin) and Abacavir. Statin response, beta-blocker response, and caffeine metabolism are also tested. The subject can bring this information to the attention of her doctor and change dosages or medications as indicated.

Finally, the test provides information about specific physical traits as innocuous as a photic sneeze response or type of earwax, and as important as cholesterol levels, leprosy susceptibility, longevity, and resistance to HIV/AIDS. Knowing your susceptibilities and sensitivities allows you to make better health decisions. For example, some people have genes that help them resist malaria, while others have a genetic makeup that can encourage serious complications if they contract malaria.

*DNA Hints at Life Expectancy*

Another specific and potentially intrusive bit of information that can be gleaned from your chromosomes has to do with biological aging. A lab can look at the length of chromosomes to determine important information about longevity.

Your body's cells copy themselves to offset general wear on the body. That process is limited by the length of DNA sequences called telomeres that protect the ends of your chromosomes. Telomeres get shorter with each copy a cell makes of itself. Eventually, the telomeres become too short to assist in replication, and the cell dies.

Telomere length, which has a significant genetic component, varies in humans and tends to be longer in women than in men. Some scientists believe that telomere length can determine longevity, but work is still being performed to test this hypothesis. Testing telomere length could tell your doctor—and also someone else—the nature of your life expectancy.

*Your DNA—Personal and Private*

Here we have only cracked open a window into the new art and science of public genetic testing, showing part of what a small sample of your genetic material can reveal. When you consider that someone who has a genetic sample from you could discover whether you are naturally inclined toward alcoholism or drug use, whether you are likely to develop Alzheimer's disease or diabetes, and whether you are a carrier for a disease that could develop in your children, then you must take seriously the threat to your privacy that analysis of your genetic material can create.

Someone looking at your DNA is likely to know more about you and your family than you know yourself, including things of a deeply personal nature. Your DNA is your past, present, and future in one tiny package. To maintain your privacy, you must control access to the many stories that your genetic material can tell. If someone gathers and analyzes your DNA, that person can learn all of these health facts about you, and more. As we will learn later in this chapter, someone holding your

DNA could test it for family or paternity information and compare it to criminal databases.

## WHO CARES ABOUT YOUR DNA, AND WHY

You have strong and legitimate reasons for wanting to know what your genes have to say about you. This knowledge can guide you and your doctor toward the most effective treatments for your health issues, and even help you spot likely health concerns before they arise. Knowing about your DNA can help you decide whether to have children.

Your DNA data can also prove beneficial to you in encounters with the law. DNA has not only been used to convict people charged with violent crimes but also to exonerate the innocent as well, leading to releases from prison of people wrongly convicted. Even early in an investigation, DNA testing can exclude you as a suspect in crimes you did not commit. Someday the plea of "genetic predisposition" may even be a recognized defense to charges in court.

DNA can help you find lost relatives and prove the relationship between family members. And of course, DNA has positive entertainment and educational value, describing your family history, national and racial origins, and maybe helping you find famous (or rich) relatives in your family tree.

However, the same DNA information that benefits you may benefit others as well, and their interests are not necessarily aligned with yours.

### Why Insurers, Employers, and Other Businesses Want Your DNA

Thanks to a recent US federal law, information gleaned from your DNA cannot be used to charge you more for health insurance, or to deny you coverage altogether. However, that law does not cover life insurance or long-term disability coverage. Suppose insurers knew that Angelina Jolie had an 85 percent chance of developing breast cancer before age sixty-five. Would they have denied her life insurance, or insisted on a double mastectomy before insuring her at a reasonable rate? Who is to say that some insurers are not peeking at this information when making decisions?

A prospective employer that tested your DNA could tell if you were predisposed to addiction, which might make them view you as a risky hire. The DNA test might reveal that you are predisposed to certain diseases that would affect the price that company is paying for employee health insurance. In either case, the company could make a logical decision not to hire you.

Other businesses or major political parties, who are already collecting records about you, would be glad to add DNA's predictive health information to their huge databases of shopping, Internet surfing, charitable giving, real estate, social media, and other behavioral data. They hope to use this information to help them make you a more profitable customer or a more consistent supporter of their candidates.

### How DNA Information Made Public Affects Your Personal and Family Life

People who hold your DNA information can also make informed decisions about how to treat your children, parents, and siblings, simply based on what can be learned from your genes. Not only the facts of genetic parentage but also information about other family members' physical traits and susceptibilities to diseases and medicines can be inferred from your DNA tests. For example, if an employer knew a woman had the gene for hemophilia, it may be less likely to hire her sons. Siblings often share the same genetic illnesses. You might be affected by the public disclosure of a family member's genetic code, even if yours is still a secret.

Through genetic testing, a prospective spouse may decide that the two of you are genetically incompatible due to a high risk of certain diseases to your children. Or a prospective spouse could be discouraged from commitment due to lifespan incompatibilities, not wanting to be left lonely for twenty years if you are likely to die first.

If made public, your genetic information may be used for identity theft, affecting everyone close to you. It may match you to a crime committed in your youth or reveal other personal information you do not want others to know, such as that the father you lived with is not your biological father.

### Could You Be Cloned?

Taking these concerns one step further, it is possible (although illegal nearly everywhere) to clone a person from samples of his or her DNA. We can envision a time when an enthusiastic Kobe Bryant fan could create her own little Kobe by stealing his water bottle, collecting a sample of his DNA, and finding the right mad scientist to grow a cloned fetus and implant it in a surrogate mother. Or, North Korea might surreptitiously obtain the DNA of the South Korean prime minister and use this knowledge to find genetic flaws to exploit.

While widely illegal and certainly unethical, these scenarios are not beyond what science can now do. If you worry about the discovery of your DNA leading to higher insurance rates, how would you feel if a few strands of your DNA in the wrong hands could lead to clones of you released into the world?

## LEGAL LOOPHOLES LEAKING YOUR HEALTH DATA

"But wait," you might be thinking. "My health information is covered by privacy laws imposing penalties on anyone who leaks my hospital or pharmacy data." And you would be correct. In every industrialized nation, health care records are treated as a special class of data that must be limited to only those people with a need to know, and they must be protected by intricate security schemes. However, significant holes in the system make it possible for your health information to still leak through.

### Protected or Not Protected?

In the United States, the Health Insurance Portability and Accountability Act (HIPAA) protects health-care information created or learned by certain classes of health-care providers and the contractors that work for them. However, if you provide biometric or health information to other people for other reasons, such as a retina scan for your employer's security function, or a DNA sample to a genetic testing company to learn about your ancestry, then the information you expose is not protected under HIPAA.

Information that other people are able to determine by studying your body is also not protected. After all, how could the law enforce a restriction on your coworkers speculating about whether you are pregnant because you are showing all the well-known signs? Similarly, if you cough and sneeze all day, friends assume that you either have a cold or that your allergies are acting up. This observational analysis is obviously not against the law.

But take it one step further. Suppose a coworker takes your disposable coffee cup out of the trash and pays to have it analyzed for infectious agents. His actions, while creepy and disturbing, also probably violate no laws in the United States.

The current strange disparity in US law covering the use of a third party's DNA is perhaps the best example of this last point. When you submit your DNA for analysis for medical research or health-care purposes, HIPAA protects the data from distribution and exposure. In fact, HIPAA is careful to treat your DNA sample as the core data model for your entire life and health. No one can see the sample unless that person has a reason to do so. Improper exposure or storage of your sample could lead to penalties in the millions of dollars. This law applies if you are a subject of a medical study or if you visit the doctor for a checkup or treatment of disease.

But what if someone other than a medical provider or medical researcher obtains a sample of your DNA? It is still the vital building block to your essential being. Is it still accorded all possible protection and respect under the law? Or is DNA just another cast-off piece of litter, disposable and not protected by the law? The United States has yet to answer this question. Canada, Great Britain, Australia, and Europe, while overall more protective of personal privacy than the United States, may also have holes in the way this data is protected.

## How Law Enforcement Uses and Stores DNA Information

Law enforcement in the United States looks upon each one of us as little more than large slogging, sloshing sacks of DNA, spilling our genes wherever we go—a lost hair here, saliva on a cup there, a nicked finger leaving blood somewhere else. Law enforcement has no problem capturing the DNA you leave behind. Since they are allowed to search our trash cans at the curb for discarded items and mine those items for information, why should they be stopped from collecting the cells that our bodies naturally discard and mining those cells for information too? Information such as whether you are really the father of the children who live at your house. Or whether you might be related to, and therefore in contact with, a known terrorist.

In most cases, law enforcement is not interested in health information derived from DNA and does not store such information. Instead, they tend to hold and inspect only abstracted segments of DNA that the police can compare with similar abstracted segments for identification purposes. In addition, law enforcement's DNA databases, while public and not always tightly regulated, tend to be guarded carefully by their owners.

For example, the FBI's CODIS system for storing and comparing DNA is based only on specific information found in thirteen spots on the human chromosomes known as alleles. These thirteen alleles are found in what scientists call "junk DNA" (spots on the human chromosome that do not produce specific proteins). Though variable among humans, under current scientific knowledge alleles do not provide significant health information about the donor of the sample.

CODIS has standardized collection and comparisons of DNA for law enforcement across the United States. Police can and do use full DNA samples to pull family information that is useful to a case; however, the vast public DNA databases are available primarily for comparison of these alleles, expressed in a mathematical abstraction. For that reason, health data is not available to everyone who uses the CODIS database.

## Expanded Police Rights to Take Your DNA

All fifty US states passed laws allowing for law enforcement to take DNA samples from people convicted of crimes. In 2013, the US Supreme Court decided on an expansive view of police rights to take your DNA and store it in a law enforcement database for later comparisons. The court majority in *Maryland v. King*[4] upheld a Maryland law allowing police to take a cheek swab and sample the DNA of any person arrested for certain crimes, then to store that DNA and use it to search for matches to past crimes that the donor is not currently suspected of committing.

In *Maryland v. King,* the majority held that while swabbing your cheek for DNA counted as a search, such a search was not unreasonable to conduct on arrested suspects, under the regime outlined by the carefully crafted Maryland law. That law allows DNA samples to be taken only from people arrested for burglary or violent crimes. The samples may not be tested before the suspect is arraigned. If the arrested person is not ultimately convicted of a crime, then the DNA sample is to be purged from the databases.

However, many people are concerned that the Supreme Court's decision in the *King* case will be viewed more broadly by police and may be used to harvest DNA from arrested people regardless of circumstances. A vocal four-judge minority of the court disagreed with the opinion, writing, "Make no mistake about it: As an entirely predictable consequence of today's decision, your DNA can be taken and entered into a national DNA database if you are ever arrested, rightly or wrongly, and for whatever reason."[5]

The minority did not see protections in the careful wording of the Maryland law, reasoning that if police see value in a DNA search to identify someone for robbery, then "you must believe that it will identify someone arrested for running a red light."[6]

On the whole, the law enforcement community likely read the message that DNA swabbing and matching is acceptable for people under arrest. A slew of new DNA samples will fly into the CODIS database, to be searched by any federal, state, or local law police throughout the country. If you are arrested, the court has allowed the ultimate fishing expedition with your DNA: it can be taken and compared to all the evidence from all the unsolved cases in the database, just to see if you match anywhere.

## Opening Pandora's Box

Generally speaking, placing your DNA into a public database such as the FBI's CODIS database is a one-way door. The databases grow and grow, and information that goes in is never deleted. And like Pandora's box, once the lid opens and the contents are released, those contents cannot be stuffed back in.

The immutable nature of biometrics such as DNA presents special problems when it comes to your privacy. While you can always change your lost password or credit card, you can't change your DNA. When DNA is lost or captured by someone you want to hold secrets from, DNA tells its tale, which will be accurate as long as you live and will follow in family linage after you have passed away.

Moreover, if the local police release information about you that they learned from analyzing your DNA, the information can reach your boss and neighbors and will not be "unheard." Protection of private information can be the work of a lifetime, but a single slip will ruin the entire life's work. So the consistency of treatment is paramount.

We cannot fight to protect DNA information in one circumstance and then build loosely guarded public databases of private DNA for another circumstance. Failing to secure the public database ruins all the protection afforded in other circumstances. Currently, the states have widely differing laws about protecting DNA in law-enforcement databases. We will never truly protect this basic health information of every person until we have consistent treatment and protection across categories.

## COLLECTORS, ANALYZERS, AND RESEARCHERS

Law enforcement is not the only entity interested in collecting and analyzing your DNA or other health information. Other government bodies also collect DNA for their own purposes. In addition, your health-care provider, your insurance companies, and your pharmacy all keep information about you. If your pharmacy is inside a bigger store such as Wal-Mart, Target, or your grocery, then information about your prescribed drugs may be stored with other data about your shopping habits. And with today's sophisticated analysis tools, those who collect your health information and habits can draw a surprisingly detailed picture of your private life. According to the website PrivacyInternational.org, more than sixty countries have created DNA databses to help fight crime. This site lists the United Kingdom as the country with the largest DNA database.

### Military and State Databases

If you are in today's military, then your DNA records are kept on file for identification purposes. The US military also likely checks a full screen of susceptibilities before you report for duty. The defense department keeps DNA records of contractors sent into dangerous theaters.[7]

Depending on their age, your children's DNA may also be in a government database. Babies give blood at birth and are tested for genetic disorders. US states mandate that newborns are tested for as many as fifty-four different conditions, and the DNA samples are stored in state labs, some for only months and others forever. States such as Florida store babies' DNA indefinitely, and parents in Texas and Minnesota have filed lawsuits to have their children's DNA removed from the public database.[8]

*Celebrity DNA Trophy Hunters*

Imagine that a celebrity visits your town in an announced trip. The world's paparazzi are focused on your town as the celebrity tastes the local fare and watches a musical in the town theater. But other stalkers are present as well: trophy hunters, searching for the celebrity's DNA.

In his mansion behind ten-foot walls and electrified gates, the celebrity can protect himself from stalkers. But here, out in the open, he is vulnerable. Trophy hunters target the cup he used for water at the local restaurant. They pay the hotel maid to be allowed in the celebrity's hotel room, then scour for hair samples culled from the celebrity's hairbrush. In little time they are gone with their trophy: the celebrity's entire genetic record.

The celebrity's DNA could be simply offered for sale on eBay to people with more money than sense. Or it could be processed and examined for everything that DNA can tell us about this person: his ancestry, his racial makeup, his susceptibility to certain diseases, and his propensity toward alcoholism or aggression. If the DNA bounty hunters do their homework, the celebrity's DNA can be compared against other people in his family or other families to confirm whether he fathered a child out of wedlock or was himself the illegitimate child of someone famous. A world of embarrassing details might be uncovered and used to blackmail or simply humiliate the celebrity.

Trophy DNA can be put to uses even more malicious and dangerous than blackmail. According an article in *The Atlantic* in 2012, a strand of the US president's DNA could be used to create a bioweapon—a virus that spreads easily, but will only be fatal to the president.[9]

To the authors' knowledge, bioweapons aimed at specific people, or specific races of people (ethnic bioweapons), have not yet been created. But trophy hunters of celebrity DNA have been around for years. In 2002, British newspapers reported on a "honey trap" conspiracy in which Prince Harry was to be seduced in Spain with the purpose of capturing his DNA and proving that he was not the son of Prince Charles, but a love child of another man.[10]

Genetic bounty hunting is not specifically illegal in the United States, Canada, or Great Britain, although certain general privacy laws might be crossed depending on how the DNA capture and examination is accomplished.

*When the Trophy Is Your Own DNA*

The capture and analysis of genetic material, now part of our celebrity-stalking culture, can be turned against regular citizens as well.

Stealing a person's DNA to find his or her embarrassing family secrets may sound farfetched, but it can be simple to accomplish. The purpose of the theft may not be blackmail, but simply the need to know if the DNA donor was the thief's real father or birth mother. In a divorce in which child support is at issue, a father could test the DNA of his own children if he suspects his wife of infidelity. Or, a mother could test her children where infidelity is established but child custody is at issue.

We may be close to a time in which any person engaged to be married is asked by her betrothed or his parents for her genetic makeup to check for potential time bombs that would exclude her from being a suitable spouse or a suitable mother. Diseases such as cystic fibrosis and Canavan disease are passed on recessive genes and may emerge when two non-symptomatic carriers of these genes have a baby. Some couples test themselves voluntarily, but what if one doesn't want to take the test? A concerned spouse or even in-laws can have the test performed against his will and without his knowledge.

Finally, we cannot ever discount the depths to which political rivals, business competitors, or tabloid journalists will sink to reach their goals. Covert genetic testing from left-behind materials may become a tool in the rivalries of the future.

## Analysis Tools Paint Your Health's Picture

George Orwell is known for saying that "at fifty, every man has the face he deserves." Our habits and health are written on our face and bodies as we age. We present our faces, voices, and bodies to the public every day, and sometimes our health conditions are obvious to people who know what to look for. This can lead to negative consequences as employers, prospective business or marriage partners, and others make judgments about us based on the health information they glean from our appearances.

Today, technology allows interested parties to take this observation a step further and make judgments about us based on perceived health conditions they could not have interpreted at a glance several years ago. Health tests have become more widely available and easier to perform. A full DNA test for two hundred traits and susceptibilities can be performed with a tiny sample such as a strand of hair. It is not necessarily illegal for police, employers, or others to perform such a test on you, although it can be problematic to lie about whose sample is being tested and why.

An employer who believes your health information is relevant to your job is likely to require your signed permission statement to test your DNA for specific factors as a condition of your employment. The system of health care in the United States is tied directly to employment, giving companies important financial incentives to maintain healthier work-forces. As more businesses adopt antismoking hiring policies,[11] and weight discrimination becomes endemic in the workplace,[12] businesses find ways to weed out potentially higher-cost, higher-maintenance workers in favor of the young workers with what they perceive to be healthy lifestyles.

Current technology allows certain significant health conditions to be determined without any tests at all, invasive or otherwise. The mathematically based science of data mining can demonstrate health issues simply by knowing some of your behaviors. With the help of predictive behavioral mathematical models, some large companies have secretly changed their methods of decision making.

For example, in 2011 Hewlett Packard tested a predictive scoring system to grade the likelihood that certain employees would quit the company, and who was most likely to leave. The company then notified managers which of their charges were likely to leave.[13] This same type of employment analysis could easily be aimed at behaviors that indicate health problems, or even the likelihood of future health problems.

Insurance companies have built actuarial charts for decades, calculating rates based on statistics about how behaviors like smoking and regular alcohol use affect life expectancy. The numbers can also show the health costs we can expect from certain smokers and drinkers in their productive years. Calculations like these at insurers and employers throughout the world are likely affecting hiring decisions. Publicizing such calculations and their effect, if any, on hiring is not in employers' best interest, so it is unlikely that the general public will read about these practices.

As described in chapter 1, retailer Target used predictive analysis to determine which of its customers was pregnant.[14] Target's analysis started with a question to an in-house statistician: "If we wanted to figure out if a customer is pregnant, even if she didn't want us to know, can you do that?"[15] The statistician watched the buying habits of women on Target's baby registry and found some triggering behaviors, such as purchases of large quantities of unscented lotion around the beginning of their second trimester, and extra-large bags of cotton balls along with washcloths and hand sanitizers prior to delivery. When analyzed together, about fifteen products correlated with being pregnant. The resulting analysis tool proved highly effective, predicting the pregnancy of at least one customer before her family knew of her pregnancy. Target uses this information to determine what coupons to send to its customers and how aggressively to push certain sales for those customers.

Nearly all large companies in the United States use predictive analysis based on what's called "Big Data" to learn more about us as consumers, employees, and prospects. They are quiet about which behaviors they study and what they learn from the statistical correlations, but you should know that these studies affect the way major companies interact with you, and some studies relate to your health conditions.

*Losing Yourself to Research*

The HIPAA laws protect the privacy of health care data for people in the United States. They also force health care providers to carefully secure the health care data of patients and research subjects so that this valuable information is not lost accidentally. In addition, the Genetic Information Nondiscrimination Act of 2008 prohibits health plans from using a person's genetic information to discriminate on insurance underwriting.

Unfortunately, these are not the only privacy protections that you might want for the records and materials that result from health care or medical research. If you are a participant in a medical study, then your biological samples and information, including all that can be learned or created from those samples and information, probably belong to the research institution and not to you.[16] While the "Common Rule" in the United States regarding health research mandates that the research subject give informed consent to the procedures and use of information, enforcement seems lax. The Citizens' Council for Health Freedom did a study on how long states keep the DNA of newborns. Many parents were shocked to learn that the DNA of their infant was taken while at the hospital, without their consent. In some cases, some states store and share the DNA with other groups.[17]

Many patients entering clinical research are at a power disadvantage in relation to the researchers and will sign any consent forms to be allowed to participate in the research. This is especially true when the research promises the possibility of a cure or remission in diseases that are otherwise untreatable. Once the research institution holds the patient's tissues and information and owns them by law or by coerced consent, the institution has no compelling reason to stop using that material as long as it can be useful in research.

We know that privacy can be shattered through the researcher's ownership of your medical information from incidents such as the case of Henrietta Lacks, which was documented in a popular book by Rebecca Skloot.[18] Ms. Lacks, a black tobacco farmer and mother of five who died in 1951, achieved posthumous fame from the way her tissue was used in medical research. A sample of her tissue, taken by doctors ostensibly to assist in her cancer treatment, was grown into the HeLa line of cells and used in research around the world. Cells from this line have been infected with viruses, shot into space for research, and used to develop important vaccines and medications. The tissue that led to this cell line was taken without her consent, and her family didn't know about the use of her cell lines until twenty years after her death. In 2013, a group of scientists sequenced the genome of Henrietta Lacks and published it.[19]

Ms. Lacks' family members were upset, as they should be.[20] Anyone with access to this raw data can send it to genetic analysis sites such as

SNPedia for processing. The result is a report similar to those provided by 23andMe and other private biotech companies.

Medical research is vital in the development of new treatments and cures for human diseases, but that doesn't absolve researchers of their responsibility to protect the privacy of the people tested. Protections should continue even when the person's tissue is being used in experiments decades later. The researcher's ownership of a patient's genetic and other biological material is a loophole in the current law that can destroy a patient's privacy.

In the seventy or so years since Watson and Crick identified the DNA molecule and how it functioned, genetic analysis has become an everyday technology, ordered over the Internet by anybody with three hundred dollars. Every day we learn more about how DNA works, what proteins it produces, and what they do in our bodies. We also unlock new mysteries of the brain and other body chemistry. As testing our bodies and knowledge about the results becomes more complete, greater opportunities exist for our privacy to be violated. The law and society have yet to catch up to the biotech revolution.

## NOTES

1. Christine Nordqvist, "Angelina Jolie Has Double Mastectomy Because of 87% Breast Cancer Risk," *Medical News Today*, May 14, 2013.

2. Bonnie Rochman, "23andMe Wants FDA Approval for Personal DNA Testing. What Can It Reveal?," *Time*, August 2, 2012.

3. See company website at www.23andme.com. Also see Steven Kotler, "What Is 23andMe Really Selling: The Moral Quandary at the Center of the Personalized Genomics Revolution," *Forbes*, December 13, 2012.

4. 569 U.S. ___ (2013), June 3, 2013.

5. 569 U.S. ___ (2013), June 3, 2013.

6. 569 U.S. ___ (2013), June 3, 2013.

7. Douglas J. Gillert, "Who Are You? DNA Registry Knows," American Forces Press Service, US Department of Defense website, July 13, 1998, www.defense.gov/News/NewsArticle.aspx?ID=41418.

8. Elizabeth Cohen, "The Government Has Your Baby's DNA," CNN.com, February 4, 2010, www.cnn.com/2010/HEALTH/02/04/baby.dna.government/index.html.

9. Andrew Hessel, Marc Goodman, and Steven Kotler, "Hacking the President's DNA," *The Atlantic*, October 24, 2012.

10. Peter Guarnieri, "Prince Harry and the Honey Trap: An Argument for Criminalizing the Nonconsensual Use of Genetic Information," *American Criminal Law Review*, September 22, 2011, citing Martin Smith, "Honey Trap Plot to Hire Beauty to Snatch a Lock of Hair from Harry; How Palace Uncovered Outrageous Sting to 'Prove' Link with James Hewitt," *Mail on Sunday*, December 15, 2002.

11. "For example, hospitals in Florida, Georgia, Massachusetts, Missouri, Ohio, Pennsylvania, Tennessee and Texas, among others, stopped hiring smokers in the last year and more are openly considering the option." A.G. Sulzberger, "Hospitals Shift Smoking Ban to Smoker Ban," *New York Times*, February 11, 2011.

12. Josh Sanburn, "Why Being Overweight Could Earn You a Lower Salary," *Time*, May 2, 2012.

13. Joel Schectman, "Book: HP Piloted Program to Predict Which Workers Would Quit," *Wall Street Journal*, March 15, 2013.

14. Charles Duhigg, "How Companies Learn Your Secrets," *New York Times*, February 16, 2012.

15. Duhigg, "How Companies Learn Your Secrets."

16. See *Washington University v. Catalana*, 437 F. Supp2d 985 (E.D. Mo. 2006), also, 490 F.3d 667 (8th Cir. 2007), finding that tissues taken by researchers in a biological study were an "inter vivos gift" to the university conducting the research.

17. Citizens' Council for Health Freedom, www.cchfreedom.org/cchf.php/385#.UkLbJBZXFgI.

18. Rebecca Skloot, *The Immortal Life of Henrietta Lacks* (New York: Crown, 2010).

19. Rebecca Skloot, "The Immortal Life of Henrietta Lacks, the Sequel," *New York Times*, March 23, 2013. The full publication of the HeLa genome has since been taken offline, but other partial publications of it may still be publically available.

20. Skloot, *The Immortal Life of Henrietta Lacks*; "Tracing the 'Immortal' Cells of Henrietta Lacks," Fresh Air interview by Dave Davies with author Rebecca Skloot, NPR, March 18, 2011; Sarah Zielinski, "Cracking the Code of the Human Genome," *Smithsonian*, January 22, 2010.

*Technology Section III*

# Home Is Where the Heart (of Surveillance) Is

Your home is your sanctuary. Your privacy must be protected there. But you are about to learn that many people are peering into your home, even if you don't sense them. Many of those people or companies looking in at you are doing it for reasons that sound almost altruistic—to help you save money, get a rebate, have a safer home, or watch over your loved ones even when you are not there. Your power company and other utilities have developed computerized "smart grids" that can read the activities in your home through the power you use. The companies you invite into your home, to play games or send you entertainment, are also taking notes about your lifestyle. If you set up a digital network in your home, you could be inviting unwanted visitors. You may not be the only person who can use those security cameras. The following chapters demonstrate these and other threats to your privacy that you encounter without ever leaving home.

# ELEVEN

# Home Sweet Home: Spies in Your Living Room

You sit in your living room sipping an iced tea and browsing the web for bargains on toasters. You're safe from the world of privacy invaders, right? Maybe not. Today the average home may contain computers, smartphones, and household appliances hooked up to Internet services that control lights, heating, and more. In this chapter you discover who is studying you after you enter your front door, and why.

> **People who understand how personal data is generated, collected, stored and used are better equipped to take control of their personal data and demand accountability from the agencies and corporations that store and use their information.**
> **—Barbara Jones, director of the Office for Intellectual Freedom[1]**

## HI HONEY, I'M HOME (BUT YOU KNEW THAT, DIDN'T YOU)?

Today there are super smart appliances, from your lighting system to your television set, that can sense where you are and what you're doing. The tradeoff in convenience over loss of privacy is a tricky one, but to make the right choice, you should know what risks accompany the convenience.

### Warmth and Light: What They Reveal about You

The temperature adjusts and lights go on. Meet the modern-day peeping Tom, and it's not your neighbor looking in your windows or tracking your location with a smartphone, the Google maps car app, a drone, or even a satellite in the sky. You let the peeping Tom into your home when you modernized it.

Turning the lights on remotely using a smartphone app leaves digital clues that could pinpoint your arrival or departure for criminals. Your habits of lights on/lights off create a series of triggers that marketing firms put to use. Marketing firms might get important information about someone who turns off the lights at 10 p.m., back on again at 2 a.m., and then off again at 4 a.m. This pattern could be the sign of sleepless nights, so it might be handy to market to you as you browse online late at night. Marketers might also offer targeted ads for sleep aids and products and services that help you deal with stress. But if you don't protect this data daily, detailed information about your habits can be handed over to law enforcement without your knowledge, or stolen by cybersnoops and cybercriminals.

Home privacy and security used to mean turning on the outside lights, locking the doors, and pulling the shades. Now your home is a series of electronic devices connected to the Internet. An entry-level Internet-connected home may contain technology as simple as an Internet and cable connection. At the other end of the spectrum is the highly connected home, also known as a "smart home." This self-aware home can be taught how to turn things on and off. The self-aware home can alert you about groceries you need to replenish or dirty HVAC filters that you need to replace.

These interconnected devices are all silently sending signals and transmitting data over Bluetooth, wireless, cellular, or broadband connections. All of those bits and bytes of your daily life and routines come together to make your house more comfortable and to add conveniences to your life. But there are unexplored challenges to these smart homes. While you learn to use and love your smart home and its gadgets, criminals are quickly finding ways to learn how to tap into your smart home too.

Cybercriminals are looking for new ways to attack your in-home technologies. They look for the ways that data is shared among your devices, appliances, and even with the companies that you trust. They look for any access control points in the neighborhood such as neighborhood cameras or smart meters. Each device in your home collects data about you, and it's up to you to know what the privacy policies of vendors are and what the vendor will do, if anything, in the event that your data on their device is breached. Remember, the gadgetry of technology often outpaces the ability for privacy and security experts to build in the core protections that you need. Sometimes the challenge is the razor-thin profit margin and not knowing if consumers will adopt the product. Other times, it's just not in the mind-set of the developers the length to which a criminal will go to steal your information.

It would be alarming for most of us to receive a phone call where a stranger says to you, "I can see all of the devices in your home and I think I can control them."[2] *Forbes* reporter Kashmir Hill, using a Google search tool and some technical know-how, cracked the code on how to control "smart" home systems. To prove her point, she called a few of the occupants of the smart homes to ask them to verify if she was indeed controlling their home smart systems from the Internet. The surprised occupants answered in the affirmative; she had indeed turned on, and then off, a light in their room.[3]

## What You Watch While Others Are Watching

You decide to relax and watch a show you download from Netflix. Who else knows about your activity besides you and Netflix? If you are using any type of cable service for viewing television, your cable company has been watching your habits for years, including when you watch, what you watch, when you record programming, and more. This information has helped the company management decide how to bundle and package services, how to keep you as a customer, and how to invest in the appropriate bandwidth for growing home markets. This type of watching TV watchers was considered OK in the early days of cable TV; however, with the advent of Internet-connected cable plans, gaming systems, and other intelligent devices connected to your TV, there is a whole new level of watching going on. If you were watching it on Smart TV, be aware that the TV might collect your TV watching habits and transmit the information back to a database. Read your privacy settings for the Smart TV carefully.

When you download a movie from Netflix, Amazon, or Hulu, these services pay attention and alert marketers to your browsing, sampling, and viewing habits. Verizon is so convinced that this is the future of getting to know their customers that they have already filed a patent for a cable box that can sense what you are doing in addition to watching television so they can send you marketing ads that target your activities.[4] It's called gesture recognition technology, and it uses audio sensors, facial recognition, and movement to learn more about you. Not only does this technology allow marketers to know what you are watching on TV, but it can guess your gender, the global location of your accent, facial features, and even the language you are speaking. These sensors may sense your moods too. If you seem angry, do not be surprised if you are offered relaxing vacation packages or anger-management self-help lessons.

If you have a newer gaming system that uses recognition cameras to give you a virtual-reality experience, those systems also know when you have entered the room and try to match you up with the player name that you chose when you played Dance Party last night.

In an even more intrusive way, companies are in a race to watch you watch TV in higher resolution. One of those companies is Intel, which is going to sell you a streaming TV service box that will watch you while you watch TV.[5] Intel indicates that by watching you watch TV, it can know you and help improve your overall TV-watching experience. By learning about you, the camera will help companies transmit targeted ads just for you. The question is, what else might they do with that data, and would groups such as law enforcement, cybercriminals, or health-insurance companies that want to monitor coach potato habits want to do with that data?

*Getting You to Give Yourself Away*

The author of a recent *Wall Street Journal* report[6] explains how marketers are using cable set boxes and other technologies to watch you in your living room while you watch television. The US Army showed different ads to various markets via cable set top boxes to understand how to tweak their ads to reach key demographics. They sent one ad featuring a female soldier and others showing soldiers of various ethnic backgrounds. They delivered different ads to different homes based on the demographics they guessed were resident in the homes.[7]

The television industry is using a matching process that involves reviewing marketing databases from your shopping habits at brick-and-mortar and online stores, your other Internet activities, and your viewing habits. Under the Cable Privacy Act, companies cannot share your personal information without your express permission. But online providers of video services do not follow the same rules. Sound confusing? To you, it's your television, but knowing who provides a show is important in understanding your privacy rights. If you want to opt out of tracking and ads, you can currently opt out at DirectTV, Tivo Inc., and Cablevision Corporation. If you have a different provider, you'll have to call them to ask if you can opt out.

Of course, some services that allow you to watch content on your television are not delivered by cable providers. Watch YouTube? Now you can snoop on your city and see what everyone else is watching using a tool called YouTube Trend Maps. You can see a map that shows you what people are watching across your city, state, and even the country. This service currently shows the last twenty-four hours of TV-watching trends. You can sort the results by age groups and gender, geographic location, and more, and even get a report on the top-ranked videos for that time period.

## HOW YOUR HOUSE SEES YOUR EVERY MOVE

Every move you make, your house is telling on you even when you stay offline. While your interconnected Internet home controlled by apps improves your life, it also broadcasts data about you to marketing firms, bad guys, and even government spies. An interconnected device can transmit the geolocation of the device and your activities real time. This information might be sent to others through radio frequencies, Wi-Fi, Internet broadband, or cell. The actual devices themselves may store an incredible amount of data that could tell on you.

### People Bug Themselves for the Convenience

When asked how US teams that must conduct covert or clandestine operations will be affected by digital devices that are connected to the Internet, General David Petraeus responded,

> "Transformational" is an overused word, but I do believe it properly applies to these technologies, particularly to their effect on clandestine tradecraft. Items of interest will be located, identified, monitored, and remotely controlled through technologies such as radio-frequency identification, sensor networks, tiny embedded servers, and energy harvesters—all connected to the next-generation Internet using abundant, low-cost, and high-power computing.
> —Former CIA director and US Army general David Petraeus (Ret)[8]

The interconnected household can make your life much more convenient. You can save on energy costs by turning the thermostat up when you're home and when you're asleep or away from home. You can improve your physical safety and assets by using remote alarm monitoring, turning lights on and off to convince would-be thieves that you are there, lighting your house when you pull in the driveway, and more. You can also keep tabs on an infant in the next room or an elderly parent who is being taken care of at home. You can check in on your pets to figure out who has been lying on your new white comforter.

Have a parent with early-onset dementia? In the UK, the government has proposed tracking granny and gramps using GPS.[9] By asking seniors to wear a device around their necks or on a keychain, they can monitor them all day long, sending their GPS location to a website roughly every five minutes. Their caregivers and family members can watch them as they go through their day and keep tabs on them.

### How Connected Are You?

> Internet-connected smart houses and security systems can be hacked and used to facilitate bad guys while hindering the home owners.
> —Jim Boxmeyer, AT & T Tech Security Principal[10]

How connected is today's home? Let's talk a virtual tour though a home to see what's happening. We'll start with your front door. Hate to fumble around for keys but do not like the idea of an unlocked door? Move to a smartphone-app-enabled key-and-lock set. Using a device that is home Wi-Fi–enabled you can lock your door and then use an Internet-based command to check the status of the lock and to also lock or unlock the door remotely. So, over the Internet and on your Wi-Fi, you are broadcasting when you lock and unlock your door.

In the just-having-fun-at-bedtime department, are you having trouble picking out a bedtime story to read to your kids? No bedtime routine with your kids is complete without a good story. In the cool-factor department a new set of pajamas is on the scene. The Smart PJs have a fun little pattern on them that include Quick Response (QR) codes. These QR codes can be scanned into your smartphone or tablet and then show a video or a story with pictures and words. Too tired to read to junior? There's an app for that, too, that can entertain your kids at bedtime by reading the story to them.

Then there is the case of the smart seat, as in smart toilet seat. One maker provides a Bluetooth-enabled toilet that can be controlled via your smartphone. The app on your phone lets you put the pesky seat down if you follow a male in the house or put that seat right up if it is in the way—all by hitting an app button instead of touching the germy seat. If that is not enough for you, you can also flush the toilet using the app, and you can keep what you left behind in the toilet diary if you so choose in their online toilet diary. Not sure if you want your doctor, insurance agency, or a peeping Tom to be able to access that private information. By the way, ethical hackers have already demonstrated they can hack into smart toilets, caveat emptor.[11]

Want to get really specific about what lights come on and off? Maybe you want to dim or brighten the lighting. This is all possible, bulb by bulb, as new lighting systems come out on the marketplace. Some of the new lighting systems allow you to track the bulb's IP address and turn them on and off. Yes, just like your cell phone or tablet uses an IP address to talk to the Internet, your home light bulbs can too. But are all these apps that you use to turn your lights on and off keeping your data secure and private?

Do you need a doctor who does house calls? You can now get a web-based house call using medical equipment that phones home to your doctor's office with your vital statistics. Each of these medical devices has a unique ID that lets your doctor's office know if the device is functioning properly and or how you are doing. But if you watched Season 2 of *Homeland* on Showtime (season spoiler alert, so move along if you have not seen this), you know that the Pacemaker was hacked and took out the vice president. Now maybe you are not a high-ranking official, but if your data is not kept private and secure, what might your home Wi-Fi, Internet, cell service, and medical devices be broadcasting about you?

One of the coolest powers that Superman[12] has is his X-ray vision. Imagine being able to beam your X-ray vision to check on your kids in the next room. A new system called Wi-VI, developed by MIT's Computer Science and Artificial Intelligence Laboratory, gets you one step closer to Superman's powers.[13] The Wi-Vi, using the reflection of Wi-Fi signals and interference between antennas, can track movement behind a wall and identify if someone is occupying a room.

Now we enter the kitchen to see the surprised shopper who learns that her Internet-enabled fridge that is connected to online ordering and her delivery team has played a trick on her. One day, a deliveryman brings to the door ten times the groceries she normally purchases. Since your smart home is just one large computer, it is probable that hackers could take over your fridge and start sending out orders for more food.

### Stickers That Track Your Every Move

Now the smart house can help you to never lose your keys, phone, or wallet again. Sounds like a little piece of heaven, doesn't it? A new device helps you track every object you typically can't find such as your keys, tablet, phone, wallet, and checkbook.

This new technology is a Bluetooth-powered sticker thinner than a quarter. Whenever you have a technology that makes life easier, you have to ask yourself, could this technology betray me? In the wrong hands, could making my wallet or keys easier to find help out a bad guy? What happens if the trackers betray you?

The technology is in the wafer-thin trackers that can now be made as small as stickers! Their internal batteries last roughly twelve months, and they are Bluetooth enabled. You tag the object that you don't want to lose by placing the sticker on it, and then you can see them on an app. The app notes the distance, and if you decide an object is too far away, you can tap the app and the sticker on the object will light up and buzz. Just remember, cybercriminals are testing how to break into Bluetooth-enabled devices every day and are prepared to capitalize on this technology. They call this "bluesnarfing," when criminals "listen in" on your Bluetooth broadcasts. It's okay if you decide to use this time-saving and potentially device-protecting technology. Just ask your manufacturer first how they protect the Bluetooth signal so it doesn't broadcast to everyone, only you.

### What's the Risk?

None of the hypothetical hacking incidents that we mention above has been reported yet, so there is time now to think before you connect and then ask questions about how your security and privacy will be protected.

And how reliable is the Internet that your smart house relies on? Many of the devices in your house depend upon cellular service for access. Those of you on 4G swear by it, and you get mad when you can't access it. You notice if your smartphone or tablet seems to move in slow motion. Well, it might upset you to learn that 4G networks are vulnerable, and just a few on-purpose steps or accidental ones could take 4G down for your town. Those 4G networks—the high-speed cellular and wireless data networks—are quickly becoming mandatory in our busy lives. But security geeks recently found that a simple technique could bring down your service, leaving you in slow-mo or, worse, with no access at all.

Researchers recently revealed that for roughly $650 and a little know how, bad-guy hackers could disable 4G for a local area.[14] They could purchase a cheap, battery-operated transmitter and an amplifier and aim it at a Long-Term Evolution (LTE) network hub and take it down. It could leave you in slow-mo on 3G and 2G networks, but even those are being phased out. The good news for all of us is these good-guy researchers filed their report with the National Telecommunications and Information Administration (NTIA). This group advises the White House on telecom and information policy. The NTIA is working with experts to study this issue further. In their report they mention roughly eight places where a bad guy could hack the network and bring it down. No known jamming has taken place yet, but it's important that you have a backup plan just in case!

Beware of counterfeit devices in your home because you may get more than you bargained for. You may not know this, but fake technology products in use at your home, at work, and by US military and government offices are at an all-time high. This could mean your devices do not work quite right but could also mean things as dangerous as short circuits in airplanes or problems firing computerized weapons. According to a newly released study, counterfeit technology goods quadrupled from 2009 to 2011. A few years ago, the FBI seized over $70 million counterfeit CISCO routers, which are commonly used at home and at work for access to the Internet. And the Department of Homeland Security said that consumer electronic counterfeits topped the pirated goods list last year, beating out counterfeit shoes for the number-one spot!

### Protecting Yourself from the Peepers

You can protect your home network by asking questions about where your technology comes from. Only buy from reputable retailers—it's not a guarantee that you will not get a counterfeit product, but you will have recourse to return the item if you do. Keep in mind that you get what you pay for. Getting technology at the cheapest price might not be the best bargain—counterfeit goods are often much cheaper than the legitimate version.

If you or a loved one believes you are a victim of purchasing counterfeit technology, please report it. You should contact the following authorities.

- Local police if you bought it from a local vendor
- FBI at www.ic3.gov
- DHS ICE at www.ICE.gov

## FEATURE: INTERVIEW WITH THE CREATOR OF SHODAN

The challenges of protecting the privacy and security of your data stored on various devices is exemplified by a search engine called Shodan (SHODAN at www.shodanhq.com). This search engine can be used to find devices connected to the Internet. A quick search might reveal unlocked webcams, printers that you can dump obnoxious printouts to, control systems for energy suppliers, and more. Your home devices may show up on Shodan too. The good guys developed Shodan, and they hope to keep it in the hands of honest people.

Basically, Shodan searches for and indexes devices connected to the Internet, ranging from webcams and printers to more exotic—and frightening—examples of security cameras and control systems for nuclear power plants. The authors were able to interview the founder of Shodan, John Matherly, to find out more about this intriguing technology.

Q: We want to alert people to the dangers of how unprotected digital devices that are collecting everyone's data could put them at risk. When we saw your search engine, Shodan, we wanted to know what inspired you to create the tool.

A: Shodan was originally developed as a website that would provide software-usage statistics for the entire Internet. You could go to Shodan and find out which web-server software is most popular, which countries prefer one type of device over another, and get a big-picture view of what's publicly available on the Internet. It was also a personal project that would let me experiment with new ideas and technologies, and it continues to help me try out cutting-edge programming techniques.

Q: Have you seen a case where major infrastructure was hiding in plain sight and either currently compromised by hackers or well on its way to becoming a target? What can you tell us about this?

A: I have seen a lot of major infrastructure that was hidden in plain sight (i.e., security by obscurity), but I am not involved in the subsequent law-enforcement proceedings. The DHS, FBI, or other agency receives as much information from Shodan as possible (for free) to track down the owner of the device and from there they handle everything. Fortunately, there's a big gap between identifying a vulnerable device and the skill required to successfully compromise it (by taking down a power grid, for example). I believe that's a substantial reason why we haven't seen more widespread attacks on the infrastructure. It's trivial to execute a denial of service attack, but invading and compromising critical infrastructure remains something that's very rare and difficult to do. [Authors' note: a denial of service attack, sometimes referred to as a DDoS, or Distributed Denial of Service, typically refers to a computer program that is designed to flood a website with demands that put it over its capacity. Many times the program slows the website to a crawl, or it can overload the site so much that it crashes and is unavailable.]

Q: Do you find various law-enforcement agencies and government groups using your tool to proactively find exposed critical infrastructure?

A: Yes, from the very start of Shodan-related discoveries, the government (ICS-CERT, the United States Industrial Control Systems Cyber Emergency Response Team, in most cases) has been in dialogue with the researchers and myself to ensure devices are properly secured as soon as possible. Over the years, law enforcement on all levels has been educated on Shodan so it can be used as a tool to help make critical infrastructure safer. Nowadays when a new vulnerability is announced, researchers immediately compile a list of potential IPs with Shodan that could be vulnerable and send it to the relevant authorities. For example, when issues were discovered in devices made by RuggedCom the ICS-CERT used Shodan to locate potentially affected devices, and many of them were taken offline within hours.

Q: What's your biggest worry as you look at the results of the Shodan tool?

A: I worry that people will get distracted by Shodan and the types of systems that are online instead of focusing on the real issue: these systems shouldn't be online in the first place. Especially with the advent of the Internet of Things, device connectivity will increase and a continued lack of security best practices will raise the problem to new heights in terms of both privacy and security.

Q: Many people might say that you are just making it easier for the bad guys too. That's the challenge, right? When you alert the public you alert the bad guys? Are you able to take steps to combat that?

A: Let me be clear about this: Shodan is not an anonymous service. With free access the user only gets a very limited number of results, and if a company wishes to obtain millions of records then they need to enter into a formal agreement with Shodan. The bad guys have had their own tool, similar to Shodan, for a long time; now the good guys have something of their own. Specifically, the bad guys can simply use a botnet to scan the entire Internet without anybody finding out (see Internet Census 2012). [Authors' note: The Internet Census 2012 was created by a hacker who infected over four hundred thousand devices worldwide with a bot that he labeled as harmless and called "Carna."[15] The hacker said that he/she created the bot and the inventory of devices to show how poorly protected devices are. Once he/she performed the Internet census, the hacker then plotted all of the unique Internet addresses of the devices so that they could be seen on a global map.]

Q: What's the scariest situation you have encountered or witnessed since you have launched the Shodan tool?

A: There was a recent incident of an elderly person getting attacked by her daughter, and all of it was caught on a webcam. Turns out a Shodan user was randomly searching for webcams and happened to see the attack live on his screen. He had the presence of mind to record everything, send it to law enforcement, and he also notified me promptly to let me know what happened. The odds of something like this happening are extremely low, and I was very happy to see that the perpetrator was brought to justice.

Q: Based on current estimates, do you have any key metrics that the "good guys" should be paying attention to? For example, the number of hospital networks wide open or the number of power plants around the globe with SCADA systems completely exposed. [Authors' note: A SCADA system, or Supervisory Control and Data Acquisition system, is typically used at an energy or textile plant but can be found at many other types of manufacturing facilities. The SCADA is used to control sensors at the plant and send sensor data to a central location. The sensors collect information that helps with maintenance concerns such as heating and cooling efficiency; it may also control the systems at the factory.]

A: It would certainly be a good metric to see how many SCADA systems are found each year and how successful the various government agencies are at making them secure (or taking them off the Internet). But people are still discovering new SCADA devices that are vulnerable and connected to the Internet, so the baseline for any metrics hasn't yet been reached. In terms of health care, the medical device industry is poised to undergo the same scrutiny and transformation that the SCADA systems industry has had to endure. On a basic level, they are both becoming more networked and connected due to business pressure and don't currently have the security expertise to adequately handle such a transition. We're already starting to see medical devices use the same technologies as SCADA systems, bringing with them the same security issues.

## WHO'S WATCHING?

You might wonder who cares about what you do online or in your home. Online transactions can be read by companies, the CIA, and cybercriminals, but how do they use your information?

### Marketing Types and Cybercriminals Love Your Data

As you go about your daily routines, Internet-connected devices are transmitting data and frequencies from your home. Data can be read by insurance companies to see if you are really as sick or healthy as you say you are, by marketing companies that want to sell you the next big product, by your gaming platform that wants you to buy and play more games, and by spies using this data to target you with a social-engineering scheme designed to steal your identity. Many of these devices are intended to make your life easier. The developers of those devices generally don't think about how bad guys might use the same technologies against you.

Your boss, marketing companies, intelligence agencies, and cybercriminals all can read your information with just a little technology know-how. Your boss can track communications that take place on the corporate network and on social-networking platforms. Marketing companies purchase large databases that are provided by phone companies, credit card companies, retailers, and others. Intelligence agencies can intercept emails, calls, videos, posts, and more for future reference. Cybercriminals specifically target communications online to see if there is something they might make use of.

*The Government Needs to Know . . . Or Does It?*

The challenge to any government that collects the calls and correspondence of its citizens in the name of security is that they may unfairly connect that data to the unsavory activities of cybercriminals.

Here are a few examples of recent increased digital surveillance by governments:

- In the UK in 2012 there was a proposed legislation that would provide the government with expanded digital surveillance capabilities. That legislation has been on and off again and is still working its way through the UK parliamentary processes.
- The government of the Netherlands has also looked into expanding the sophistication of their digital surveillance techniques. The Netherlands is seeking permission to bolster their Intelligence Act to assist them in the better collection of emails and phone calls. They would also like to allow the Dutch police access to the computers of crime suspects, even if they are based outside of the Netherlands.
- In the United States, in June 2013, it was revealed that the surveillance of domestic Internet and cell phone traffic was collected and stored at a more extensive rate than previously understood.[16] Documents, provided in response to Freedom of Information Act requests, reveal that the governing authority, the Foreign Intelligence Surveillance Court (FISC), had previously warned the NSA to change their surveillance process. The FISC was uncomfortable with how the NSA was using phone-call data.[17]
- India's government demanded that BlackBerry provide them with the capability to monitor real-time communications, with the exception of those that originate from the manufacturer's corporate-focused BlackBerry Enterprise server.[18] Essentially this means that consumer traffic on BlackBerry devices will be monitored.

In the days following the revelation of the extent or digital surveillance by the United States in June 2013, the Pew Research Center and the *Washington Post* conducted a poll for four days. The poll reached roughly 1,004 adults, and 56 percent of the Americans that took the survey responded that they believe that the National Security Agency's (NSA) programs that track cell phone calls of Americans is an acceptable way for the government to investigate terrorism. It is important to note that 41 percent responded that they consider it unacceptable.[19] The poll also indicated that 62 percent of the Americans responding said that even if the US government has to intrude on personal privacy, it is more important for the United States to research and analyze possible terrorist threats. When asked about US government officials tracking US citizens on the Internet, the poll showed that 45 percent agreed that the US government should be allowed to monitor and collect everyone's Internet activities if that information were being used to prevent future attacks. Roughly 52 percent did not want the US government to deploy Internet tracking of US citizens.[20]

Although US officials have tried to explain that phone calls are not being listened to and that emails are not being read without a warrant, the idea that all of the details about every call made are being stored in a huge database in perpetuity was unsettling to US citizens and citizens of other countries. The commentary from Europe's press and citizens, still smarting from vivid memories of previous government-sponsored snooping by totalitarian regimes, was quite negative. It's clear that the collection of data for future analysis presents a modern-day conundrum. Christopher Swift, an attorney with the Washington firm of Foley and Lardner and former Treasury Department investigator, commented on the balance he sees the US government trying to keep since the 9/11 attacks.[21] When asked about the recent revelations of the US intelligence community participating in deep data collection and analytics of phone calls and other Internet traffic, Mr. Swift has stated that he believes the laws in place are being followed but also said there are operational challenges at stake:[22] "To the extent that I have a problem with this, it's whether our intelligence and law-enforcement agencies are being overly broad when they seek this data. At some point, it's too big to be useful for what they claim they're using it for."[23]

Mr. Swift is quick to point out that when something bad happens, such as the April 15, 2013, Boston Marathon bombings, US citizens are "boiling mad and asking why the Federal agencies didn't stop them." He sees a real conflict, not just for the analysts and agents collecting the data, but also for US citizens. He says, "You can't have absolute security and absolute privacy."[24]

Whatever your personal opinion is on this matter, of greater concern to the coauthors is that we know that no network of data is immune to a cyberattack. None. The best, locked-down networks have suffered breaches. So, while all this data is being collected about you and your loved ones in the name of security, not only are your civil liberties at risk, but so is your data.

## The Privacy Debate

In America, following the Boston Marathon bombings on April 15, 2013, the media speculated about what the government knew and when they knew it. One reporter for the *Washington Post*, Sari Horwitz, wrote a piece about Katherine Russell, the wife of the bomber who died, Tamerlan Tsarnaev. In her article she mentioned that law enforcement at the federal level had access to Katherine's phone calls. "Officials said that Russell called her husband when she saw his photograph on television—following the FBI's release of the pictures of the suspects."[25]

In addition to US citizens learning of this surveillance of phone calls in the *Washington Post*, if they tuned into Erin Burnett's show on CNN, they would have seen the following interchange between Erin Burnett and Tim Clemente, a former FBI counterterrorism agent. An excerpt of that interview follows:[26]

> **Burnett:** Tim, is there any way, obviously, there is a voice mail they can try to get the phone companies to give that up at this point. It's not a voice mail. It's just a conversation. There's no way they actually can find out what happened, right, unless she tells them?
>
> **Clemente:** No, there is a way. We certainly have ways in national security investigations to find out exactly what was said in that conversation. It's not necessarily something that the FBI is going to want to present in court, but it may help lead the investigation and/or lead to questioning of her. We certainly can find that out.
>
> **Burnett:** So they can actually get that? People are saying, look, that is incredible.
>
> **Clemente:** No, welcome to America. All of that stuff is being captured as we speak whether we know it or like it or not.

The fact is that countries are rushing to add more and more surveillance of private citizens in an effort to the protect them. In the UK, regulators worked on the Communications Data Bill, which would provide the UK law enforcement the ability to gather more information from Internet Service Providers with fewer roadblocks. That data would be stored for up to one calendar year. When pressed by UK privacy groups, the government responded that they are doing their best to protect the privacy of citizens because they are not going to read nor listen to full messages. They will just obtain subject lines, who called whom, date and time of calls, and who was involved in the conversation, but not the actual content of the conversation.

For now, just assume that any conversation you have via electronic or digital methods (cell phones, home phones, faxes, email, chats, and more) are all collected in a variety of databases that could be tapped into by the bad guys to co-opt your identity, or by law enforcement in an effort to protect you.

And don't forget about those drones flying overhead and surveillance cameras that are also tracking you. At least you know you are never really "alone."

## THE SMARTGRID PRIVACY MOVEMENT

Anyone looking at digitized power usage numbers can understand the activity that is happening in that home via something called the "smart-grid."

> **While the Europe-wide rollout of smart metering systems may bring significant benefits, it will also enable massive collection of personal data which can track what members of a household do within the privacy of their own homes, whether they are away on holiday or at work, if someone uses a specific medical device or a baby-monitor, how they like to spend their free time and so on. . . . Patterns and profiles can be used for many other purposes, including marketing, advertising and price discrimination by third parties.**
> **—European Data Protection Supervisor (EDPS)** [27]

As utilities move toward the smartgrid and improve their ability to track your usage statistics, they will also capture your behavior patterns. If a house takes longer than normal to cool off, it might be a wayward HVAC that needs tuning, or you might have a lot of visitors. This information could be interesting for marketers, but also to snoops.

What can you do to better protect your data? Do you have to go off the grid, or is there another option? There is one emerging that was created by the Future for Privacy Forum (FPF) and a privacy and security company, TRUSTe. These two organizations have worked together to create a privacy program to help consumers identify companies they can trust. The privacy program will be available to any energy company or company that uses energy information to go through a series of reviews of their privacy policies. The reviews will examine how they treat energy data for consumers relative to privacy and security. Those companies that meet the standards of the FPF and TRUSTe program will receive a privacy seal of approval. [28]

Some privacy advocates worry about how these tracking programs help Big Brother to make decisions for you. In the European Union (EU), there are concerns about a new proposal to manage high-peak demands on the grid. The proposal provided by the National Grid, a private power company in the EU, was to install smart devices that could help them balance their loads by shutting off freezers, ovens, and refrigerators until they can get out of a peak-demand situation. [29] This proposal works in tandem with another proposal to install smart meters across the UK by 2019.

## CABLE TV IS WATCHING YOU

Cable television knows your viewing and computing habits and is proposing technology to watch whatever your eyes see.

It used to be that cable TV was competing against itself and network TV for your eyes and attention, but now the web is a player, too. That's why the cable TV industry has stepped up their surveillance to learn more about your purchasing habits. The competition is so fierce that Nielsen recently adjusted how they rate show popularity by adding in web-linked TVs and programming. Many households around the globe have dropped regular programming from their cable and local providers and have moved to being only web connected to get their programming. Nielsen felt they had to integrate in the "Internet only" TV-watching households because so many have dropped cable programming.

Why do entities begin to track your Internet usage? Advertisers want to be where the consumers are online so they can reach them at the point where they are most likely to purchase a product or service. Those consumers may only watch shows they can stream on their gaming system. Some may only watch shows that they can grab via Hulu, Netflix, You-Tube, or Amazon. Even the Billboard music ratings have added YouTube streams when calculating rankings of the most popular songs.

Samsung released a model of television that brings new meaning to "Smart TV." The model has face tracking and speech recognition, an internally wired camera, and more. Does this mean that Samsung or other Samsung-affiliated companies would be able to watch you watching TV? How is your personal information stored along with your unique device ID? Could viewing patterns that suggest younger viewers are watching let people know when you have left your tween-age kids home without a sitter so you can enjoy dinner out? Could a hacker watch to see if you have a dog to determine how risky it would be to physically break into your home?

## THE GAME'S AFOOT

Xbox and other gaming systems use facial recognition to know which family members enter the room and what they are doing.

For example, Microsoft Kinect is fun. You can create a virtual likeness of yourself on the platform. The system follows you and tracks your every move and translates those moves into playing a computer game.

How you move speaks volumes about you, maybe even more than words. In one study, scientists at Cornell University used a Kinect to accurately detect actions in the home such as cooking, hair brushing, or taking medications. Using their model and the Kinect, they hit an 84 percent accuracy rate of correctly guessing the subject's activity.[30] Think that's too simple a task? How about having that same model predict that a new person is visiting your home and guessing his activities. If you don't think your Kinect takes notice of who is in the room, then look at the patent they filed to count the number of people in the room. In future, when you want to watch a pay per view show, this technology could count all the people in the room and make you pay per person for the pay per view.

## TELEPHONE SURVEILLANCE OF YOUR HOME

Rules and laws apply, so the government can't just snoop on your home phone . . . or can they? The reality is that if the government wants to, it can perform telephone surveillance of your home. In May of 2013 it was revealed that the Associated Press had their phones monitored by the Department of Justice. Even more shocking was that the personal home numbers of reporters were also under surveillance for two months.[31] In July of 2013, *Le Monde*, a French daily newspaper, reported they found that France's external intelligence agency was intercepting phone and Internet signals to create diagrams of who was talking to each other.[32]

Surveillance of home phones is nothing new. Back in 2010, the *Washington Post* reported that the NSA stores roughly 1.7 billion emails, phone calls, and other forms of digital or electronic conversations on a daily basis for future review.[33] Law enforcement may also send subpoenas to phone companies to request your phone records.

As more citizens in the United States, the UK, France, Germany, Canada, and other countries drop their home lines and only use a cell phone, this creates a new set of rules and laws to follow. Ce -phone conversations can be much easier to intercept by the government and others, depending upon the technology used. Some law-enforcement organizations use a stingray device that creates a virtual cell phone tower that your phone connects to, which allows them to listen in on your conversations. If you use a Bluetooth-enabled handset, your government can hack into your communications using a hacking technique called "bluesnarfing," and so can the bad guys.

Another technique called "phone cloning" involves incoming calls coming to you and to a clone phone. The perpetrators can send, receive, intercept, and listen in on calls as if they were you.

At times, spying on your phone calls is based on the tools you use. For Apple phone fanatics, Siri, the pocket personal assistant on the iPhone 4S and later models, can be asked any question and will provide an answer. Apple recently revealed that they store all those searches you do on Siri for roughly twenty-four months.[34] When you talk to Siri, your request gets matched up against Apple's databases and information contained on the World Wide Web.[35] Apple explains that they anonymize the data, meaning that they note that a search has been performed but not the identity of the device or person searching, but anonymization is not always foolproof. Think twice before you share your secrets with Siri; clearly, she will blab them back to the Apple database.

You can take steps to help mask your identity on the Internet. There are services that can make your Internet traffic look like it came from another location. There are also services that can anonymize your email address, keeping your name secret. There are different ways to protect or cover your personal identity to allow you to be more anonymous, but be aware that no method guarantees 100 percent foolproof anonymity.

A recent review of over one hundred thousand scam emails, also known as phishing, was conducted by the security firm Trusteer Inc. They found that phishing emails were often responded to by consumers, and over two thousand of the responses to the scam emails came via the consumer's smartphones.[36]

Andrew Carter, a Miami attorney, learned how much a crook could do when he can spy on your smartphone. Andrew misplaced his phone during the Christmas vacation season. He did not have an automatic screen lock and password on his phone, and when the bad guys found his phone, they were able to withdraw two thousand dollars from his bank account. The bad guys used various tactics such as email password resets, searching his phone for clues, and attempts to hack into his Facebook account.[37]

Do not lose faith in your ability to combat thieves like those who targeted Mr. Carter. You can protect yourself from incidents like these with just a few steps.

- Set the auto lock on your phone for five minutes or less.
- Create an email address that you ONLY use for banking and use a completely different address for your social media accounts.
- Set up strong and different passwords for all of your accounts.
- Set up automated texting alerts that tell you when changes are made to your bank account and/or when your bank records deposits or withdrawals.

## NOTES

1. Deborah Caldwell-Stone, "Do You Know Who Is Tracking You? Choose Privacy Week Is May 1–7," ALA OIF, April 18, 2013, ndlaonline.org/ifblog/?cat=7.

2. Kashmir Hill, "When 'Smart Homes' Get Hacked: I Haunted a Complete Stranger's House via The Internet," *Forbes*, July 26, 2013.

3. Hill, "When 'Smart Homes' Get Hacked."

4. Katherine Bindley, "Verizon Files Patent for DVR That Watches Viewers, Delivers Targeted Ads Based on What It Sees," *Huffington Post*, December 7, 2012, www.huffingtonpost.com/2012/12/05/verizon-dvr-patent-spies-tv-advertising_n_2246973.html.

5. Bill Ray, "Intel's New TV Box to Point Creepy Spy Camera at YOUR FACE: One Day We're Gonna Watch You Like It's 1984," *Register*, February 13, 2013, www.theregister.co.uk/2013/02/13/intel_tv/.

6. Simon Constable, "How Your TV Is Watching You," *Wall Street Journal—Digits*, March 7, 2011, online.wsj.com/article/848DE868-1C36-4CC8-A731-A519DD4A7E5C.html#!848DE868-1C36-4CC8-A731-A519DD4A7E5C.

7. Constable, "How Your TV Is Watching You."

8. Rob Waugh, "The CIA Wants to Spy on You through Your TV: Agency Director Says It Will 'Transform' Surveillance," *Daily Mail*, March 16, 2012, www.dailymail.co.uk/sciencetech/article-2115871/The-CIA-wants-spy-TV-Agency-director-says-net-connected-gadgets-transform-surveillance.html.

9. Maria Cheng, "UK Police to Track Dementia Patients Using GPS," *Ledger-Enquirer*, May 1, 2013.

10. Jim Boxmeyer, "Help, I Was Betrayed by My Cloud Enabled Smart Fridge!," AT & T's *Networking Exchange Blog*, att.com, April 11, 2012, networkingexchangeblog.att.com/enterprise-business/help-i-was-betrayed-by-my-cloud-enabled-smart-fridge/.

11. Ms. Smith, "Privacy and Security Nightmares: Hacking Smart Toilets, Smart Toys, Smart Homes," *Network World*, August 4, 2013.

12. www.dccomics.com/superman

13. Randall Marsh, "Wi-Vi system uses Wi-Fi to see through walls," *gizmag*, July 1, 2013, www.gizmag.com/wi-vi-see-through-walls/28120/.

14. David Talbot, "One Simple Trick Could Disable a City's 4G Phone Network, High-speed LTE networks Could Be Felled by a $650 Piece of Gear, Says a new Study," *MIT Technology Review*, November 14, 2012, www.technologyreview.com/news/507381/one-simple-trick-could-disable-a-citys-4g-phone-network/.

15. Anthony M. Freed, "CARNA Botnet Conducts Biggest Internet Census to Date—Findings are Troubling," *Tripwire Blog*, March 19, 2013, www.tripwire.com/state-of-security/it-security-data-protection/cyber-security/state-of-security-carna-botnet-ipv4-census-nsa-offensive-cyber-powers-2013-threat-report/.

16. "Opinion Roundup: Edward Snowden and the NSA Leaks," NPR—The Opinion Page, transcript from *Talk of the Nation*, guests James Woolsey and Brian Fung with Host Neal Conan, June 10, 2013, www.npr.org/2013/06/10/190398617/opinion-roundup-edward-snowden-and-the-nsa-leaks.

17. Scott Shane, "Court Upbraided N.S.A on Its Use of Call-Log Data, *New York Times*, September 10, 2013.

18. Mahesh Sharma, "India's BlackBerry Monitoring System 'Ready for Use,'" ZDNet.com, July 11, 2013, www.zdnet.com/in/indias-blackberry-monitoring-system-ready-for-use-7000017937/.

19. *Washington Post*–Pew Research, "Majority Views NSA Phone Tracking as Acceptable Anti-terror Tactic," *Washington Post*, June 10, 2013, www.washingtonpost.com/politics/polling/majority-say-nsa-tracking-phone-records/2013/06/10/96049508-d20c-11e2-9577-df9f1c3348f5_page.html.

20. *Washington Post*–Pew Research, "Majority Views NSA Phone Tracking as Acceptable Anti-terror Tactic."

21. Carl Prine and Andrew Conte, "NSA's 'Anti-terrorism' Tactic Appears to Be Blow to Civil Liberties, Opponents Say," *Tribune Review*, June 8, 2013.

22. Prine and Conte, "NSA's 'Anti-terrorism' Tactic Appears to Be Blow to Civil Liberties, Opponents Say."

23. Prine and Conte, "NSA's 'Anti-terrorism' Tactic Appears to Be Blow to Civil Liberties, Opponents Say."

24. Prine and Conte, "NSA's 'Anti-terrorism' Tactic Appears to Be Blow to Civil Liberties, Opponents Say."

25. Sari Horwitz, "Investigators Sharpen Focus on Boston Bombing Suspect's Widow," *Washington Post*, May 3, 2013.

26. "Widow Spoke to Bomb Suspect after FBI Released Picture," *Erin Burnett Out in Front*, CNN Transcripts, CNN.com, May 1, 2013, transcripts.cnn.com/TRANSCRIPTS/1305/01/ebo.01.html.

27. Jamie Doward and Caroline Mortimer, "Energy Smart Meters Are a Threat to Privacy, Says Watchdog," *Observer*, June 30, 2012, www.guardian.co.uk/environment/2012/jul/01/household-energy-trackers-threat-privacy.

28. Rick Armstrong, "European Advertising and Media Industry Launches a New Trust Seal of Approval," *TRUSTe Blog*, July 15, 2013, www.truste.com/blog/2013/07/15/european-advertising-and-media-industry-launches-a-new-trust-seal-of-approval/.

29. Russell Myers and Martin Beckford, "Big Brother to Switch Off Your Fridge: Power Giants to Make Millions—But You Must Pay for 'Sinister' Technology," *Daily Mail*, April, 27, 2013, www.dailymail.co.uk/news/article-2315863/Big-brother-switch-fridge-Power-giants-make-millions--pay-sinister-technology.html.

30. Jeremy Bailenson, "Your Kinect Is Watching You," *Slate*, March 7, 2012, www.slate.com/articles/technology/gaming/2012/03/kinect_research_the_amazing_disturbing_things_your_gaming_console_can_learn_about_you_.html.

31. Timothy Lee, "In AP Surveillance Case, the Real Scandal Is What's Legal," *Washington Post*, May 14, 2013.

32. Angelique Chrisafis, "France 'Runs Vast Electronic Spying Operation Using NSA-style Methods,'" *Guardian*, July 4, 2013, www.guardian.co.uk/world/2013/jul/04/france-electronic-spying-operation-nsa.

33. Ellen Nakashima, "NSA Stops Collecting Some Data to Resolve Issue with Court," *Washington Post*, April 19, 2010.

34. "Apple Admits to Storing Siri Data for Two Years," *Mobile Marketing Watch*, April 19, 2013, www.mobilemarketingwatch.com/apple-admits-to-storing-siri-data-for-two-years-31654/.

35. Robert McMillan, "Apple Finally Reveals How Long Siri Keeps Your Data," *Wired*, April 19, 2013, www.wired.com/wiredenterprise/2013/04/siri-two-years/.

36. Adam Levin, "13 Incredibly Careless Things That Make Your Smart Phone Dumb and Vulnerable to Identity Thieves," *Forbes*, May 28, 2013, www.forbes.com/sites/adamlevin/2013/05/28/13-incredibly-careless-things-that-make-your-smart-phone-dumb-and-vulnerable-to-identity-thieves/.

37. Tony Winton, "Experts: Smartphones Another Avenue for Hackers," AP, May 15, 2013.

# TWELVE

# Risks of Computer and Phone Networks

A home network is an excellent way to allow multiple devices to connect to the Internet wirelessly. Networks are incredibly convenient and cost effective for modern homes because they allow you to use one Internet connection to watch TV, play games, share devices such as a printer, and more. You can run a home-security monitoring system using your network and even look at what's going on in your home when you're not there. Public Wi-Fi systems and smartphones offer additional convenience when on the go.

However, your home network carries with it certain risks, as it opens the door to other Internet users who may use it to spy, download malware, or circumvent your security. Traveling with your computer, storing data in the cloud, and using your smartphone also pose risks.

## UNPROTECTED COMPUTER NETWORKS: WHAT COULD GO WRONG?

Sometimes it feels as if you need a computer science degree to set up your home network in a way that is private and secure.

The "bad guys" go where the action is. A press release about a recent achievement, award, or expansion of your business catches their eye. They surf the web looking for winners of contracts for government projects. They actively track and profile companies, prominent political figures, celebrities, and the wealthy to target scams. They exploit weaknesses, not just in our technology protection, but also in our human nature.

Cybercreeps and cybercriminals are expert at understanding what makes a person click on a link, open an attachment, or visit a particular website. They target their victims by mimicking their daily activities and trap them into letting them into their devices, computers, and networks. It used to be that if you put in place the best, leading-edge technology that you could fortify your digital life for your company and your personal life, and then you could be "safe." That is no longer the case.

The points of entry that the bad guys can take to invade your privacy are increasingly sophisticated. The authors have witnessed cybercriminals who use sophisticated spear phishing, a focused email scam, to target a specific person or entity. We have read how some cybercriminals hijack press releases of legitimate companies and create a false press release that may show up in your search engine and convince you to click or download information. Another set of cybercriminals are particularly expert at getting search engines to add fake press releases or websites bearing malware into their search results. This is called poisoning search-engine results. Cybercriminals are fond of using current news events to set a malicious software trap. Any hot news topic, from the death of Morgan Freeman (who is not dead, as of this writing) to the exploits of Julian Assange at Wikileaks, presents a perfect opportunity to poison search results.

## Roaming Wi-Fi Dangers

For those who live in the UK, a recent study that indicates that roughly one in four of their Wi-Fi networks is not secure may be of interest.[1] The study was run by James Lyne, who works at the security firm Sophos. He rode a bike around London and equipped it with equipment he could use to pick up any WiFi networks. He found over one hundred thousand WiFi networks while on his wanders, and almost all of the networks used the default name that came with the equipment when it was purchased. Many of the networks were left wide open with no passwords and no encryption, especially at coffee shops and hotels. By leaving the WiFi network open, many businesses make it easy for their patrons to shop and surf while on their premises. But this trusting and open access makes it easy for a cybercriminal to gain access to a network to snoop on user IDs and passwords, grab sensitive information, and provide access to devices connected to the network to infect them.

## Home Networks Aren't Immune

If you own a WiFi network at home, you can take a few extra steps to protect yourself. Go through the user manual and look for directions on how to change the network name. Make it something you can remember. Then look for directions on how to set up the security protocols, and choose the strongest options that your WiFi hardware provides. Next, set up a "guest" account so that anyone that is not a member of your family or is a guest at your business can use that account. Choose a strong password for both the main account and the guest account. You can restrict Internet usage hours on most WiFi hardware and choose that option as well to prevent cybercriminals or your kids from being online when they should not be. Change the password; do not use preset passwords. Criminals can buy password-dictionary software that they run to break your WiFi network's password.

In one case, police in Spain said they found a thirty-four-year-old man who was alleged to have broken into his neighbors' Wi-Fi and used that unauthorized access to their home traffic to record their personal and private activities.[2] They accused him of recording thousands of hours of personal and private moments of his neighbors. Some of the footage included his neighbors having sex. Police believe he guessed passwords or hacked into the Wi-Fi systems and then installed malware that let him control the webcams on his neighbors' digital devices. Many of his neighbors had their digital devices in family areas but also in bedrooms and bathrooms. In addition to controlling their webcams, he also snooped on their hard drives and copied files that he found interesting. Police also believe that he would snoop on their online conversations via social networks and chat. When the police reviewed his computer, in addition to the evidence that he was snooping on his neighbors, they found roughly five hundred images of child pornography.

Don't forget about the dangers of social media and how cybercriminals use that platform to try to infect your home network. Sixty-seven percent of people polled by Sophos, a software security company, said they had been spammed via social networking.[3] Facebook seems to have a scam story or survey regularly.

## MAKING YOURSELF SAFER FROM OUTSIDE ATTACKS

You can do quite a lot to protect your data and privacy by educating those who use your computer or network about risks, using tools on your network and computer to block hackers and malware, and using software protections such as firewalls and antimalware software.

### Protections for Home Networks

If you are a do-it-yourself type, you can install and maintain our suggested list of protections for your home network. Keep in mind that as new threats emerge, newer versions and reactive newer tactics to fight back against the bad guys will be created. This list is an illustration of what you might want to put into place for your home network. It's not intended to be an exhaustive list, and keep in mind that no amount of technology can give a 100 percent guarantee that you will not be hacked. However, our advice should make you somewhat safer and more aware. Awareness is a critical part of protecting your privacy and security.

Educate everyone at your home on online risks and the threats. Just starting a conversation about a news headline helps with awareness. A resource that you can use to start the conversation is www.OnGuardOnline.gov. They have free Internet safety games. Take time to play those games and then spend time talking about the experience. An informed family member could be your best defense.

Provide your family with ground rules such as "Never put sensitive data on a thumb drive (also called a USB stick or Flash drive) unless it's encrypted" or "Ask me before you click on a link and type in personal data."

If you have a business that handles secure data or if you have a celebrity in your family, free protection tools may not be for you, so you should consult with a firm that can help you develop good policies and procedures. However, many companies and households can probably get by with the resources at www.OnGuardOnline.gov that can help you create "Do's and Don'ts" that are best for your company and your household. You can also use the FCC website to create a checklist that works well for you: www.fcc.gov/cyberforsmallbiz.

Using your computer's firewalls and adding network firewalls are a helpful way to control traffic coming to and going from your network. Often your favorite antivirus or antimalware software also provides firewall products. *PC Week* magazine (www.pcweek.com) regularly reviews the best firewall products for home use and is a good source to check for features, functions, and prices.

The key to a successful firewall strategy is to set up one with a strong password and then read the instruction manual to find out what types of rules you can implement. For example, if you do not want your kids or bad guys using your Internet between the hours of midnight and three a.m., some firewalls will let you shut down traffic during those vulnerable sleeping hours. If there are certain sites that you don't want anyone to visit, some firewalls let you set up those rules. At a minimum, use the firewall setting in your computer's operating system to control access to your device and data.

If you have a lot of home Internet-connected devices, you may want to consider adding a Unified Threat Management (UTM) tool to the mix. These are often used in organizations to sit in front of the Internet front door to a network looking at traffic, blocking bad traffic, and looking for data that might be leaving your network, unauthorized by you.

*Computer Settings and Tools to Ensure Privacy*

Beyond protecting your network, consider tools you can use to protect individual computers. Here's a useful checklist:

- To stop a website from doing a "drive-by download" while you are not looking, disable auto run and auto install on your operating system.
- To avoid a digital disaster from a hard drive crash or virus, back up your data regularly.
- To stop a criminal from hanging out on your home network, pay attention to the number of devices connected to your home network.
- For the strongest layers of protection, keep your operating system, software, and browsers up to date on the latest versions.
- Consider having more than one email address to keep those you don't know personally out of your personal email. Use one email address with your banks and nobody else, a separate one for health care, another for family and friends, and so on. Use a "catch all" email when asked to provide an email for newsletters, subscriptions, travel confirmations, and other interactions with businesses.
- Don't let the scammers trick you into giving away personal information. If you receive an email from a company, even if you do business with them, never click on the link in the email and provide personal information. Call the business's main customer service line to discuss the email if you believe it is legitimate.
- Whenever it is offered to you, leverage two-factor authentication and or the use of a security standard known as secure sockets layer (SSL). An SSL helps your device determine that it is talking to the intended recipient. SSL was developed to help transport sensitive information like your ID and password or credit card numbers. Without SSL, that information might be sent in plain text, which means a cybercriminal with some skills could see your information and snoop in on your transactions. You can request SSL by setting that feature on your browser. Many of your favorite cloud applications such as Gmail and Facebook let you set an option on your account so that all communications with them are via an SSL.
- You may want to consider disabling Java on your computer and using it only when necessary. Although the makers of Java are working tirelessly to keep their software up to date and to fight off the hackers, cybercriminals go where the action is, and Java is a hot area for them. A high percentage of cybercriminal attacks target Java, so this is a great first step, and you can find step-by-step instructions and tips at www.Disable-Java.com. Also remember to keep your Java as up to date as possible. Java releases new im-

provements for many operating systems and browsers on a regular basis.

## *Make Use of Free Anti Malware Tools*

Malware, ranging from viruses to spam and keystroke-tracking software, is one of the biggest threats to your privacy. To stop or detect downloaded malware on your computer, you can use antimalware software. There are a variety of tools to choose from, some free and some at a yearly subscription rate that includes regular updates for emerging threats. Make sure before you download a "free" tool that it is from a reputable company. You can find some free tools to try at these online addresses:

- www.Sophos.com
- www.Microsoft.com
- www.McAfee.com
- www.Symantec.com

Antivirus, anti malware, and antispam tools are important, but do not get a false sense of security after you've installed them. The cybercriminals are releasing new tactics for hacking into your accounts and any device connected to the Internet. Statistics vary on how much of the bad stuff these software appliances can filter out. Think of them as your home network's multivitamin. They help boost your immunity to some of the bad elements on the Internet, but they don't guarantee a life free from disease.

## *Going Above and Beyond*

Beyond computer settings and antimalware software, there are still more options for protecting your privacy.

Encryption can add another layer of security. Encryption is the process the creator of a message uses to encode the message so that only an authorized recipient can read it. Using software or hardware, the method of encryption is built with the goal of preventing an unauthorized person from listening in or opening the message. When purchasing software or hardware, ask if it comes with an encryption feature. For example, you can use encrypted thumb drives to store tax data offline, or you can consider encrypting your digital devices. In many cases, you may have an encryption option on the services you use. Go to the "help" feature and type in "how do I use encryption" to learn more about your options on your computer, web browser, email, and even your smartphone. Encryption is not a guarantee that your data cannot be read by anyone, but it will make it tougher for the average Sally or Joe to snoop on your data.

You can install website checkers and URL-content filtering on all of your devices. These tools can check the safety of a website before you open it. Again, these are not foolproof, but they can provide important warnings for sites that have been recently hacked or that regularly download files to user devices.

Intrusion-protection systems might be a good fit for the household network that has lots of digital devices connected to it. The intrusion-protection system can monitor traffic on your home network to look for suspicious activity such as large downloads of data or usage of your home network when you are typically away from home or asleep.

Runtime protection solutions will wake up when you turn on a device. The runtime solution will see if a program on your system is trying to modify your operating system without your express permission. It will also look for applications trying to install themselves behind the scenes. If the runtime software detects an unauthorized program running, it might alert you or stop the program. An example of runtime protection is a buffer overflow prevention system (BOPS). This software looks for attacks directed at your computer's or phone's operating system software and installed applications. The moment that software detects any attempt to overload your device, it will alert you.

A virtual private network is a kind of network that allows you to set up requirements with other networks (such as the Internet) and use features such as requiring a user ID and password to sign in.

Are you using Wi-Fi for your home network? You should secure your Wi-Fi to avoid leaving your Wi-Fi connection option to cybercriminals that may snoop or use your connection to infect your home devices. One technology that you can use is Wi-Fi Protected Access V. 2 or WPA2. WPA2 lets you lock down what devices can connect to your network and gives you privacy settings that you can use to help protect your network traffic.

---

**TOOLBOX**

**Here are five quick tips for maintaining a safer home Wi-Fi network:**

- **Change the name: When you turn on your Wi-Fi router, change the network name (SSID) from the default name.**
- **Change the user ID and password: Make sure you change the default user name and password.**
- **Select the highest level of security feature: Look for a feature called WPA2 and turn that feature on.**
- **Enable every device you own: Enable WPA2 security features on each device that you own; check your user manual for step-by-step instructions.**

> • **Stay current: Install or update your firewall, antivirus, and antimalware software.**

## LIVING SAFELY IN THE CLOUD

"The cloud" is the term used to describe data stored online rather than on your local device. You are in the cloud already whether you've provided or posted information on sites such as YouTube, Facebook, Gmail, or Hotmail, or somebody else has posted information about you.

What should you know before you store your personal secrets and identity information in the cloud? Read the privacy settings first. You need to understand if the data remains your property or becomes the service's property to do with what they will. If you post in an online diary and decide one day to quit the service, can you export all your information and then leave their service without leaving data behind in their database? If you post pictures on Facebook or Instagram, the policy today says that the pictures are both yours and theirs. One day, they could tweak that policy again and use your photos in ads without seeking your permission first. They have already started to test the waters with this. They have held back so far due to privacy concerns but will eventually move forward with this practice.

## STAYING PRIVATE ON THE GO

When you travel from your home or office, you need to take a few extra steps to protect your privacy and data. Consider the fact that many of the places you visit offer free Wi-Fi. This sounds convenient, but is it secure? While visiting a coffee shop that offered Wi-Fi, I asked how they set up their Wi-Fi. The coffee house manager pointed to a nearby residential condo unit and said how cool it was that one of their customers offered to let them piggyback on his network. He even renames his home Wi-Fi network to their coffee shop name so the shop could offer free Wi-Fi. He gets free coffee and you get free Wi-Fi. Let's hope that customer is honest!

Often criminals will set up a Wi-Fi hotspot with the same or a similar name to a local business and people hop on and browse the web happily, never knowing that they just invited a snoop onto their device.

If you must stay connected via a public Wi-Fi network and can't use your cell phone's connection, consider purchasing your own mobile WiFi device. Mobile WiFi might come in the form of a card that you plug into a computer, or it could be a peripheral that can act as a personal WiFi hub, providing Internet access via a cellular phone network for several devices. You can also set up a Virtual Private Network for your communications to add another layer of protection.

If you must use that free WiFi, don't type in passwords or do any financial transactions such as making a credit card payment or logging into your bank account. If you travel with your device, keep it with you at all times. If you must leave your laptop or tablet behind, make sure it's powered down, password protected, encrypted, and locked up.

## SECURING YOUR SECURITY SYSTEMS

Whether for your camera or mobile device, there are many solutions to security out there today. You need to understand how you're being put in harm's way and what tools are available to protect you.

### *Out-of-Date Camera Apps*

Sometimes devices that are supposed to make us safer can put us in danger. If you install a camera and leave the admin password as the default, criminals may easily guess that password and gain visual access to your home. In addition, webcam owners may forget to go to the Internet to update the cameras with the latest operating systems. This action is critical to insure that the latest security protections are in place.

### *Security Apps for Mobile Devices*

There are benefits to being connected, and one of those benefits is the plethora of emergency apps that have hit the smartphone and tablet market. In the event of a real emergency, nothing should replace calling 911 in the United States or the emergency number for your country first. But sometimes events don't require 911, or you need assistance beyond 911. There are now lots of apps to help you in emergencies.

Before you choose the app that is right for you or your loved ones, here are a few considerations.

Start with apps that are age appropriate. Think about who you need to connect with. If an incident involves small children or the elderly, think through whether or not your loved ones are old enough or tech savvy enough to be able to use these apps effectively in the event of an emergency.

The saying "practice makes perfect" is key in an emergency. Read the app reviews carefully to make sure apps work as advertised. Before buying the apps, read user reviews to determine if these apps are right for you. Once you buy and download apps, try them out periodically so you and your family get used to using them. There are many apps out there, but here are a few examples that you may find of interest.

TOOLBOX
Here is a list of some tools that you might want to explore that can make you safer online:

- My Aircover (www.myaircover.com). My Aircover is a family location tracker. A tracker allows you to register specific devices to a master account that you can find via the location of those devices. Each tablet, computer, and phone, when it is connected to the Internet or a cellular network, can broadcast the geographic location of the device. This is more of a proactive tool to help prevent emergencies or to use in emergency situations. There is a free version of the app available for a limited time. With this app you can proactively track and see the location of your loved ones. Using My Aircover you can send out and receive an Emergency Alert. You can also set up "safe regions"; if loved ones enter or exit the region you get an automated notification. The app even gives you "safe place" access such as the nearest hospital, fire department, or police department.
- Guardly (www.guardly.com). During an emergency you can connect with those in your life quickly using this app, which also allows you to send photos to loved ones or your insurance agent to update them about the situation. The app also includes a sound blasting siren to either scare an attacker or alert others in the area.
- My Force (protect.myforce.com). This app is free to download but it comes with a monthly subscription fee. A quick tap on the app interface will automatically make a call for you when you sense danger or an emergency. The app also offers a silent alarm that you can trigger. Once you choose the silent alarm, the phone will quietly begin recording any sound on your end of the call and will automatically dial 911 for you. It will also alert any contacts you have set up in advance.
- Hollaback!    (www.ihollaback.org/resources/iphone-and-droid-apps/). The Hollaback! app allows you to report inappropriate behavior. You can text or send pictures to report incidents that will then show up on a map. Reports go to local authorities and officials who will review whether or not there are hot spots for issues in their town. This app is free but not yet available in all locations, so check their available maps first before downloading.

## NANNY CAMS AND HIDDEN CAMERA NETWORKS

Many of you have heeded our advice about the Internet and you are using it in ways that are positive and protect your safety. But what happens when you think you are offline and random parts of your everyday life at home and at the office are set up to spy on you? This use of technology isn't the material of spy novels. It's real, affordable, and might be in your living room.

Most of you know that phones and emails reveal your secrets, and some of you have even stopped posting some photos online to maintain a sense of security and privacy. But many people don't realize just how pervasive digital devices are in our lives and how they are recording everything we say and do. (Make sure you live the Golden Rule at all times because your actions might end up on YouTube!)

Spying techniques may start with programming your phone, laptop, or tablet to spy using simple apps that will record pictures, videos, or audio. This surveillance is all silent and hard to detect. The spy may also buy what looks like a toy airplane or helicopter and launch it above your house, acting like a personal drone and recording hours of video and audio. Also easily available are everyday items such as stuffed animals, plug outlets in a wall, thumb drives, clocks, calculators, pens, and glasses that can now be equipped with chips that can record images, text, photos, and videos.

This spying technology can be helpful. You could use an online service such as Dropcam as a way to double check on things at home while your kids are there and you're away. A webcam might be helpful if you are worried about theft while away from home.

But this viewing technology can be co-opted and used against you. How can you protect yourself from digital spies? Start by disabling video cameras on phones and tablets when not actively in use. You should also keep social networking platforms turned off from video or voice mode when you're not using those features. At home, pay attention to devices such as webcams; they may sport a strange red or green blinking light to indicate a wireless connection or that they are recording. If you have digital devices with cameras, you may want to consider an old-school method for protection by covering the lens with tape. That method does not stop audio recording, but you can prevent criminals from snooping in on you.

If you think someone is spying on you, you can also buy some antispy gadgets. One example is the radio-frequency (RF) bug detector. These devices can scan a room looking for the frequencies that a video camera would emit. They may also pick up a Wi-Fi network, so be sure before you point the finger at someone that you verify what the RF bug detector found. Another technology to check out is the spy-camera detector. These devices look for cameras that might not transmit a frequency. They actually look for the small glass viewfinder of a camera and alert you to its presence. There are several products out on the market, many of which you can find with a quick search on Amazon.com. One vendor, AGPtek®, provides various models that can find listening devices and spy cameras. Another is the vendor DD1203, which provides a handheld bug detector to scan for any hidden listening or recording devices.

If you are a victim of digital surveillance, talk to local law enforcement and seek legal counsel to discover your legal options. Before you set up any kind of digital surveillance at home or in the workplace, you should familiarize yourself with the laws governing this activity. A good place to start is: www.ncsl.org/issues-research/telecom/electronic-surveillance-laws.aspx.

## SMARTPHONE SMARTS

Smartphones aren't immune to dangers. One big danger is that you'll lose your phone or have it stolen. When that happens you will wish you had taken steps to be able to find your phone and protect the data on it.

### *Locating a Lost or Stolen Phone*

It's happened to all of us. You misplace your phone at home or at work. Sometimes you leave your phone in a public place and it ends up in someone else's hands. You can use a location service, such as Apple's Find My iPhone, to locate your phone, but often finding your phone is not enough to get your phone back.

Some ingenious app developers have gone a step further to stop would-be thieves from running off with phones permanently. What if the phone took a picture of someone trying to unlock the code and emailed the owner with the geographic location and a picture of the thief? Well, that idea is a reality and it's been helping many owners reunite with their phones. The great thing about these apps is that they are low cost. If a do-gooder has found your phone or a would-be thief tries to unlock your phone, there are apps out there, such as Lookout, which will provide various methods for notifying you that your phone is in someone else's hands. Many of these apps can take a picture, grab the geographic location of a thief, and send an email to a predetermined email address. If your phone is missing but really in the hands of your toddler or hanging out next to the family dog, then the location service may send you an email with a picture of your dog or toddler. At least now you have found your phone.

---

**TOOLBOX**
**Some sample apps that you might find of interest are:**

- iGotYa: igotya.com/
- Best Phone Security Pro by RV AppStudios LLC: www.rvappstudios.com/
- Lookout by Lookout, Inc.: www.lookout.com
- Norton Anti-Theft: https://antitheft.norton.com/offer
- Thief Face Trap Mini: https://play.google.com/store/apps/details?id=com.terboel.tfth&hl=en
- GadgetTrak (also available for Mac laptops): www.gadgettrak.com/

---

*Protecting the Data on Your Phone*

You can also protect yourself by using the encryption that comes with your phone model. As with computers, no encryption is foolproof, but it will help to protect your data in many cases. In fact, some encryption can be so complicated that it gives law enforcement fits when trying to crack a case. Some law-enforcement agencies have stated that they have a tough time when it comes to the Apple iPhone's encryption. Sometimes law enforcement has to enlist the aid of Apple to override the security controls on seized devices. There is even a waiting list as of the writing of this book keeping law enforcement waiting up to eight weeks for Apple to help them with identifying or collecting data about a particular phone.[4] The US Drug Enforcement Agency (DEA) has also mentioned that messages that are sent via the Apple's Messages App are difficult to wiretap.

Not convinced that you need to protect your phone from snoops? Symantec conducted the smartphone "Honey Stick" project in 2012.[5] They intentionally "lost" fifty smartphones in Ottawa, Canada; New York; Washington, D.C.; San Francisco; and Los Angeles. They installed twelve fake decoy apps to make it look like sensitive banking data and other private information was contained on the phones. Of the twelve apps installed, people who found the lost devices accessed an average of six of the decoy apps. Seventy-two percent of those who picked up a lost smartphone looked at photos, and 60 percent snooped on social media accounts. Fifty seven percent looked at emails and files with the word "password" in their names, and 53 percent looked at emails and files labeled with the terms "Human Resources" or "HR." A whopping 96 percent of those who picked up the lost smartphones snooped on sensitive information such as online banking or HR salaries, and only half of those who picked up a smartphone tried to turn it in.

Your smartphone safety measures should include:

- Making settings to automatically lock your phone after a period of inactivity
- Requiring a password to access your phone
- Asking your phone vendor if the phone model has an auto-locate and auto-wipe feature
- Being careful about what information is on the device and if you have a backup of that data, such as contacts
- Being careful what you click on and download so that you do not introduce a rogue app or virus onto your smartphone

## NOTES

1. Warwick Ashford, "More Than a Quarter of London's Wi-Fi Networks Are Poorly Secured," *Computer Weekly*, September 6, 2012.

2. Lee Moran, "Pedophile Computer Expert Spied on Hundreds by Hacking Neighbors' Wi-Fi: Cops," *New York Daily News*, May 2, 2013.

3. Sophos Security Threat Report 2011, www.ihrim.org/Pubonline/Wire/Mar11/sophos-security-threat-report-2011.pdf.

4. Andrew Cunningham, "Apple Will Reportedly Unlock Your iPhone for Police, but There's a Wait List," *Ars Technica*, May 10, 2013.

5. "The Symantec Smartphone Honey Stick Project," Symantec, 2012, www.symantec.com/content/en/us/about/presskits/b-symantec-smartphone-honey-stick-project.en-us.pdf.

*Technology Section IV*

# Where Do We Go from Here?

Technology will not stop evolving and expanding. You are likely to bring more Internet-connected computers deeper into your life in coming years. Simply extrapolating from what technology is used now, this section predicts the new threats to privacy for the easily foreseeable future. Computerized clothing, accelerated drone programs, pervasive biometrics, and television that watches you will fill our future with more and deeper invasions of privacy. Technology can see into your brain right now and interpret what you are thinking without you saying a word. Are you prepared to protect your own thoughts in real time?

This section also looks at the current state of the law in many countries, and what might be done to protect our privacy from the technological onslaught. The law tends to lag behind changes in society, but we can implement rules to keep our liberties protected while we decide how much intrusion is too much. This section discusses the tools at our disposal to manage the growth of intimate technology and its capture of information about us.

# THIRTEEN

## The Future of Technology and Privacy

While many of the technological intrusions discussed in this book seem like a science-fiction fantasy, all of the technology we have described is currently in use today. But technology is like a flowing river, changing constantly, so it is important to look into what the near future holds. Even in this futuristic chapter we do not make wild speculations about time travel or mind melds. We simply extend the current technology to its next logical step, or examine existing technology that may be more commercially available in the coming years.

### MANY STREAMS FEED THE RIVER OF CHANGE

Often technologies grow and change, or burst into our homes, simply because computing power is now cheaper, smaller, and stronger, and can do more things that we need at a more affordable price. Other times a popular use is found for a technology—what used to be known in the industry as a killer application or "killer app." The public's desire to use the technology for this killer purpose drives the adoption of the technology.[1] Still other times, a new application of a technology, such as microwave ovens or VCRs, proves popular enough to earn a place in many homes.

A variety of forces—personal, corporate, and economic—can widen channels to the market, which is how consumer technology becomes widely adopted in our society. For example:

- An influential company champions a decade-old technology, breaking political and standards log jams that held it back (the iPod).

211

- Advances in computing and software make a naturally great idea into a practical consumer item (smartphones).
- The business world, or special portions of it, enlists a technology to help efficiency and effectiveness, and the technology bleeds over to the consumer world (personal computers).

We know that change will be constant, and we are always looking for the next big tool to help our lives. With hundreds of companies across the world competing to improve our current technology and bring us the next big thing, we should not expect the current state of technology to last much more than a few months. Before we know it, a better version of a familiar household item, or a completely new thing, will invade our lives.

## CHEAPER AND MORE PERVASIVE

The technologies we use will change in certain directions over the next ten years as the various technologies become less expensive, enabling more people to take advantage of them. This trend will play out in a number of ways. Less-expensive computing means not only that your standard computer of today will be able to do more things tomorrow, but that powerful computing will become smaller and more portable. It means the mobilization of nearly everything that you currently do on a computer at home. It means expecting computers to exist in places in our lives where there are no computers now. It also means that both new and old types of computing will become more pervasive, now that a greater percentage of the world population can afford them.

We do not need the predictive powers of Nostradamus to foresee that this change will occur. It has been happening since the invention and commercialization of the computer transistor in 1958, and the trend of the past half-century will not grind to a sudden halt. The trend of rapid growth in computing power and reduction in cost is called "Moore's law." Gordon Moore, the cofounder of the Intel computer-chip-manufacturing company, wrote in 1965 that the number of circuits on an affordable integrated computer chip would double every two years for at least a decade. This means that computerized technology will become significantly more powerful for the same price every two years. It also means that we could buy the same technology two years from now for roughly half the price.

Moore's prediction has been remarkably accurate over time, to the point that computer companies have built their long-range plan on the expectation that Moore's law will hold true. In forty years, computers have shrunk from building-sized behemoths to handheld devices much more powerful than that early huge monster. And while the natural, physical limitations on the size of computer chips may mean that the pace of change described in Moore's law is slowing without significant technology changes, we can still expect computers to be cheaper, smaller, more powerful, and more deeply connected to each other, with more applications being written to take advantage of the progress. So expect to see a cascade of new technologies that use this growth and ubiquity to insinuate computers even deeper into your life.

## Mobility Goes Crazy

The first decade and a half of the twenty-first century will likely be marked as the time that computing power truly left its desktops and office docking stations and provided mobility to the masses. While some form of laptop or lug-able computing has been around since the personal computer was invented, the advent of the Internet allowed those computers to be truly useful for people on the go. Then it took a few years of Internet growth and the emergence of omnipresent wireless access and cloud computing for companies to develop products designed for true mobility—not just lighter desktop computers—but truly mobile devices optimized to interact with people as they move. This time frame has seen a shift of computer models, moving from your laptop computer that contained all of the power and memory it needed in its box to a handheld device that operates best by accessing vast computer information, storage, and even applications stored at remote computers and operated by Amazon, Google, Apple, or other companies.[2] So in the past fifteen years, a world of desktops and heavy laptops has become a world of computing on smartphones, tablets (three primary sizes), and paper-thin laptops. The next ten years will continue this trend to almost absurd lengths.

In a survey conducted in 2012, 87 percent of American adults said they owned a cell phone, and nearly all of them claimed that they could not go a single day without their device.[3] Half of all Americans sleep with their phone next to them like a teddy bear, including more than 80 percent of eighteen- to twenty-four-year olds.[4] According to the same survey, 56 percent of Chinese respondents admitted to using text messages to set up a rendezvous with a lover, and 57 percent of the respondents in India said that they would always need the latest technology.

Our mobile connection devices are not likely to fade as important parts of our lives, only to grow. In 2008, technology analyst Mary Meeker expected mobile data use to expand by more than 4,000 percent by 2014, and that by 2014 mobile access points to the Internet would outnumber fixed access points.[5] So the trend is toward more deeply integrated mobile computing in our lives, and professional industry watchers see dramatic growth in mobile computing worldwide. This trend is likely to express itself in ways that continue to intrude more deeply into your private life, as mobile technologies burrow further into everything we do.

*Recent Developments Lead to the Future*

The nascent field of wearable tech is one clear area where we can examine the trend toward more intrusive personal, mobile, Internet-connected computing technology. It is likely that no one you know owned a wearable computer while this book was being written. And yet within seven years of its publication, we believe that more than half of Americans will own some item of clothing or body-adornment that is connected to the Internet.

This is not a wild prediction; it rises from already existing technology being adopted into current consumer trends. We have seen the current and likely future growth of mobile computing, and as each of us becomes more comfortable with being connected to the Internet at all times—and many people find it deeply desirable—we will accept helpful new ways to connect and use those connections.

Another important trend in computing that will drive the acceptance of wearable Internet nodes is the growing movement toward more natural human–computer interfaces. We are rapidly learning what we should know by common sense—there is no reason that a keyboard should be the dominant interface with a computing system. While most serious business computers are still driven by keypad entry, in nonbusiness applications interfaces are changing to integrate with the way we naturally move.

For example, computerized gaming systems have long used buttons and joysticks to allow humans to interact with the game. But for the Christmas buying season of 2006, Nintendo introduced its Wii game console, which allowed players to interact with the computer using a wireless, handheld controller. The controller could not only be a pointing device, but would detect movement in three dimensions and project that movement into the game. When a player swung her arm in a tennis motion, her virtual racquet moved accordingly onscreen.[6]

In 2009, Microsoft improved on this concept in a way that demonstrates how the coolest, most useful advances are often the most intrusive into your personal life. The Xbox 360 allowed the game user herself to be the controller, without having to hold or point any handheld piece of equipment. Instead, a set of sensors—cameras, motion sensors, and microphones—observes where the game player stands in the room. Her body movements become the Xbox's control mechanism. The Xbox 360 also includes biometric facial-recognition and voice-recognition technology, so that it knows which player is giving instructions and can call up your personalized characters and favorite games, right where you left off last time. But this also means that the Xbox recognizes exactly who is in the room at any given moment. The full body and voice interface is not only used on the games but also allows users to control the system with a wave of the hand.

Smartphones are also integrating more natural human interfaces than a keypad and touch screen:

- Introduced in 2009, Apple's Siri software includes both a voice interface that learns your speech patterns and a knowledge navigator that helps discern what you are asking your iPhone to do.
- Google Now offers a similar interface for Android phones with the full search power of the Google engines behind the technology, so asking questions like "How far from here to Pittsburgh?" or "Show me a video of how to cut a mango" will yield fast, effective results.
- Samsung Android phones are incorporating hand-waving motions as controls and front-facing cameras to note whether your eyes are still locked on the screen, so the device can stop a video when you turn away and start it again when you face the screen again.

One more tech trend that supports the growth of wearable Internet connections is the maturation of Radio Frequency Identification technology (RFID) and other sensors. RFID uses radio waves to send and receive signals to transfer data. Tiny RFID chips are used in many industries and are working their way further into consumer products. Airbus uses RFID tags to track parts through the assembly line, and Walmart announced a huge initiative to make suppliers affix RFID tags to pallets and packaging on goods. RFID technology can help a retailer tell what inventory is on its shelves and in the warehouse by simply waving an RFID-reading device in the right direction.

On the consumer side, RFID devices are currently placed beneath the skin of millions of American pets to track their movements and find the pet when lost. Some schools require that children wear RFID-enabled badges so the school knows where they are at all times of the day.

If RFID technology becomes pervasive, a thief might be able to find what RFID-tagged merchandise sits in your home by scanning inside your house from a car driving down your street. When teamed with the kinds of sensors currently used in smartphones, an RFID-enabled device could sense movement, location, or heat, sending signals of its readings to waiting devices. Other wireless technologies using other parts of the spectrum, such as Bluetooth technology, could be used the same way.

*Wearable Technology*

Chapter 6 mentioned the first signs of a wearable-technology trend that may result in a wave of Internet-connected items for you to slip over your head or affix to your body. Two of the first examples—eyewear and wrist wear—are natural choices that have been described in science fiction for years.

Google Glass, projecting Internet information and applications right in front of your eyes as you move, is the first wearable item to be tested and distributed by a major hardware company. Google announced that Google Glass will not be allowed to run facial-recognition programs or voice-recognition software, thus limiting the privacy invasion of having a person wearing Internet-connected glasses look deep into your eyes and ask his glasses to tell him your name and history.[7]

If Google Glass is successful, other manufacturers will offer their own i-eyeware products,[8] and they may not be so careful as to limit intrusive applications. Even if Google doesn't offer face- or voice-recognition programs to the general public, we can image a hack that provides this capability for government agents, in Mission Impossible fashion. Someone only needs to pull the various existing pieces together.

While Google Glass is touted as an enhanced reality for moving through your everyday world, similar technology is currently used to create full battle simulations for training of police and soldiers. Motion Reality, Inc., makes full motion-capture outfits now, complete with motion-captured guns. The outfits turn a group of ten officers moving down a flat field into a battle simulation projected onto the visor of each participant, so that his movements and actions (such as firing his gun) are captured by the simulation system. Within the simulation, he is allowed to interact with his nine teammates, plus the virtual characters that the computer places into the simulation with him. Future generations of this technology could project computer-generated worlds on the space right before our eyes, while our every movement is captured by small sensors placed on our bodies. This type of gaming, likely to be in the immediate future of wearable technology, will collect and store your every movement, so you can watch replays of yourself as you slay the dragon.

The other most obvious wearable technology is the watch phone, in which a cell phone, or even smartphone technology, is crammed into a small enough space to be worn on your wrist. Wristwatch cell phones are available for purchase, and some even have cameras. However, wrist telephones or wristband smartphones are not likely to catch on with the general public. The screen is too small to function in many ways we expect of our smartphones, and the small element worn on the wrist makes it difficult to hold a private conversation. It is awkward to hold your wrist next to your ear and talk into it at the same time. This problem may be addressed by software, but it seems like a difficult sale to make to the teenagers and business people who drive the mobile smartphone market. Of course, if Apple creates a product that proves to be useful and excites people like the iPhone, then the Apple iWatch may change this analysis entirely.

Even if wristwatch phones do not become popular consumer items, they might be marketed as specialty products in certain work environments. For example, emergency medical technicians need to keep their hands free while they communicate and do not need privacy in their work conversations in the way that most private citizens would. Also, a wristband could house the core communication and computing elements of a small, wearable computer system. Match the wrist computer with a Bluetooth-enabled earpiece and a microphone hung close to the mouth, and the system might appeal to anyone who wants to travel very light and operate hands-free. Once again, advances in the voice interaction technology could make this system functional and effective for many people.

Eyewear and wristbands are only the most obvious wearable technology we are likely to see and purchase in the coming years. Other options are only limited by our imaginations. For example, the following technologically enhanced clothing either exists in working prototype or is currently offered for sale:

- GotWind technology company created a thermoelectric boot that turns heat from your feet into electricity to charge your smartphone.[9]
- Vodofone offers power shorts that turn body heat and movement into a full charge for your mobile device.[10] Just plug your phone into your clothes.
- Brando Workshop offers a Wi-Fi Detection Cap that uses LED lighting to notify you of the availability and strength of wireless signals in your immediate location,[11] so finding a place to connect to the Internet may be as easy as putting on a cap when you leave your house in the morning.
- Social media is attached to at least two items of clothing: a vest that squeezes you for a real hug when someone sends you a hug over Facebook,[12] and the ElectricFoxy Ping garment, a hooded wrap that gives you a "tap" if your friends message you on social media.[13] The wrap also allows you to respond to these messages by turning body motions into messages.

Active solo sports may very well engender the first real markets for wearable technology, as demonstrated by the following new and on-the-horizon products:

- A Redmond, Washington, company called Heapsylon sells fitness socks with special textile sensors that communicate with a matching anklet.[14] The socks and anklet feed data to a smartphone application, tracking a runner's steps, distance, speed, and calories used, as well as providing advice on improving the runner's stride.
- Similar sensors sewn into jackets or riding/ski pants could read the wearer's heart rate, pulse, breaths per minute, or other vital signs, and send the information via Bluetooth to the wearer's smartphone or Google Glass for constant health monitoring.
- At a recent technology show, Motorola demonstrated a snowboarding jacket with telephone controls built into the sleeve and con-

nected by Bluetooth to the boarder's phone in a pocket.[15] The jacket vibrates to signal phone calls, and it includes speakers in the collar of the jacket's hood with a microphone mounted on the jacket's lapel.

- Apple has applied for patents on sensing and communicating shoes, shirts, and sweatpants, so it may be looking to build the future of wearable sports computing.[16]
- In the near future, a biking or motorcycle helmet could easily be outfitted as an entire smartphone, then programmed to call a loved one or 911 when the helmet is in a particularly hard crash. Even if the biker could not speak, the helmet could immediately send the geolocation coordinates to the police or medical evacuation unit.
- In addition to the same smartphone functionality, skiing gear could monitor the body heat signature of its wearer, warning the skier or others of impending hypothermia.
- Any of these clothes could tell the wearer how fast she was traveling, how far she had ventured that day or on that particular trip, and how many miles or feet to the nearest coffee shop.

Such monitoring technology will likely be available for purchase now or in the near future. Runners, skiers, bikers, swimmers, and other athletes will soon take comfort with being in touch with the world and completely wired during their workouts.

Clothing that includes body sensors is not just significant for exercise, but may also become a vital health care tool that can allow more patients to go home from the hospital early, safer in the knowledge that their socks or bracelet will be reading their vital signs and sending data back to the doctor's computer at regular intervals. Jewelry for diabetics could read exhalations or skin changes to warn of an oncoming blood-sugar crisis early enough to avert problems. Health-monitoring clothing could help the elderly remain in their homes longer.

Outside of the sporting and health industries, wearable technology may find a market in children's clothes, allowing parents to keep track of kids with sensors that could send a text to Mom every time her child left the authorized zone or appeared within a block of horrid little Tommy Morrison's house. GPS-enabled shoes or underwear for junior may be the next step in helicopter parenting.

Given that many changes in both fashion and technology are driven by teenagers, it is likely that teens will lead at least part of the wearable technology revolution. Products like the iWatch or Google Glass may need to come down in price before becoming status symbols in high school, but telephone jackets, or sweatshirts with microphones in the lapel and speakers in the hood, seem like natural high school fashion statements. Any new way to enjoy music on your own or to blast music with friends will be a quick hit with the high school set. Imagine a jacket or bracelet that lets you bump wrists with friends to share songs or pictures. Imagine a T-shirt with a picture of the kid's favorite band, and technology that comes preloaded with the band's newest release.

All of these items could be available now, and they will likely be sold in our near future. Nearly all gather more information about their users than has been gathered in the past. Wearable technology, especially those clothes or adornments connected to the Internet, add to the vast stores of private information that may be dropped into company databases and combined with other data about us. However we wear it, this future mobile technology is likely to be more intrusive, rather than less so.

## CURRENT TRENDS ACCELERATE

The uses of technology by government, business, and organized crime described in earlier chapters are not temporary or isolated events. Each of the important trends discussed—accessing your computer and your power/cable usage as a window into your life and home, developing and deploying equipment to record your movements in the real world, measuring your body and accessing your health data, building enormous databases to capture this information, and developing more sophisticated ways to read and interpret all of your data—will continue to accelerate. The people of Generation Y are digital natives, exposed to personal computing and the Internet their entire lives. It may be difficult for them to understand that we are still in the early stages of development of this medium, so all of the trends that meet the needs of business or government will continue to grow.

### Data Grows, Connections Increase

While the idea of data mining has been around for at least two decades, now the amount of data collected and stored is significant and the analytical tools are sophisticated so that business and government greatly benefit from the deep analysis of all the data available to them. The crop of databases and the ways to reap value from this bounty will continue to grow. One educated estimate stated that, if printed in CD-ROMs, the amount of stored information in the world in 2013 would stretch to the moon in five separate piles.[17] And the amount of data available for analysis seems to be growing geometrically. One data business predicts that the amount of data held by business in 2020 will be more than thirty times larger than the amount collected in 2012.[18]

Government is at the beginning of its Big Data journey. The "Big Data Factsheet" released by the Obama administration on March 29, 2012, lists eighty-five examples of federal agency data mining as part of the government's Big Data Research and Development Initiative. Director of White

House Office of Science and Technology Policy John R. Holdren issued a statement saying, "In the same way that past Federal investments in information-technology R and D led to dramatic advances in supercomputing and the creation of the Internet, the initiative we are launching today promises to transform our ability to use Big Data for scientific discovery, environmental and biomedical research, education, and national security."[19] As the United States moves forward with the Affordable Care Act, the government will aggregate an unprecedented amount of data. The challenge is that identity thieves go where the action is, and they will target not just the US government but any vendors or state agencies that they believe have access to the treasure trove but lesser defenses.

The federal government has only just begun its collection and use of all types of data, and 2012 was its kickoff celebration. Similarly, the states and municipalities have barely started the big data efforts that could address a panoply of local problems, despite New York City's celebrated "Geek Squad."[20] These databases and the ways to analyze them will continue to grow. It is important to stay aware that, with limited exceptions, the data collected by government is public record that can and will be used by others.

Industry's appreciation of the value that analyzing huge databases brings is also on the rise. According to a 2011 report by the McKinsey Global Institute, "If US healthcare were to use big data creatively and effectively to drive efficiency and quality, the sector could create more than $300 billion in value every year. Two-thirds of that would be in the form of reducing US healthcare expenditure by about 8 percent."[21]

The same report stated that users of services enabled by personal-location data could capture "$600 billion in consumer surplus."[22] So, not only does this highly respected consulting company see drastically increased use of information about your location gleaned from your smartphone and car, it also sees the money in your wallet as "consumer surplus" to be harvested by business.

Companies such as Google and Amazon base their entire business model on increasingly effective use of large data sets. As deep analysis becomes institutionalized, more companies will start or grow the depth of their data mining. Simply put, we can expect more entities, collecting more of our information, and using it to predict and influence our actions in more ways.

*Better Data-Collection Tools*

In the digital world, software will continue to become more sophisticated in eliciting, collecting, and using measurable reactions from you. For example, in 2013, your interest in an advertisement, website, or television show could be most easily captured when you clicked your mouse on an interesting item or typed its name into the computer. This is an affirmative voluntary response that you choose to make. But advertisers know that even before you choose to click the mouse, your body expresses interest in things in many measurable ways. Efforts are currently underway to capture and measure the involuntary responses that your body makes without a conscious act.

The most likely example to reach mass consciousness over the next ten years is eyeball-capture technology. Verizon has applied for a patent covering a television set-top box that not only serves as a standard digital video recorder but also includes a camera to watch the eyes of viewers.[23] With this technology, already available to Microsoft in its Xbox 360, Verizon could both calculate how many people are in the room when a certain television show is being displayed and record how long each person's eyes are affixed to the television screen. Eye-movement capture becomes more important in a world of infinite distractions, where people watch television while texting on their smartphones and looking up information on tablets. Verizon, Microsoft, and others want to find a better measurement of your interest. All mid-market and above tablets and smartphones now sold by major manufacturers include front-facing cameras, and these cameras can easily be enlisted to read your eye movement. Expect all tablets and smartphones to use this tool in the near future.

The trend toward measuring involuntary reactions can go beyond eye movement. Scientists know that your voice displays clues to your mood and intentions, so some companies use voice-pattern analysis for customer-service calls to notify the service representatives or their managers when the customer is becoming frustrated or angry with the service solution provided. Other uses of voice-measurement technology may find the best time to offer an "upsell" of a higher-profit product when you are ordering over the phone or in person at a store.

In malls and markets, body language and body placement are already being recorded and analyzed to read whether a person is likely to steal from a store. As camera systems continue to digitize their video, the recordings become easier to analyze by computer algorithm, so that more useful information about your body can be taken from these cameras. With the wearable technology described above and even with handheld devices, sensors could begin to measure not only your gaze with front-facing cameras but also your heart rate, pupil dilation, breathing, skin temperature, and other up-close-and-personal changing attributes useful to a retailer or the person on the other end of your phone call. One of these physical measurements is likely to break through as easily measurable and effective over the next ten years, so expect more biocapture of your body data.

The same will be true as data-capture tools extend their reach throughout the physical world. As the technology becomes easier to install and cheaper to use, smaller and smaller towns will find the money to implement traffic and other surveillance cameras tied to a central database. Digital video surveillance is also becoming much more cost effective for businesses, so expect your local chicken stand to start using a nine-camera setup that is much less expensive, but not much less intrusive, than the system your bank branch has been using for years.

We can also expect more drones. Drones in the hands of federal, state, and local government. Drones in the hands of business. And unless proscribed by a new series of laws, drones in the hands of your neighbors and the press. Given that two excellent cameras share a tiny space with dozens of other gizmos in your smartphone, we know that small cameras on drones can also take excellent pictures and video, and that this video can be saved in a small space or even radioed to a remote capture and viewing device. We also know that unmanned air technology gets smaller and more manageable all the time. You can currently buy decent remote-controlled fliers at Radio Shack and online.

Governments will be able to use drones that fly for miles with state-of-the-art cameras and weaponry. In May of 2013, the Canadian Mounties claimed to have saved a man's life using a drone to find him.[24] There will also be paparazzi and dirty old men that use drones to capture candid pictures of their targets. Drone technology has not left its infancy, and we can expect drones to capture more of our private lives in upcoming years.

*Technologies Merge*

The Internet has insinuated itself into many corners of our lives, and the trend will continue and accelerate over the coming years at a cost to our privacy. We have discussed how Internet-enabled clothing expands the types of data taken from us, but other common items are likely to be affected too.

A highly touted technology trend expected to explode in this decade is "the Internet of Things," focused on connecting machines to each other, rather than connecting them to people. GSMA, a global mobile-industry trade group, reports that while there were nine billion devices connected to the Internet in 2011, by 2020 there will be twenty-four billion connected devices, half of them mobile.[25] The FTC held an Internet of Things workshop on November 19, 2013, to discuss the implication of this coming trend on consumer privacy.

The Internet of Things is already upon us as more of our everyday items become Internet-enabled and connected, not just to us and to our telephone companies, but also to each other:

- Medical devices are starting to connect to each other online.
- Bank ATMs have communicated in networks for many years.
- Stoplights are beginning to sense the traffic and communicate timing.

- Our cars are the first everyday "thing" belonging to regular citizens to become connected in this way.[26] Cars are connected to their manufacturer, to a safety organization that can help in crashes, and in many cases to our insurance companies. Soon cars may be connected to each other, feeding information about distance and speed for safer driving.
- Our house security systems are already connected online, but each appliance could be connected, sharing safety information and functionality and effectiveness data so that you know when your furnace is about to break rather than waiting for it to happen.

As you can imagine, all of this connectivity generates data about you and how you live your life, data that will be collected and used by someone.

The merging of television with the Internet will continue over the next few years, until we reach a time when you may not remember when your picture was not digitized and couldn't be manipulated. An early step in this trend took place when television began to be served as a digital signal, rather than an analog signal. This allowed the content to be served across a network just like other digital data. Then Web TV and Smart TVs appeared to integrate further flexibility and Internet aspects into the television feed.

Television-content providers began serving shows on the Internet, often for free. Now many people no longer feel the need to contract for a cable or satellite television service because all they want to watch is available online. As more companies like Netflix, Google's iTunes, and Amazon Prime offer freshly produced content available only on the Internet, this trend should accelerate. Finally, if Apple, Amazon, Google, or another Internet company could offer a package of live sports and live local news online, then many more people might take a similar plunge into an Internet-only television world, simply connecting the Internet to their wall-mounted screens and watching from Hulu or other services. Now the cable/satellite companies are fighting back by offering live sports on any Internet device anywhere, as long as you have a subscription.

Expect the merger of television and the Internet to continue, and possibly be complete in the next five to seven years. As a result, even more companies will have knowledge of your television-watching habits, as those habits move to the web.

## YOUR BIOLOGY BECOMES AN OPEN BOOK

The biological readings discussed in this book are also in the infancy of their public use, with enormous room to grow in the coming years. Fingerprint readers are good tools for identification purposes, but a tool that can read the vein patterns under the skin of your fingers is better. Vein patterns are not only unique, they also provide proof of life in the reading. Similarly, though iris patterns are unique, retina patterns are unique, can't be replicated with current technology, and also provide proof of a live subject. Companies that truly need strong security will probably begin moving to these more sophisticated measurements in the near future.

Abstractions of biometric data are as effective as a picture of the biometric imprint—a fingerprint or iris scan—and the abstractions are much safer. You cannot change your fingerprint if a picture of it is lost, but you won't have to change it if the information taken from it was abstracted into a mathematical algorithm before it was lost. If stolen, the abstraction can be changed and used without giving away the basic information. These innovations can make biometric security stronger and safer for the public.

Yet as biometric readings and interpretations become more sophisticated, they can also become more intrusive. For example, it is now possible to read brain signals, or brainspray, from outside your head and interpret those signals into learning your intentions or your attitudes. Much work has been done in the field of capturing and applying directed brain signals. At least two companies sell games that are controlled by brainwaves focused and captured by headsets.[27] In February 2013, University of Pittsburgh researcher Andrew Schwartz's years of brain research paid off, as surgeons implanted four microchips in a paralyzed patient's brain that translate her brain's signals into movement in robotic equipment, so that she can feed herself ice cream through brain signals sent to a robotic arm.

Each year, researchers learn more about capturing directed brain waves and create new programs that allow directed thoughts to move objects in real or virtual worlds. Soon amputees should be able to receive a set of chip implants to drive a prosthetic arm. Though this sounds like an entirely positive benefit at first, the maker of the arm would probably push to own the information collected by the chips. In that case, actual thoughts of the prosthetic recipient would become data for processing by others.

Using functional Magnetic Resonance Imaging (fMRI) technology, it is also possible to read the brain's reactions to stimulation and learn whether the observed person has a positive or negative reaction to what he sees. With current technology, the patient must sit perfectly still in a huge fMRI machine for the exercise to work. But if and when the technology becomes cheaper and easier to use, then discretely placed fMRI "cameras" could add the ultimate set of data—a direct line into a person's brain reactions. This would be helpful to car salesmen and suspicious police officers.

The future of intrusive technologies is likely to be a simple acceleration of current trends. More data collected about us by businesses, people, and government. More ways to analyze and use all this information, and more aspects of our private lives stripped bare. To avoid this, we can hide from the technology, or we can look to governments to set rules that protect our privacy.

## NOTES

1. Merriam-Webster's online dictionary defines "killer app" as "a computer application of such great value or popularity that it assures the success of the technology with which it is associated; *broadly*: a feature or component that in itself makes something worth having or using." Some people argue that email was the original killer app, driving people onto the early Internet so that they could trade email with family and friends, or that Milton Berle's show was a popular killer app, pushing people to buy television sets.

2. The cloud computing model is not new. It is a throwback to the earliest days of computing, when a bank or engineering company had powerless "dumb" terminals on the desks of workers and kept a huge mainframe "big iron" computer in the basement or in its own hurricane-proof building. The model is the same: the human interfacing machine taps a remote and vast source of computing power to grant the human problem-solving assistance. However, the entire setup has evolved, allowing people anywhere to access the whole world's knowledge base, rather than being limited to desk-bound employees accessing their own company's database.

*What can you do to prepare for the future?*

The pace and change of technology integration into our everyday lives reminds us all how important it is to guard our own online identities. Less is more when you think of the next time you post something on a blog, a social media page, or websites of companies who solicit your information. There is more information online about you than you think. You don't need to make it any easier.

3. Nancy Gibbs, "Your Life Is Fully Mobile," *Time*, August 16, 2012.

4. Gibbs, "Your Life Is Fully Mobile."

5. Mathew Ingram, "Mary Meeker: Mobile Internet Will Soon Overtake the Fixed Internet," *GigaOM*, April 12, 2010.

6. This motion-capture technology was not new and had been used for doctoring golf swings for more than ten years before the Wii was released to the public. But the Wii was the first immensely popular motion-capture device that brought this type of computer interaction into American homes.

7. Clive Thompson, "Googling Yourself Has a Whole New Meaning," *New York Times*, August 30, 2013.

8. We expect to see Apple eventually offering the i-Eye, or its higher-end version, the i-Eye Captain. It is most likely that either Microsoft, Sony, or one of the other game-making software/hardware companies will make electronic eyewear that can also play video games while linked to other players online.

9. www.gotwind.org/orange_power_wellies.htm.

10. Daniel Perez, "Vodafone's Power Shorts Uses Kinetic Energy to Charge Your Smartphone," *Ubergizmo*, June 19, 2013.

11. Russell Winslow, "Brando Workshop WiFi Detecting Hat," CrunchWear.com, August 24, 2009, www.crunchwear.com/brando-workshop-wifi-detecting-hat/.

12. MIT student Melissa Kitchow created this vest "to feel the warmth, encouragement, support or love that we feel when we receive hugs," advancing the Facebook "like" button a significant step. Charlie Osborne, "Weird Wearable Technology," ZDNet.com, June 3, 2013.

13. Sharon Vaknin, "Your Hoodie Just Updated Your Facebook Page," c/net.com, April 14, 2010.

14. Taylor Soper, "These Sensor-Infused Socks Track Your Steps and ID Injury-Prone Running Styles," GeekWire.com, May 21, 2013, www.geekwire.com/2013/heapsylon-wearable-socks/.

15. Mike Hanlon, "Motorola and Burton Unveil Bluetooth Snowboarding Jacket, Helmet and Beanie," gizmag.com, January 9, 2005, www.gizmag.com/go/3598/.

16. Michael Gorman, "Apple Patents Clothes That Track How You Wear Them, Tell You When It's Time to Update Your Wardrobe," engadget.com, January 17, 2012, http://www.engadget.com/2012/01/17/apple-patents-clothes-that-track-how-you-wear-them-tell-you-whe/.

17. Viktor Mayer-Schonberger and Kenneth Cukier, *Big Data: A Revolution That Will Transform How We Live, Work and Think* (New York: Eamon Dolan/Houghton Mifflin Harcourt, 2013).

18. CSC Corporation, Big Data Universe Beginning to Explode, csc.com, 2012, www.csc.com/insights/flxwd/78931-big_data_universe_beginning_to_explode.

19. Quoted in Nancy Scola, "Obama, the 'Big Data' President," *Washington Post*, June 14, 2013.

20. Alan Feuer, "The Mayor's Geek Squad," *New York Times*, March 23, 2013. The article shows how city statisticians use government data to assist in problems like grease-clogged sewers.

21. McKinsey Global Institute, James Manyika, and Michale Chui, *Big Data: The Next Frontier for Innovation, Competition, and Productivity* (New York: McKinsey Global Institute, 2011).

22. McKinsey Global Institute et al., *Big Data*.

23. Christopher Zara, "Is Your Cable Box Spying on You? Behavior-detecting Devices from Verizon, Microsoft and Others Worry Privacy Advocates," *International Business Times*, July 26, 2013.

24. Carl Franzen, "Canadian Mounties Claim First Person's Life Saved by a Police Drone," *The Verge*, May 10, 2013.

25. Om Malik, "Internet of Things Will Have 24 Billion Devices by 2020," *GigaOM*, October 13, 2011, gigaom.com/2011/10/13/internet-of-things-will-have-24-billion-devices-by-2020/.

26. We are not counting smartphones for this purpose, because they serve as our connection to the Internet, and we act through them. In the Internet of Things, the things will be connected for their own reasons and our use of that connection to check movie times or directions will be secondary.

27. Grown-up toy store Hammecher Schlemmer sells a "Telekinetic Obstacle Course" that uses focused brain waves to maneuver a ball through an obstacle course.

# FOURTEEN

## Laws and Regulations That Could Help Preserve Privacy

As we have seen in these pages, the privacy that we have come to expect on our computers, during our phone calls, in our homes, and even with our bodies is rapidly disappearing. But little of this change is due to huge government programs designed to spy on us. Instead, the change has crept upon us with new and exciting technology that added comfort, convenience, and safety to our lives. With each new security camera, biometric reader at an amusement park, or mobile shopping app, the veneer of obscurity protecting our lives chips away. And yet many new technologies have proved so useful, an entire generation cannot live without them. Our smartphones do so many tasks for us that our need for them is a forgone conclusion—all that is left is to pick a color and a brand. Smashing our gadgets like luddites or living unconnected in the woods like hermits would deprive us of the great advantages life in our own era offers: the advantages of infinite knowledge at our fingertips and constant connection to those we love.

Though the loss of privacy may make us feel helpless at times, we do not need to completely lose our private selves in exchange for the benefits of modern technology. Now that we know what is at stake, we can do something about it. In this concluding chapter, we explore the legal limits that currently exist on intrusion into our privacy. We examine ways that other nations view personal information and protect it under the law. Finally, we outline simple ways to limit intrusions into our personal data without placing significant restrictions on business or law enforcement.

## THE LAW DEFINES OUR PRIORITIES

We live in a civil society operated by laws, rules, and regulations. While those laws necessarily lag behind social and technological growth, they always can be changed to reflect our values. The law and civil rules represent our only method of maintaining a check on the continued growth and access of ever-expanding, cross-referenced, self-sustaining databases of personal information about you.

If our society values its privacy, then we can change the rules so that government cannot tap into our electronic messages or study our varying locations without a judicial process that requires a good reason for needing the information. If our society values its privacy, then businesses can be further limited from the type of information they take and share with each other (and with the government), and what they can do with all of that data. Complete loss of privacy is not inevitable. Some people on this Earth fight to create laws that protect their dignity, even while using the most modern of technologies.

*When Priorities Clash . . .*

Our priorities depend to a large extent on the roles we take in family, community, and work life. It's natural for priorities to occasionally conflict between those who take different roles. For example, your priorities as a parent might conflict with your teenager's priorities when it comes to using social media. Such conflicts are best resolved when each party can recognize the other's priorities, and when you set clear limits. Similarly, certain work roles in society, such as law enforcement or retail advertising, have their own priorities that impact our privacy. When conflicts arise, it is important for us to state our priorities and set clear limits.

Law enforcement has shown itself to be voracious about the amounts and type of information it needs to access. We understand, because it is the police's role in our society to solve and stop crimes using all the resources available to them. They will always push for more leeway and more resources, but they will also honor the limits. We just need to set the limits at a level at which we are comfortable that law-abiding citizens are not constantly surveilled as part of a wider enforcement scheme.

Business behaves similarly, taking full advantage of all the resources available to companies for profit and competitive advantage. We should not expect companies to hold themselves back from exploring the data we deliver to them every minute of every day.

Sun Microsystems CEO Scott McNealy, a tech superstar in his day, famously said in the Internet's early days, "You have zero privacy anyway. Get over it."[1] While Mr. McNealy may have believed this statement to be true, it is entirely self-serving for a technology executive who would like to remove all barriers to gathering data. If he can lead the public to believe that all privacy is lost, then the public is less likely to press their legislators for protections that shackle his company.

### . . . It's Up to Us to Set Clear Limits

We cannot be surprised or upset with the starving tiger that attacks a person for food. This is how tigers eat. We can, however, keep tigers in a restricted environment, far from the temptation of feasting upon our children. Similarly, rather than condemning business and police from pushing the boundaries and infringing on our privacy, we need to set rules around what they can see and what processes are required for them to move beyond their basic level of access.

If we let the tigers roam free in town, we know what will happen. If we do not apply sensible rules to business and law enforcement, then we should not be surprised that they push into our private lives. That is their nature.

## IS PRIVACY A HUMAN RIGHT?

Among industrialized countries, the United States is the most deferential to business and law enforcement, valuing the interests of police stopping terrorists and business innovation over general protections of a citizen's privacy. Other industrialized democracies treat the private information of citizens in a much different manner. In the European Union (EU), Canada, and Mexico, personal and sensitive information belongs to the person the information describes, not to anyone who happens to be holding it. Under the laws of these countries, the ability to say what happens to information about you is an important human right, and neither government nor business can take and use this information about you without your permission.

### How US Law Addresses Personal Privacy

US law does not ignore personal privacy; instead, it focuses on a few very specific areas that legislators have found most important to protect. Specifically, financial-account information, health-care-provider data, and any information intentionally taken from children are protected as private.

So your credit card number and your latest blood-test results are protected as private under both federal and state laws. Other items of information that we might consider to be private, such as our locations at any given moment, our visit to the My Little Pony website, or the fact that we bought a box of condoms at the grocery store, are not protected as private data by US laws. But there is no reason that this must be true. Other countries do protect this type of information from being disseminated and distributed into databases, and we can, too, if we choose.

The United States bases all laws and regulations on a Constitution that was written and ratified by the country's founders well over two hundred years ago. The founding fathers knew nothing of DNA markers or GPS on cell phones. They would have found the concept of electronic surveillance of criminal suspects ridiculous. The mechanical printing press was the most advanced communication technology of the day. To achieve absolute privacy, a person in the days of the Constitutional Convention simply needed to exit the company of other people, an easy proposition on a huge and sparsely populated continent, and made easier by the absence of electric lights, the lack of ability for anyone to climb higher than the nearest tree, and the fact that communications could not travel faster than the speed of a burdened horse.

So while the US Constitution specifically protects a number of liberties that can only reach their full fruition through privacy, the document never mentions privacy as a fundamental right or even an important concept. In a number of cases, the US Supreme Court has found a right to a certain amount of privacy in the "penumbra" of the other rights granted to citizens, including rights over your own body and rights to avoid unreasonable search and seizure. And yet, despite this tenuous finger hold as an essential right in limited circumstances, privacy is not accorded the same respect as other rights in the US Constitution or the laws that have emerged from it.

The United States is a representative government. We each have state and federal representatives who are elected in our district and who answer to us for their votes and positions on issues. These legislators are sensitive to the balancing of interests necessary in any society. They hear from all elements of their constituencies and receive donations from many of them. They listen to the concerns of all these interest groups. When congresspersons hold town hall meetings in their districts, they expect to hear about the issues that are important to voters.

Despite the fact that privacy bills have been introduced and debated every year for the past decade, regular people have not been loud enough about protecting their privacy interests to drive Congress to pass protective legislation. As of this writing, the last federal bill to protect the general privacy of electronic information was passed in 1988, before the Internet came into wide use. Louder voices on this subject may be accorded more attention.

We enjoy convenient, inexpensive, and innovative products and services; we need to be protected from criminals and terrorists; and we want to maintain a base level of privacy in our lives. These goals push against each other until it seems as if we cannot increase support for one without diminishing the others.

When we tell legislators that privacy is a priority for us, we may be told that more privacy necessarily comes at the cost of increased prices, or of reduced security, convenience, and innovation. But sometimes this is a false choice. When technology reaches a certain stage, negligible increases in cost and convenience can buy significant privacy protection.

We need to define and push for the privacy we need. Then we can measure the costs, if any. Law enforcement is pushing the legislature for as much leeway as possible in gathering data. Business interests are pushing for no limits at all on their ability to gather and use your personal data. If people who care about maintaining their privacy never push back, then we will lose our privacy, and we will never know how little it would have cost us to protect it. Our system works through interest groups advocating for their needs and desires. The voices of individuals who value their privacy are quiet and unorganized compared to the opposition.

Current laws and regulations are effective in their fields, so there is no reason to believe that broader laws would be less effective. For example, as health care data is regulated and protected in the United States, we see very little improper sharing of health care information. In fact, the primary fines administered by federal regulatory agencies relating to health information are levied for sloppy care and handling of the data, not intentional sharing outside the bounds of the law.

Where business limits are clear, companies tend to stay within those lines. We should place the lines in a manner that protects areas of privacy where we are losing the most privacy the fastest, such as geolocation. Addressing location privacy now would keep US businesses from building business models around collection of that data.

## How Privacy Is Viewed in Europe and Other Democracies

After World War II, privacy was recognized legally and culturally as a fundamental human right in Europe by the European Convention on Human Rights.[2] and the Universal Declaration of Human Rights[3] Each nation in the EU enacted legislation implementing these official statements. Recently, EU member states adopted the Lisbon Treaty Establishing the European Community,[4] which protects privacy as a fundamental right of all people, and the Charter of Fundamental Rights, which adds protection of personal rights and freedom in the processing of personal data as a fundamental right.[5]

Under the current Data Protection Directive,[6] all EU nations have privacy protections built into their national laws and agencies focused on the use of personal information. The directive specially protects personal data related to certain sensitive categories, including racial or ethnic origin, political opinions, religious or philosophical beliefs, union membership, health, and sexual activity.[7]

How did the impulse to treat privacy as a human right arise in Europe, and not in the United States? Many Europeans would argue that privacy is a fundamental requirement for exercising human rights. Unlike the United States, which has been a democracy generally protective of individual liberties for centuries, much of Europe is not more than a generation or two from fascist or communist dictatorships, in which the government strove to know all the secrets of its citizens. Under those regimes, general knowledge of certain private facts, such as a person's practiced religion, political leanings, or sexuality, could lead to imprisonment or death.

Understandably enough, these countries are sensitive to how important privacy can be in regard to the state or to business, because they have recently seen the evil that flourishes when privacy is not protected. Without such visceral recent reference points, the United States is content to allow its regulation with regard to privacy drift with the winds of business, protecting the most obviously vulnerable data and leaving the rest uncovered.

## Treading the National Boundaries of Privacy Laws

As the Internet captured personal data and ignored jurisdictional boundaries in the 1990s and early 2000s, the United States' more cavalier attitude toward privacy of electronic data caused a rift between the United States and the EU.

European rules require that personal data may only be transferred to third countries if those countries provide an adequate level of protection for the data. The United States was essentially considered a noncivilized country with regard to personal privacy, and the EU threatened to stop allowing personal data from Europe to flow into the United States.

To avoid this fate, the United States negotiated a collection of methods for its companies to adopt that would make EU governments comfortable that their citizens' information would be adequately safeguarded. The most famous of these methods, called the International Data Safe Harbor, was developed and is currently operated by the US Department of Commerce in consultation with the various privacy offices of the EU.

The Safe Harbor is a set of principles and practices that US businesses must publically agree to if they want to receive personal data from EU countries. A company that undertakes the required steps and files its agreement with the US Commerce Department is considered to be Safe Harbor Compliant.

The EU Data Safe Harbor requires companies to comply with the seven principles of European data protection:

- People must receive notice that their data is being collected and notice about how it will be used.

- They must have the choice to opt out of the collection and transfer of data.
- A company many only transfer the data to another company that follows these rules.
- The company must protect the data with reasonable security measures.
- The data must be relevant for the purpose of its collection and use.
- The data subject must be able to access the information and correct or delete inaccurate data about him or her.
- There must be a means of enforcing the rules.[8]

So while US business is regulated at home under relatively lax federal data laws, any company that collects data in Europe must comply with the more protective laws there.

Canada also recognizes a fundamental human right to protect and control personal data about you and has passed laws enacting this principle into practice.[9] While the Canadians have not officially restricted the flow of personal information to the United States, Canadian companies are aware of their obligations to protect data and work to impose those restrictions on companies that they do business with. Canadian businesses also tend to be careful about entering into cloud-computing contracts with US companies, citing concern over the access to private information that US law enforcement is allowed under the law.

## Not All Countries Respect Privacy and Human Rights

Many countries in the world have much less rule of law than the industrialized democracies. Others have rule of law but with much less concern for the basic human rights of their people. Many people live in theocracies that filter all rights through the prism of religion or ideology. Because those cultures' norms are far from the respect for individual rights found in countries where democracy flourishes, this book does not examine their laws for comparative treatment of personal privacy.

In countries that the United States calls friends and allies, privacy is generally considered a fundamental human right, to be protected at significant cost.

## Establishing Privacy as a Right

As we have seen, the current state of US law regarding protection of sensitive personal data is not inevitable. In fact, the United States is an outlier among industrialized democracies in not passing a comprehensively protective personal-data privacy law. We can find examples of broader privacy protection by simply looking across our borders and to our closest trading partners.[10]

To limit the ever-increasing intrusion of technology into our lives, we could recognize a constitutional right to privacy, or we could grant a similar broad right through federal statute. US citizens could then sue companies and governments that infringed on their newly recognized rights, forcing those companies and governments to justify the privacy intrusions or drop the practices altogether. This would raise awareness of the need to protect individual privacy in both the private and public sectors.

## PLACING LIMITS ON BUSINESS

Even without granting a fundamental right of privacy recognized under law, the United States could take strides to protect its citizens from the intrusions created by new technology. Legislators could take aim directly at business, outlining certain areas of information that are off limits for collection, analysis, and sharing.

One easy example would be to restrict information relating to geolocation of people using a company's technology. For example, Congress could pass a law limiting the collection or retention of location information from people's cell phones or wearable computers.

A variety of companies are eager to collect location data from your smartphone. Of course, your telephone company, your data provider, and the company that provides the software infrastructure, such as Apple, Google, or Microsoft, collect location information. But many apps also require or request location data to work optimally. Other app companies simply take location data along with everything else they collect, whether it is needed for functionality or not. When you make purchases from your cell phone, the seller is likely to note your location. The same is true for other types of transactions, such as when you use online banking or an app that identifies a song you hear on the radio.

If we do not want unknown companies learning about us from our travels and daily routines, we can define restrictions on how they collect and use this information.

### Restrictions on Data Collection

A law to restrict the spread of your location information could target collection. The law could specify that only certain types of companies can accept information about your whereabouts from your smartphone, that they must need that particular data for their app to work, and that they can only collect it with specific permission granted by you, the smartphone's user.

The law could also include an expiration of permission. Once every ninety days, you would need to look at the permissions you have granted for capturing location data and choose which ones to renew. That way, you can restrict permission to companies that are still relevant to your daily life.

Having to renew expiring permissions might be mildly annoying, but it would save you from granting permission for a one-time use of an application, only to trigger tracking from that application for years on end, whether you remember about it or not. This law would add to privacy protections while being minimally intrusive into the lives of citizens and the business models for most smartphone companies.

### Restricting Data Storage and Use

Another type of regulation would target storage and use of location data after it has been collected. The law could allow all permitted geolocation information but limit its use only to functions required for the phone and software to function correctly. That way, companies could not collect this data and then store it to analyze and use for data mining at a later date.

To cement this last point, the law could forbid saving location data any longer than needed for the designed function within the application. Companies would be required to create regular programs for dumping location data when it is no longer necessary for immediate functionality. Dumping the data reduces both the size of collecting companies' databases and their temptation to use this information to spy on consumers.

Once again, this type of prohibition is narrowly tailored to protect the privacy of smartphone owners while minimizing the business impact on companies that create software and services for smartphones.

### Defining How Data May Not Be Used

Finally, an even more narrow law could allow companies to capture and retain geolocation data from smartphones, at the same time carving out a list of specific functions that could not be performed with this data.

For example, this law could simply prohibit the use of geolocation data taken from smartphones, cars, or wearable computers to be used to track that user without his or her permission, to assist in identifying the technology user, or to otherwise be combined with unrelated data about the user.

Even this very limited restriction would significantly reduce the growth of databases following our every move and extrapolating meaning from those movements.

*Similar Restrictions for Other Personal Information*

Location data is only one type of consumer information that companies are reaping from smartphones and other mobile technology. Any of the laws and regulations outlined above could be aimed at all the different personal data collected by mobile technology.

Some states have already introduced bills to restrict the capture and use of biometric information. As apps continue to develop to measure heart rate and other vital signs, Congress could pass laws to restrict use of medical and health information taken on mobile devices. Currently this data is not protected under the Health Insurance Portability and Accountability Act (HIPAA) unless it is specifically taken for provision of health care by a provider or other triggering circumstance.

*Transparency for More Informed Buying Choices*

By choosing to buy the safer products that intrude less on our private data, we can use our purchasing power to push business to be more attentive to personal privacy concerns. If privacy is worth fighting for, then it is worth paying more for products and services that protect privacy. This method speaks with dollars, rather than votes. Laws and regulations can help in this case too, by requiring app providers to provide us with the information we need to make informed buying choices.

Today, few of us understand how apps or other tools collect, store, and use data about us. Companies like it this way, because the mystery means that you will be unlikely to reject an app for its data policies. To address this situation, Congress or the Federal Trade Commission (FTC) could require each app provider to publish a statement with their products about how the app uses location data and other consumer information. The statements should be uniform, so consumers can easily judge whether an app collects and uses too much data. With those disclosures, we would all have a useful tool to judge how to protect ourselves. Without them, we simply do not know if the technology is taking more data than we are comfortable giving.

This type of consumer-information law, similar to the law requiring nutrition information to be consistently displayed on packaging of prepared food, would be an excellent step in protecting our privacy from encroaching technology.

## PLACING LIMITS ON LAW ENFORCEMENT

Law enforcement plays a unique role in our society, as the one power with a monopoly on the use of force and the one power with the ability to restrict our movements into a prison or even sentence us to death. For this reason, the government is especially restricted under the US Constitution to avoid abuses of this power. The Constitution does not allow the government to arrest or imprison citizens without probable cause that the citizen has committed a crime. The Constitution places restriction on making people testify against themselves and promises security of a person's home from government intrusion without good reason.

Still, the police wield awesome power and authority in our society. By allowing surveillance that was once impossible to be performed cheaply and easily, technology is increasing that power. The police hold and continue to build vast databases of faces, fingerprints, DNA, and other biometric readings of citizens for use in crime solving. Police are able to tap into the records of telephone companies, not only to find what calls have been made from a particular mobile phone but also to name all the locations that the phone has visited in the relevant time period. Police can capture from your computer which websites you visited and how long you stayed at each.

In each of these cases, technology provides the police with new resources granting insight into a suspect's movements, motives, or intentions. This information was totally unavailable to law enforcement twenty-five years ago. Now its use is a daily check taken for granted by most police departments.

### Officer, You Need a Warrant for That

Our legal system is based on rules and process. The rules dictate that in order for police to see a protected item of information, they must go through a process to prove the need for the information and the appropriateness of their request. Usually this means showing a judge probable cause to receive a warrant to search for information inside a house or a car trunk. It can also be a warrant to place a tracking device on a suspect's vehicle or to plant listening devices into the suspect's telephone. If the police can show that a piece of information is needed for an investigation into a crime or a terrorist plot, they almost always are granted the right to access the information.

We make the rules that define the difference between data that law enforcement can freely obtain and data that law enforcement is restricted from accessing without a warrant or court order. The legal philosophy of our system is based on the idea that certain searches are particularly intrusive into the lives of ordinary people. Asking a law-abiding person questions is not intrusive, but searching her house is intrusive, so the police need a warrant to search her house.

Thanks to technological advances, police today are able to access a wide variety of communications between suspects, from text messages and chat-room comments to telephone voice data. And when a new technology is introduced into society, the police generally assume that a warrant or other court order is not needed to take advantage of the evidence offered by the new technology. Only after a court determines that evidence from a new technology is protected by the process will government agents tread more carefully around the new technology. If we want to place limits on what the police see, our courts or legislatures can increase the number and types of information that law enforcement need a warrant to see.

For example, the US Supreme Court recently ruled that police do not need a warrant to take the DNA of an arrested suspect. In addition, many states do not require a warrant for law enforcement to see a suspect's mobile-phone records. Others do not require warrants to view Internet-surfing data. We could change the law so that a warrant or special court order is needed for police to take and store DNA samples, or to see a month's worth of telephone or location records from the person's mobile-phone company. New technologies will be less able to invade our privacy when officers and agents need to show probable cause that a suspect was the perpetrator of a specific crime before they are allowed to make those kinds of searches.

As it stands now, the telephone companies give up mountains of information on regular people to the police based on millions of data requests each year,[11] including police demands for "tower dumps" that drop all of the data from one cell tower into police hands, regardless of whose information is contained in the dump.[12] Requiring warrants to receive this data and forbidding generalized searches such as tower dumps will help protect our privacy. Despite their protests to the contrary, such restrictions will not place an undue burden on law enforcement, which is becoming comfortable with the ability to grab any technical information available.

### Changing Presumptions with New Technology

Another way to protect privacy from the increasing intrusiveness of advancing technology would be to create a presumption that police need a warrant to gather evidence arising from new technology. This is vastly different from the current situation, in which police assume that they have a right to all information amassed by smartphones, digitized power grids, or DNA testing until they are told otherwise.

Currently, police actively collect and use data from new technology before a court or legislature even has considered or debated the wisdom of allowing such intrusion into private lives. Our privacy would be better protected if we created a presumption that collecting evidence from new technologies always requires a warrant. Then police would have to justify why the law-enforcement value outweighed the intrusion on privacy as each new technology comes into use.

This approach also makes sense because the police have a stronger legislative lobby and judicial presence than advocates for personal privacy. So law enforcement is in a much better position to fight for its desired results than the general public is in to advocate for more privacy protection. If we *begin* using new technology under an assumption that privacy is protected, then we are less likely to automatically lose our personal and sensitive information before we even know it is threatened.

## Placing Limits on Storage of Biometric Information

We can also use the law to protect our privacy from new technology advances by placing strict limits on whose DNA or other biometric information could be kept in police databases. For example, the government adds DNA samples from people who served in our military to their law-enforcement databases, seeming to make a tacit accusation that our military heroes are criminal suspects upon their return to civilian life. We can create a set of rules that allow DNA matches with convicted criminals, but we do not allow bolstering those databases with biometric information from law-abiding citizens, or with people who have been arrested, but not convicted, of crimes.

As it currently stands, your DNA may be checked against crime scenes if you have been convicted of a traffic violation in some jurisdictions, or simply arrested in others. Warrants are not required to place an arrested person's DNA into the criminal database. The FBI's CODIS database started with sex offenders, but it has moved far past that point, including information from more than ten million offender profiles and well over a million arrestee profiles.[13] A law limiting the type of data that could be included in this and other law-enforcement databases of personal physical characteristics could protect privacy while setting reasonable limits for law enforcement. Currently the FISA courts that the NSA approaches to receive approval for certain surveillance techniques operates with only one side arguing a case before the judge. The differs considerably from our normal conception of courts. In most instances, two opposing sides make an argument before a court, and the court weighs the presentation of both parties before making a decision. If only one party is allowed to argue, it is only natural that the court will agree with the presenting party nearly all the time. Therefore, Congress should appoint an ombudsman to represent the privacy and other constitutional rights of US citizens in FISA courts. This ombudsman can oppose NSA data gathering requests and argue for more privacy and less government intrusion. The FISA court would then function with the natural checks and balances that US citizens expect from their government.

## NOW IS THE TIME TO ACT

This book has not revealed secret scientific discoveries or confidential military programs, and has discussed only technological data already in use, for sale, or analyzed in public fora. The authors, who may have some inside knowledge of additional privacy intrusions, have only reported on technologies, business data mining, and government programs well-covered by the media. We hope to have made the point that it is not just governments that track our everyday habits, commercial companies track us too, and to a much greater extent. They track us through everyday technology and conveniences that we have become highly dependent upon. During the writing of this book, the federal government was forced to admit spying on its citizens through massive volumes of telephone metadata, and spying on others by tapping the data of the top Internet application providers. We all knew that Google was amassing warehouses of information about each of us, but until June of 2013 we could not report that this information was shared with the US security apparatus. Other deep intrusions beyond what is reported here surely exist. We just don't know about them yet.

So we can safely assume that someone in the government; the business community; a political, religious, or charitable group; or even a fraudster or stalker knows much more about you than you would like them to know, because your technology betrayed you. Your Internet searches on religious subjects gave someone enough information to correctly surmise your leanings. Examination of your power usage demonstrates an interest in home cooking or questionable indoor botany. Your car signaled that you were away from home. Your grocery store VIP card shows that you have bought many baby products recently.

As we enjoy the convenience the technology brings, the technologies burrow deeper into our behavior patterns, and the databases of our activities grow larger every day. How long before we take the loss of privacy seriously?

> **They who can give up essential liberty to obtain a little temporary safety, deserve neither liberty nor safety.**
>
> —Benjamin Franklin[14]

Many of our essential liberties—from free speech to free assembly, from security in our person to freedom of religion—depend on privacy, obscurity, and anonymity to reach their full expressions. Privacy is important for human dignity, for freedom from coercion, and for true freedom of action, as we all behave differently when we know someone is watching us.

We have spent the past decade allowing intrusive technologies to crawl deep into our lives without making a stand for limiting their reach. The time has come for all of us to raise our voices and alert our leaders that privacy is a value that is important to us, because trading this fundamental right for convenience and cost would be a tragedy. It would be even worse if we cared for our privacy and watched it slip away because we were too hypnotized by shiny new technology to pay attention to what was happening all around us.

## NOTES

1. Polly Sprenger, "Sun on Privacy: 'Get Over It,'" by *Wired*, January 26, 1999.
2. Convention for the Protection of Human Rights and Fundamental Freedoms, art. 8, Nov. 4, 1950, 213 U.N.T.S. 221.
3. Universal Declaration of Human Rights art. 12, G.A. Res. 217 (III) A, U.N. Doc. A/RES/217(III) (Dec. 10, 1948).
4. Treaty of Lisbon amending the Treaty on European Union and the Treaty Establishing the European Community art. 16B, Dec. 13, 2007, 2007 O.J. (C 306) 5.1
5. Charter of Fundamental Rights of the European Union arts. 7–8, Dec. 18, 2000, 2000 O.J. (C 364) 10.
6. Directive 95/46/EC on the protection of individuals with regard to the processing of personal data and on the free movement of such data.
7. Directive 95/46/EC at 8(1).
8. See the US Commerce Department website describing export controls and the EU Data Safe Harbor, found at export.gov/safeharbor/eu/eg_main_018475.asp.
9. The Canadian government agencies are limited by the Privacy Act of 1983, while businesses and other organizations are restricted in data usage by the Personal Information Protection and Electronic Documents Act.
10. Mexico, Japan, Australia, India, and Brazil also have much more comprehensive national laws protecting personal privacy than the United States, although, unlike the EU and Canada, some of these nations do not have robust enforcement schemes in place to truly guarantee personal-data protection in most situations.
11. Eric Lichtblau, "More Demands on Cell Carriers in Surveillance," *New York Times*, July 8, 2012, citing US Congressional findings by Edward J. Markey, who requested data from nine mobile-phone carriers.
12. Andy Greenberg, "Here's How Often AT & T, Sprint, and Verizon Each Hand Over Users' Data to the Government," *Forbes*, July 9, 2012.
13. CODIS–NDIS Statistics, *Measuring Success*, United States Federal Bureau of Investigation Internet site, accessed June 8, 2013, www.fbi.gov/about-us/lab/biometric-analysis/codis/ndis-statistics.
14. As published in the "Memoirs of the Life and Writings of Benjamin Franklin" in 1818. Attributed to him around February 17, 1775 as he prepared for the Pennsylvania Assembly.

# Index

10 minute mail, 66
123People, 83
23andme (DNA analysis service), 156–158
*60 Minutes*, 122

ABI Research, 130
absolute rights versus process rights, 9
account hijacking, 60
Adams, Jared, 38
adware, 22–23, 31, 81
Aerovironment, Inc. (AV), 120
Affordable Care Act, 69, 220
Afghanistan: biometrics used to identify escaped prisoners, 145; drones hacked by insurgents, 122; government surveillance in, 41
AGPtek (security products), 205
*Air Force Times* , 123
airline-reservation systems, 12
Akamai, 39
Alberta Provincial Privacy Commissioner, 27
Albine, 82
Al Jazeera, 123
al-Qaeda, 121, 148
Amazon.com, 58; Amazon Prime service disruption, 61; government and law enforcement record requests, 36; recommendations and privacy of choice, 6
America Online. *See* AOL (America Online)
American Civil Liberties Union (ACLU) : on drones for surveillance, 120; on facial recognition software, 151; on U.S. government tracking citizens, 114
analytics, vii, viii, 39, 186
Android, 88, 103, 105, 108, 215

anonymity, 2
Anonymouse, 81
anti-malware software, 200
anti-virus software. *See* anti-malware software
AOL (America Online), 58; tracking chat and messages, 43. *See also* email
AP (Associated Press), 190
Apple computers and phones: encryption on iPhones and Messages, 207; FaceTime, 43; Siri, 99, 190; targeted by spyware, malware, and hackers, 32, 103
Apple, Inc., 11, 31; collecting personal data, 13, 38; government and law enforcement record requests, 36, 37; smart garments in development, 100, 218
apps : controlling home systems, 177–178; health data collected by, 236; in the cloud, 58; location data collected by, 234; safe use of, 89; security for mobile devices, 203–204, 207; on smart phones, 97; as spyware, 63
AT&T, 36, 106
*Atlantic* , 165
attachments, 23
Australia, 46. *See also* right to privacy
Automated Biometric Identification System (ABIS), 52
Automated Wait Time monitoring (TSB), 104
automobiles. *See* smart cars
Aviva, 132
Aviv, Adam, 100

Back Orifice, 24
backups, 180, 208; offsite storage, 58
Baltimore, Maryland, 116

banking online, 67, 191

*Bazemore v. Savannah Hospital*, 16n2

behavioral advertisers, 79; disclosure standards for, 81; and social media, 85–86

behavioral biometrics, 140

behavioral science. *See* social science

Belize, 96

Benghazi embassy attack, 37

Berk, Richard, 15

Berwin High School, xi–xii

BestBuy, 118

Biden, Joseph hacked, 62

big data, 7–8, 37; analysis of, vii; Big Data Research and Development Initiative, 219; biometrics databases, 141, 143; cell phone call data storage, 186; charities' use of, 7; commercial purposes of, 6–7; and constitutional rights, 38; economic value of, 220; government collections of, 37, 89, 162, 190; growth rate of, vii, 219; law enforcement collections, 14; placing legal limits on collection and storage, 239; political parties' use of, 7; privacy and security of, viii; thieves' use of, 8; voice conversation collections, 90; vulnerabilities of, 37, 90, 149, 163–164. *See also* data collection

Big Data Research and Development Initiative, 219

Bill of Rights. *See* Constitution (U.S.); right to privacy

Bin Laden, Osama, 123

Bing, 40. *See also* search engines

Binney, William, 44, 45

biometric identification, 122. *See also* biometrics

biometric identification machines. *See* biometric readers

biometric identification regimes, ix

biometric identifiers, 139–142. *See also* biometrics

biometric readers, 139, 140; calibration issues, 141; DNA readers, 140; fingerprint reader, 140; voice analyzers, 140. *See also* biometrics

biometrics: benefits of, 143–147; capturing brain waves, 224; eyeball-capture technology, 221; false results, 142, 147–148; future trends, 223–224; handheld digital scanners for identification, 145; HIPPA privacy protections, 161; identification by, 139–141, 142–143, 145, 145–146; immutability issues, 149; legal limits on collection and storage of, 239; locking mobile devices, 153; physiological versus behavioral, 140; silicone "fake fingers", 148; traits that can be measured, 142; voice-pattern analysis, 221; vulnerabilities of databases, 149. *See also* data collection; DNA; facial recognition software

biosurveillance, 49

Blackberry, 11, 185

black boxes in cars, 128–130

Bloustein, Edward, 4

bluesnarfing. *See* Bluetooth: vulnerabilities to intrusion

Bluetooth: on mobile devices, 104; stickers to track personal objects, 179; and traffic control, 131; vulnerabilities to intrusion, 104, 108, 190

Bork, Robert, 5

Boston, 113

Boston marathon bombers, 47, 48, 83; camera images used to identify, 116; crowdsourcing used to identify, 97; on terrorist watch list, 48; YouTube channel of, 83. *See also* Boston Marathon bombing

Boston Marathon bombing: digital tracking aids law enforcement, 89; phone call access by law enforcement, 186–187; public opinion affected by, 114. *See also* Boston Marathon bombers

Boxmeyer, Jim, 177

Brando Workshop, 217

Brazil, 73, 122, 148, 241n10

breaches. *See* data breaches; security breaches

Brenner, Joel F., 105
Brookings Institute, 119
*Brooklyn Paper*, 134
Brossart, Rodney, 121
browsers. *See* Internet browsers
browsing the web. *See* Internet
    browsers
buffer overflow prevention system
    (BOPS), 201
Buffett, Warren, 82
Bureau of Alcohol, Tobacco, and
    Firearms (ATF), 89
Burger King, 61, 62
Burke, Terri, 114
Burma, 41
Burnett, Erin, 187
Burns, Larry, 62
Business Climate Survey, 40

cable companies, xiii, 176, 188–189
Cable Privacy Act, 176
Cablevision Corporation, 176
California State University – San
    Marcos, 62
cameras: on cell phones, 99;
    government access to private
    camera networks, 115–116; in home
    computers, xi, xii, 10, 197, 203; and
    spyware, 29, 65. *See also* surveillance
    cameras
Canada: Canadian Freedom of
    Information and Protection of
    Privacy Act, 28; Canadian Legal
    Information Institute (CANLII), 44;
    Canadian Legal Records, 44; drones
    used by law enforcement, 120;
    privacy in the workplace, 27–28;
    rights to privacy, 8–9; tracking
    travel to, 46
CANLII. *See* Canada: Canadian Legal
    Information Institute
Cardozo, Nate, 129
car insurance companies, 2
Carnivore, 26
cars. *See* smart cars
Carter, Andrew, 177
cDc Communications. *See* Back Orifice
cell phones: cell-tower triangulation,
    98; law enforcement's access of

records, 35, 38, 106; location
    functions, 13, 97–98; metadata on,
    96; safety measures for, 89, 107–108,
    191; utility sensors on, 100;
    vulnerability to tracking and
    hacking, 10, 35, 43, 98, 99, 107, 190,
    191. *See also* cameras; data
    collection; mobile devices;
    stingrays; tracking
cell-tower triangulation, 98, 107
cellular Internet service, 180
Central Intelligence Agency, 37, 51
Centralized Monitoring System
    (India), 50
Central Processing Unit (CPU), 30
Chapman, Peter, 72
Charter of Fundamental Rights (EU),
    231
chat logs vulnerability to spying, xii
Chicago : Chicago Police Department,
    49; surveillance cameras in, 113, 116
Child Exploitation Tracking System, 73
Child, Lee (*A Wanted Man*), 51
child pornography online. *See* children
    and teens; pornography
children and teens: cell phone use,
    73–74; hiding online behavior from
    parents, 70; identity theft and,
    70–71; Internet risks to, 69–74; social
    media use, 71; targeted by sexual
    predators, 71–74
China: attacks on U.S. computer
    systems, 14; government
    surveillance in, 40; intrusion on
    computers and mobile devices, 105
choice and privacy, 1
Chrome (Google), 23. *See also* Internet
    browsers
CIA (Central Intelligence Agency), 37,
    51
circles of privacy, xi–xiii
Cisco Systems, 12, 31, 180
CISP (cyber security information
    sharing partnership), 40
Citizens' Council for Health Freedom,
    168
Clapper, James, 37, 105
Claypoole, Theodore, viii–ix
Clemente, Tim, 187

Clinton, Hillary, 61
cloud computing, 58–60; cloud-based
    services, range of, 58; Cloud
    Security Alliance, 59; data
    ownership, 61; history of, 225n1;
    storage services, 59; vulnerabilities
    and self-protections, 59–60, 61,
    62–64, 67, 202. *See also* big data, data
    collecting
Cloud Security Alliance, 59
Cohen, Jared (*The New Digital Age:
    Reshaping the Future of People,
    Nations and Business*), 63
Colorado and drones, 113, 120
Comcast, 36
Committee to Protect Journalists (CPJ),
    41
Communications Assistance for Law
    Enforcement Act (CALEA), 45
Computer Sciences Corporation (CSC),
    vii
computer sensor, 29
computers. *See* personal computers
computers in cars. *See* smart cars
Congress (U.S.), viii; new privacy laws
    proposed, 230, 234, 236; report on
    cell-phone surveillance, 106
Constitution (U.S.), 9, 230. *See also* right
    to privacy
Consular Consolidated Database
    (CCD), 52
cookies, 78
Coviello, Arthur, Jr., 59
Crespo, Xavier Orlando, 72
criminal behavior predicted, 47
criminals. *See* cyber-crime
crowdsourcing, 89
Cuba, 41
Cult of the Dead Cow, 24
cyber-attacks, 66
cyberazzi, 77, 81
cyber disruption, ix
cyber espionage, viii
cyber threats, ix
cyber-crime : cybercriminals' points of
    entry, 174, 195–196, 196; Java code
    on browsers, 199; law enforcement
    challenges, 57; scams and hacks, 22,
    60

cybercriminals. *See* cyber-crime
cyber-security: of infrastructure, 182;
    legislation regarding, viii; strategies
    to address, vii, viii, 198

*Daily Beast* , 124
*Daily Mail*, 123
databases, 13–14. *See also* big data; data
    collection
data breaches, ix, viii, 9, 57, 186; in big
    data, 90; in the cloud, 59; in medical
    records, 69
data-capturing companies, 11. *See also*
    data collection
data collection, 11; by automatic toll
    collection systems, 134; from credit
    card swipes, 87; and data mining, 6;
    by drones, 118–121; FBI's CODIS
    system, 162; of health, DNA and
    biometric information, 143, 164–169,
    220; from home devices, 87–88,
    173–174; international protocols for
    commerce, 232–233; from mobile
    devices, 88–89, 100, 101, 186; rapid
    expansion of, 219; from smart cars,
    129–131; tools for, 220–222; while
    traveling, 104–107; by U.S.
    government agencies, 11, 51. *See also*
    big data; biometrics
data loss, 59
data mining, 6. *See also* data collection
datamization, 11
data points, 11, 12, 13, 14. *See also* data
    collection
Data Protection Directive (EU privacy
    protections), 231
data-protection regimes, 8
data sources, 12–13. *See also* data
    collection
dating services, 86
DEC. *See* Digital Equipment Corp.
DD1203, 205
DDoS. *See* distributed denial of service
DeadDrop, 81
deep packet inspection, 40
deep packet sniffing, 42
Deer Trail, CO, 118
Defense Advanced Research Projects
    Agency (DARPA), 49, 90

Defense Department. *See* Department of Defense

Deibert, Ron, 105

Dell Inc., 31

denial of service attacks, 182

Department of Defense: collecting biometrics, 52; social media policies, 49

Department of Energy, 106

Department of Homeland Security, vii, 69; Advanced Passenger Information System, 46; Analyst's Desktop Binder, 44; biosurveillance program, 49; on counterfeit consumer electronic goods, 180; use of drones for border patrol, 120; email triggers, 44; hiring hackers, 106

Department of Justice, 106; monitoring journalists' phones, 190; surveillance camera effectiveness study, 115; use of warrants for GPS tracking, 135

desktop computers. *See* personal computers

DHS. *See* Department of Homeland Security

Digital Advertising Alliance, 78

Digital Equipment Corp., ix

digital surveillance technology. *See* spyware

digital tracking. *See* data collection; tracking

DirectTV, 176

Disconnect, 81

Disney (The Walt Disney Company), 108

distributed denial of service (DDoS) attacks on web sites, 182

District of Columbia, 114

Dixon, Pam, 117

DNA (Deoxyribonucleic acid), 155–158; 23andme analysis service, 156–158; analysis of, 140, 144–145, 157, 157–158, 158; as a biometric identifier, 141; cloning possibilities, 160; DNA-specific bioweapons, 165; employers' interest in, 159, 166–167; government storage and uses, 164; insurance companies' interest in, 159; law enforcement storage and uses, 162–163; marketers and political parties' interest in, 159; newborns' DNA collected, 164, 168; ownership of, xv; privacy issues, ix, 10, 161, 168; trophy hunters, 165–166. *See also* biometrics

DoD. *See* Department of Defense

*Douglas v. Stokes*, 16n2

Douglas, William O., 46

Dowler, Milly, 103

DownRightNow.com, 61

Dragan, Zenon, 120

Draganfly, 120

Dragon Dictation, 99

Drizin, Steven, 145

Droid Dream, 103

Droid KungFu, 103

drones: anti-drone devices and clothing, 123; benefits of, 121; criminal use of, 121–122; data collection by, 118–121; journalists' use of, 121; law enforcement's use of, 115; government and business's use of, 222; use outside the U.S., 119–120, 121; shooting down drones, 119; vulnerability to hacking, 120, 122

Dropbox, 36, 38, 60

Dropcam, 205

Dudzhan, Amir Abu, 83

eavesdropping statutes, 28

eBay, vii

EFF. *See* Electronic Frontier Foundation

Electronic Frontier Foundation (EFF), 36, 129, 130

Electronic Privacy Information Center, 152

email: accessed through spyware, 25, 30; attachments; cloud-based services, 58; multiple addresses for security, 199; searched and tracked, 80–81; subpoenas to providers, 35

encryption, 200, 207

Energy Department (U.S.), 106

England, 43

e-readers. *See* mobile devices

erotica. *See* pornography

EU. *See* European Union

European Convention on Human Rights, 231

European Court of Human Rights (ECtHR), 45

European Data Protection Supervisor (EDPS), 188

European Network and Information Security Agency (ENISA), 41

European Union: government surveillance in, 41; International Data Safe Harbor, 232; right to privacy in, 8–9, 231–232; smart grid controlling home energy use, 188; travelers' PNR data shared by, 46

Evans, Jonathan (MI5 Chief), 40

Evernote, 60

eyeball-capture technology, 221

EZPass tracking. *See* passcards

FAA (Federal Aviation Administration), 119

Facebook, 8, 42; access to records in the European Union, 41; data ownership, 61; Facebook Home, 86; Graph Search, 83; subpoenas to, 38. *See also* social media

facial recognition software: blocking, 122–123, 152; in gaming systems, 214; for mobile device security, 153; privacy issues, xiii, 36, 149–150; at state Departments of Motor Vehicles, 152; at stores and shopping centers, 116; at Super Bowl XXXV, 151. *See also* biometrics

FARC (Fuerzas Armadas Revolucionarias de Colombia), 121

Faull, Greg, 96

FBI (Federal Bureau of Investigation), 10; access to cell phone records, 106, 186–187; use of biometric data for identification, 52, 151–152; CODIS system for storing and comparing DNA, 162; fingerprint identification by, 141, 148; Internet surveillance by, 26; use of keystroke-monitoring software, 26; *Mayfield v. United States*, 148; SAR (Suspicious Activity Reporting Initiative) list, 44; scams and fake warnings, 22; Sex Offender Registry, 44; warrantless GPS tracking by, 135

FBI.gov scam, 22

FCC (Federal Communications Commission), 198

Federal Aviation Administration (FAA), 119

Federal Communications Commission, 198

Federal Security Bureau (FSB) of Russia, 48

Federal Trade Commission (FTC), xii, 77, 88

Federal Wiretap Act, 27

Feinstein, Dianne, 118

Ferdaus, Rezwan, 121

Ferraz Vasconcelos Hospital, 148

financial records on personal computers, 20

fingerprints: as biometric identifiers, 141; fingerprint readers, 140; used for security, 140, 148. *See also* biometrics; FBI

Firefox (Mozilla), 23. *See also* Internet browsers

firewalls, 23, 197–198

First Amendment (U.S. Constitution), 9. *See also* Constitution (U.S.)

FISA court. *See* Foreign Intelligence Surveillance Act (FISA) court

Flickr. *See* social media

*Forbes*, 105, 134, 175

Fordham University, 100

Ford Motor Company, 128

Foreign Intelligence Surveillance Act (FISA) court: checks and balances on, 239; and NSA access to phone-call data, 185; purpose of, 37

Foursquare, 98

Fourth Amendment (U.S. Constitution), 9; and big data, 38; and Facebook, 50; and facial-recognition software, 151; and GPS tracking, 135. *See also* Constitution (U.S.)

France, 37; General Directorate for External Security, 50; tracking web browsing and social media, 47, 50

Franklin, Benjamin, 240

freedom and privacy, 1

freedom of choice: and free expression, 3; and privacy, 3

Freedom of Information Act (FOIA), 44

free software and services risks, 23, 33–34, 60–62

FTC. *See* Federal Trade Commission

gaming systems: facial and voice-recognition software in, 214; natural human-computer interfaces for, 214; tracking home activity, 175, 189

Geek Squad, 31

General Directorate for External Security (France), 50

Genetic Information Nondiscrimination Act, 168

geolocation, 10, 13. *See also* GPS

Germany: use of drones by law enforcement, 119; government surveillance in, 41

gesture recognition technology, 175

Ghostery, 82

GigaOm, 37, 86

global positioning system. *See* GPS

Goan, Crystal, 28

Google, 11, 14, 31, 69; access to records in the European Union, 41; Android phones hacked, 103; blocked in China, 40; data set collected by, 13; Google Chat, 43; Google Chrome, 23; Google Drive, 38; Google Glass, 108, 150, 215–216; Google Latitudes, 98; Google Voice, 99; mobile facial recognition tool, 150; self-driving cars, 128; transparency report, 34, 37, 39. *See also* email: cloud-based services; search engines

GotWind, 217

Government Communications Headquarters (GCHQ), 37

governments: agencies collecting personal data (U.S.), 51–52; checks and balances (U.S.), 37; most wanted lists, 44; service providers providing information to, 36; spying on citizens, 6, 38, 185, 240; spying on journalists, 190; surveillance in countries outside the U.S., 39–41, 51; surveillance in the U.S., 36, 42–43, 43–47, 48–50. *See also* big data; data collection; law enforcement; tracking

GPS (global positioning system), 92; big data collections, 39; on cell phones, 98; devices used to track people with dementia, 177; warrants required for tracking, 135

Great Wolf Resorts, 109

Greece, 68

Grosso, Andrew, 151

Guardedly, 204

*Guardian*, 37, 38

Guatemala, 96

hacking, 25, 61–62; attacks on cellular Internet services, 180; "Carna" bot, 183; exposure of SCADA systems to, 183–184; vulnerability of mobile devices to, 103, 104. *See also* cyber-crime

Hall, Ashleigh, 72

Harvey, Adam, 123

Hasan, Jalil, xii

Hassan v. Lower Merion School District, xii, xvin1

health care, 69. *See also* Affordable Care Act

health records: effects on insurance and hiring decisions, 167; ownership by medical research, 168–169; privacy of, 8–9, 161. *See also* Affordable Care Act

Heapsylon, 217

Hide My Ass, 81

Higgins, Parker, 131

Hill, Kashmir, 175

HIPAA (Health Insurance Portability and Accountability Act), 161, 168

HM Revenue and Customs, 68

Holder, Eric (Attorney General), 47

Holdren, John R., 219

Hollaback!, 204

home gaming systems. *See* gaming systems
home networks: security on, 196–197, 197–198, 200–202; vulnerabilities of, 195–196, 197
homes: counterfeit electronic devices in, 180–181; data collected from, 174, 175–176, 176, 177, 184; gesture-recognition technology in, 175; government surveillance of phone use, 190; interconnected devices in, 177; Internet-connected devices in, 178–179; tracking by cable and satellite dish companies, 176; privacy issues in data collected from, 3; vulnerability of internet-connected devices in, 181–184. *See also* gaming systems; children and teens; data collection; smart grids
Horwitz, Sari, 186
Hotmail, 43, 58. *See also* email
HTC America, 88
Hulu, 58
human-computer interfaces replacing keyboards, 214–215
human dignity and privacy, 4
Human Rights European Convention, 45
Hunt, Ira Gus, 37
HushMail, 66, 81

IBM, 31
identity theft, viii, 70–71
Identity Theft Assistance Center (ITAC), 70
Immigration and Custom Enforcement (ICE), 71
IMSI-catchers, 115
India, 37; biometrics used to verify citizen identities, 146–147; Centralized Monitoring System, 50; digital surveillance through Blackberry devices, 185; government access to private camera networks, 116; and the right to privacy, 8; tracking social media, 50
Indiana Wiretap Act, 27

Industrial Control Systems cyber Emergency Response Team (ICS-CERT), 182
Information Technology Act (India), 116
*Infoworld*, 107
Instagram, 50, 58
insurance companies, 132
Integrated Automated Fingerprint Identification System (IAFIS), 52
Intel Corporation, 176
Intelligence and Security Committee (UK Parliament), 40
Internal Revenue Service. *See* IRS
International Criminal Court, 44
International Data Safe Harbor, 232–233
Internet browsers: blocking cookies and tracking in, 80; Java-targeted cyber-attacks, 199; safety and security settings, 23–24; tracked while using, 78
Internet Census 2012, 183
Internet conferencing systems, 43
Internet Explorer, 23. *See also* Internet browsers
Internet of Things, 12, 222–223
Internet Protocol (IP) address, 78
Internet Watch Foundation (IWF), 71, 72
INTERPOL Terrorism Watch List, 44
intrusion-protection systems for home networks, 201
IP address, 78
iPads, xii, 10. *See also* mobile devices
Iran, 41
Ireland, 43
IRS (Internal Revenue Service): authorized e-file providers, 67; filing taxes online, 67
ISP (Internet Service Providers) providing data to law enforcement, 187
Israel, 8
Ivory Coast, 116

Japan, 8
Java, 24, 199
Jolie, Angelina, 155

*Jones v. U.S. See U.S. v. Jones*
Jones, Antoine, 135
Jones, Barbara, 1
Juniper Networks, 103
Justice Department. *See* Department of
   Justice

Kaspersky, 31
Kennish, Brian, 82
*Kent v. Dulles*, 46
keyboards, 214. *See also* keystroke
   capture
keystroke capture: keystroke loggers
   (hardware), 26, 27, 29; law
   enforcement's use of, 26; laws
   pertaining to, 27, 28; passwords
   captured by, 26; spyware that
   captures keystrokes, 26; in the
   workplace, xii, 27. *See also* laws and
   regulations; spyware
keystroke loggers. *See* keystroke
   capture
kids. *See* children and teens
killer apps, 211, 225n1
Killock, Jim, 42
Kinect:. *See* gaming systems (home)
Kirkhope, Timothy, 46
Kogakuin University, 152

Lacks, Henrietta, 168
Lambda Labs, 150
laptops. *See* personal computers
law enforcement: access to cell phone
   and mobile device data, 106, 175,
   186–187; access to DNA samples,
   162–163; access to smart car data,
   129; biometric data shared between
   agencies, 151–152; Boston Marathon
   bombers tracked by, 89;
   Communications Assistance for
   Law Enforcement Act (CALEA), 45;
   cyber-crime and local law
   enforcement, 57; data collection by,
   14, 34, 89; drones used by, 115, 119,
   120–121; *Maryland v. King*, 162–163;
   setting legal limits on, 228, 236–239;
   use of license-plate scanners to track
   cars, 116, 133–134; use of past
   actions, 45; use of social media, 43,

49; warrants required (or not) to
   access data from technology,
   237–238. *See also* governments
Laws and Regulations:
   Communications Assistance for
   Law Enforcement Act (CALEA), 45;
   eavesdropping statutes, state and
   federal, 28; Federal Wiretap Act, 27;
   human dignity protections under
   the law, 4; Indiana Wiretap Act, 27;
   litigation under federal wiretapping
   laws, 28; new laws and regulations
   proposed, 227–240; state law vs.
   federal law on right to privacy, 9;
   technology's pace of change
   outpacing laws, 1, 10; Stored
   Communications Act, 27; Video
   Privacy Protection Act of 1988, 5;
   *See also governments; law enforcement*

*Le Monde*, 190

Leibowitz, Jon, 77
Leo, Richard, 145
library archives storing digital
   information, 43
Library of Congress, 43
license-plate scanners, 116, 133–134.
   *See also* tracking
LinkedIn, 36. *See also* social media
Lithuania, 68
location. *See* geolocation
Locke, John, 3
loggers. *See* keystroke capture
London (England), 113
Long-Term Evolution (LTE) network
   hub, 180
Lookout, 103
loopt, 36
Lower Manhattan Security Initiative,
   113
Lower Merion School District, xi–xii
loyalty cards, 13
Lyne, James, 196

Macklem, Timothy, 3
MacScan, 32
Madrid train bombings of 2004, 148
Magic Lantern, 26

Malik, Om, 86
malware, 200. *See also* hacking; cyber-
    crime; spyware
*Maryland v. King*, 162–163
Massachusetts Institute of Technology
    (MIT) : identification by location
    study by, 13, 35; Computer Science
    and Artificial Intelligence
    Laboratory, 179
Mastria, Lou, 78
Matherly, John, 181–184
Matsko, Lindy, xi
Mayer, Marissa, 36
*Mayfield v. United States* , 148, 154n16
Mayfield, Brandon, 148
McAfee security software, 31, 200
McAfee, John, 95–96
McGregor, James, 40
McKinsey Global Institute, 220
McNealy, Scott, 228
medical records: HIPPA privacy
    protections, 161; stored in
    databases, 13; stored online, 68–69
Meeker, Mary, 213
Mercedes Benz, 128
metadata, 96, 187
Metropolitan Transportation
    Commission (San Francisco), 134
Mexico, 8
MI5 (UK), 40, 51
microphones on personal computers,
    29
Microsoft Corporation, vii, 11, 15;
    government and law enforcement
    record requests to, 36, 37; security
    software, 31, 32, 200
Mijangos, Luis, 25–26
MIT. *See* Massachusetts Institute of
    Technology
mobile devices: Bluetooth on, 104; e-
    readers and tablets, xii, 88;
    government intrusion on, 104–107,
    185; locating lost devices, 206–207;
    privacy abusers targeted by the
    FTC, 88; privacy issues when
    accessed in court cases, 102; privacy
    issues when used for work, 101–102;
    remote access through, xiii; security
    measures for, 104, 108, 203–204,

207–208; trends and innovations in,
    213; ubiquity of, 213; vulnerability
    to hackers, 103. *See also* cell phones
mobile networks, 12
mobile phones. *See* cell phones; mobile
    devices
*Mobile Security Report* (Juniper
    Networks), 103
mobile Wi-Fi, 202
Moore, Gordon and "Moore's Law",
    212
Morton, John, 71
Mossad (Israel), 51
Motion Reality, Inc., 216
Motorola, 217
Mozilla's Firefox, 23. *See also* Internet
    browsers
Mueller, Robert, 67
Mugr, 150
Murray, Timothy, 129
Mutsuraev, Timur, 83
My Aircover, 204
My Force, 204
MyFord Touch, 128
MyLincoln Touch, 128
MyMagic+, 108
MySpace, 26, 43. *See also* social media

nanny cams, 205–206
NASA (National Aeronautics and
    Space Administration), 90
National Archives Records
    Administration (NARA), 43
*National Biometrics Challenge*, 52
National Counterterrorism Center
    (NCTC), 45, 47, 48
National Highway Traffic Safety
    Administration (NHTSA), 129
National Institute of Informatics
    (Tokyo), 152
National Public Radio, 40
National Security Agency (NSA),
    37–38; Data Center, 39, 51; and FISA
    courts, 240; personal data collected
    by, 11, 36, 190; tracking cell-phone
    calls, 185; warrantless snooping, 35
National Telecommunications and
    Information Administration
    (NTIA), 180

Negobot, 73
Netflix, 58, 61
Netherlands, 104, 185
networking of data sources, 13
networks. *See* home networks; Wi-Fi
   networks (public); mobile devices;
   mobile Wi-Fi
News Corporation, 103
*News of the World* , 103
New York City, 113
New York Federal Reserve Bank, 49
New York Police Department (NYPD),
   113
*New York Times*, 6, 145
*New Yorker*, 81
Next Generation Identification (NGI),
   52, 151–152
Nietzche, Friedrich, 32
Nintendo. *See* gaming systems
no-fly list, 44
normal behavior, 5
Northern California Regional
   Intelligence Center (NCRIC), 133
North Korea, 41
Norton, 31
NotCompatible, 103
NPR (National Public Radio), 40
NSA. *See* National Security Agency

Obama, Barack, 71, 106
Obamacare. *See* Affordable Care Act
Obama, Michelle, 62
Office for Intellectual Freedom, 173
Office of Community Oriented
   Policing Services, 115
OKCupid, 86
Olson, Ken, ix
OnGuardOnline.gov, 196–198
online banking, 67, 191
online identity, creating, 63–64
online profiling, 47
OnStar telematics system, 130
Open Rights Group, 42
operating system security, 23

Parkland Regional Library, 27
passcard, 13, 134
passphrases. *See* passwords

passwords: for cloud computing, 63;
   fingerprints used in place of, 140;
   for home network and personal
   computer security, 31, 196, 198; for
   mobile devices, 100, 108, 191;
   obtained by keystroke capture, 26,
   27; and online banking security, 191
Patriot Act (USA), 148
Pauley, William III, 50
Payton, Theresa M., viii–ix
*PC Week*, 198
Pentagon, 49, 106
personal computers: business finances
   on, 20; controlled by others, 24–25;
   family information on, 20; personal
   finances on, 20; proliferation of, 12;
   remote access to, xiii; security
   practices and tools, 199, 200;
   vulnerabilities to hacking and
   spyware, xii, 19, 25. *See also* mobile
   devices
personal data, viii, 8
Personally Identifiable Information, 14
PestPatrol, 24
Petraeus, David, 177
Pew Research Center, 185
phishing, 60, 191, 196
phone cloning, 190
PhotoBucket, 58
photo-sharing sites, 58. *See also* social
   media
physiological biometrics, 140. *See also*
   biometrics
Piedmont, California, 133
Pinterest, 50. *See also* social media
Pipl, 83
PNR (Person, Name, Record), 46
Poison Ivy, 24
Police Executive Research Forum, 57
political parties (U.S.), 7
pornography: child pornography,
   71–72, 72, 104, 197; spyware ads for
   pay-for-pornography sites, 23
portable computers. *See* mobile
   devices; personal computers
Powell, Colin, 61
Powell, Lewis, 5
power companies, xiii
Predator drones, 120

privacy: behavior when privacy is lost, 3; and choice, 1, 3, 4, 6; circles of privacy, xi–xiii; data's role in loss of, 6–8; eroding protections of, 34; establishing p. as a right in the U.S., 233–234; and freedom, xiv, 1, 3, 6; in the future, xv; and human dignity, 4; importance of, 1–6, 240; legal limits in the U.S., 227, 229–232; "loss of privacy" under U.S. law, 10; Privacy International, 34, 115; threats to privacy, xv; and the U.S. Supreme Court, 28. *See also* big data; biometrics; data collection; health records; homes; laws and regulations; mobile devices; rights to privacy; smart cars; social media

privacy laws. *See* laws and regulations

Privacyrights.org, 69

privacy statements, 61

process rights vs. absolute rights, 9

profiling. *See* online profiling

Progressive Snapshot, 132

property records, 13

protecting data and yourself. *See* backups; children and teens; cyber-crime; home networks; passwords; security settings; toolboxes

*Quartz*, 40

QuoremEx, 95

Radio Frequency Identification technology (RFID), 12, 134, 215

radio frequency (RF) bug detectors, 65, 205

ransomware, 22

Rapid Information Overlay Technology (RIOT), 38

Rate My Drive (Aviva), 132

Ratters. *See* Remote Administration Tools (RAT)

Raytheon, 38

Reagan, Ronald, 5

registration screens, faked, xii

Regulation E, 67

Remote Administration Tools (RAT), 24

remote capture programs, xii

remote monitoring software, xii

*Rene v. G.F. Fishers, Inc.*, 27, 32n6

Renesys, 39

Repository for Individuals of Special Concern (RISC), 52

retinal scans, 141

Revolutionary Armed Forces of Colombia. *See* FARC

RFID. *See* Radio Frequency Identification technology

Ridge Schmidt Cyber, vii

right to privacy, 8–10; and the First Amendment (U.S. Constitution), 9; and the Fourth Amendment (U.S. Constitution), 9; legal issues regarding, 10; process rights versus absolute rights, 9; in the United States, 9; in the U.S. compared to other democracies, 8–9, 229–232. *See also* privacy

Rigmaiden, Daniel David, 47

RIOT. *See* Rapid Information Overlay Technology

RISC, 52

*Robbins v. Lower Merion School District*, xi–xii, xvin1

Robbins, Blake, xi–xii

routers, counterfeit, 180

Royal Canadian Mounted Police (RCMP), 120

RSA, 59

runtime protection solutions for home networks, 201

Russell, Katherine, 186

Russia: Federal Security Bureau (FSB) of, 48; intrusion on computers and mobile devices, 105

*Russia Today* , 45

SABRE airline-reservation system, 12

Samsung, 174

SAR (Suspicious Activity Reporting Initiative) list, 44

Sarkozy, Nicolas, 47

Saudi Arabia, 41

SCADA (Supervisory control and Data Acquisition systems), 183–184

Scalia, Antonin, 135

scam artists, 22

scareware, 22. *See also* malware, spyware

scent as a biometric identifier, 141

Schmidt, Eric (*The New Digital Age: Reshaping the Future of People, Nations and Business*), 63, 69

Schmidt, Howard A., vii–ix

Schwartz, Andrew, 224

Science and Technology Council, 52

Scorfo, Nicodemo, 26

Scorfo, Nicodemo, Jr., 26

Scotland, 43

Scotland Yard, 44

search engines: data collection and bundling by, 79; government and law enforcement access, 34, 36, 37; poisoned results from, 196; search terms tracked, 79

secret police, 6

security breaches, 60

security cameras. *See* surveillance cameras

security companies, 31

security programs, 30, 32

security settings : for browsers, firewalls, and operating systems, 23; for mobile devices, 108; security apps for mobile devices, 203–204

Sex Offender Registry (FBI), 44

sexual predators: Chapman, Peter, 72; Crespo, Xavier Orlando, 72; targeting children and teens, 71–74; use of cloud computing, 71

sexual trafficking, 73

Shear, Bradley, 82

Shodan, 181–184

Shutterfly, 58

Silent Circle, 66

Simple Nomad, 96

Singer, Pete, 119

Siri. *See* Apple computers and phones

Skoot, Rebecca (*The Immortal Life of Henrietta Lacks*) , 168

Skynet, 40

Skype, 43

*Slate*, 123

smart cars: automated software updates for, 128; black boxes in, 128–130; data collection privacy issues, 129; driving patterns tracked by insurance companies, 132; driving while connected to the Internet, 130; law enforcement accessing data from, 129; self-driving cars, 128; telematics systems in, 130–131; vulnerabilities of built-in Bluetooth, 131

smart garments. *See* wearable computers and technology

smart grids, xiii; privacy issues, 188; proposals to control home energy use through, 188. *See also* homes

smart homes. *See* homes

smart phones. *See* cell phones; mobile devices

Smith, Sarah, 73

Smug-Mug, 58

SnapChat, 66

Snapfish, 58

snooping. *See* spyware

Snowden, Edward, 11, 37, 40

SNPedia, 168

social media: accessed through spyware, 25; activities that trigger investigations, 50; use by behavioral advertisers, 85–86; blocking facial-recognition software in, 123; use in the Boston Marathon bombing, 83, 89; bundling profiles for advertisers, 85; crowdsourcing through, 89; dangers of linking accounts, 63; Department of Defense policies, 49; facial recognition and privacy issues, 149–150; government access to, 36, 37, 40, 48–50, 50, 68; home networks infected through, 197; and online identity, 64, 83–84; privacy issues on, 82–83; privacy settings for, 202; search tools for, 83; and sexual predators, 71, 72; as a source of child pornography images, 72; tracking through "share" icons, 79; wearable technology linked to, 217; wanted posters on, 43

social networking. *See* social media

social science, 14–16

Social Security Administration, 69

Sonic.net, 36
Sophos, 196, 197, 200
Sotomayor, Sonia, 107
spam: anti-spam tools, 200; through
    Bluetooth, 104; used to propagate
    viruses, 103; through social media,
    197
Spider Oak, 36
Spitz, Malte, 41
Spokeo.com, 83
SPRINT, 92
Spybot—Search and Destroy, 24
spy-camera detectors, 205
spying: on teens, xi–xii; through
    personal computers, xii; through
    rented computers, xii. *See also*
    spyware
Spynet, 24
spyware, xii, 19–32; accessing personal
    data, 24–25; anti-spyware programs,
    31–32; Back Orifice, 24; commercial
    vs. targeted, 28; CPU resources
    consumed by, 30; ethical
    implications of, 21; used for
    extortion, 25–26; legality of, 20; used
    by marketers, 22; on personal
    computers, 19, 32; protecting
    against, 23–24, 28–31, 65–66, 205;
    removing, 23, 31–32; security
    programs disabled by, 30; task
    manager disabled by, 30. *See also*
    keystroke capture; malware; homes
SSL (security sockets layer), 199
Staples, Inc., 78
Stasi, 6
statistics: used to predict behavior, 15
Stephens, Paul (Privacy Rights
    Clearinghouse), 87
stingrays, 46–47, 190. *See also* cell
    phones
storage capacity, 13
Stored Communications Act, 27
Strongbox, 81
student council election hacked, 62
sUAS (small Unmanned Aerial
    System), 120
subpoenas, 35; and cell phone records,
    38; and the Fourth Amendment, 9
Sugar Land, Texas, 133

Supreme Court (U.S.): and GPS
    tracking, 135; *Kent v. Dulles* , 46;
    *Maryland v. King,* 162–163; privacy
    rulings, 28, 46, 106, 162, 230, 238;
    and the right to privacy, 9, 230; *U.S.
    v. Jones,* 106, 135
surfing the Internet, 20
surveillance cameras: effectiveness in
    reducing crime, 115; and facial-
    recognition software, 122; use by
    government and law enforcement,
    115–116; prevalence in urban areas,
    113–114; privacy risks from,
    114–115; public opinion about, 114;
    reading license plates, 116, 133–134;
    at stores and shopping centers,
    116–117; at the workplace, 117–118.
    *See also* cameras
Suspicious Activity Reporting
    Initiative (SAR) list, 44
Swarthmore College, 100
Swift, Christopher, 186
Switzerland, 8
Symantec, 31; anti-malware software,
    200; "Honey Stick" project on
    smartphone security, 207
Syria, 39; Syrian Computer Society, 39;
    Syrian Telecommunications
    Establishment, 39

tablets. *See* mobile devices
Target stores, 6–7
task manager, 30
taxes, filing online, 67–68
technology: benefits of, xiii–xiv;
    increased interconnection between
    devices, 222–223; nature of
    innovation, 211–212; pace of
    change, 10, 212, 219
teens. *See* children and teens
Terrorist Identities Datamart
    Environment (TIDE), 48
Terrorist Screening Database (TSDB),
    44
Terrorist Watch List, 44
Tibet, 105
Tiburon, California, 133
Tien, Lee, 90
Tivo Inc., 176

Tiwi, 131–132

Toolboxes: tools to foil snoopers, 66; tools to locate and secure mobile devices, 207; tools to manage online identity, 64; tools to monitor home computers, 21; tools to protect privacy of browsing history, 81–82; tools to search social media, 83; tools to secure home networks, 202; tools to store data in the cloud, 59; tools to track driving patterns, 131–132

Tor (The Onion Router), 66, 80–81

tracking: by automatic toll collection systems, 134; by behavioral advertisers, 79; by cable companies, 188–189; by car insurance companies, 132; through email, 43, 80; through Internet browsers, 78, 79; through Internet conferencing systems, 43; by license-plate scanners, 133–134; outside the home, 46–47, 77; public opinion about, 185; types of personal information tracked, 51. *See also* Bluetooth; Boston Marathon bombings; data collection; GPS; social media

Transportation Safety Board (TSB), 104

Travis, Steven, 47

Trojan horse, 24

Trusteer, Inc., 191

Tsarnaev, Tamerlan. *See* Boston Marathon bombers

Tucson Border Patrol, 52

Twitter: and big data collection, 39; tweets stored by Library of Congress, 43. *See also* social media

two-factor authentication, 199

Tynan, Richard, 115

U.K. *See* United Kingdom

Unified Threat Management (UTM), 198

U.S. Congress. *See* Congress (U.S.)

U.S. Constitution. *See* Constitution (U.S.)

U.S. Supreme Court. *See* Supreme Court (U.S.)

United Kingdom (U.K.): Border Agency, 46; Communications Data Bill, 187; data sharing with U.S., 37; use of drones in, 115, 119, 122; filing taxes online in, 68; government surveillance in, 40, 185; library archives of digital information, 43; public Wi-Fi network security in, 196; tracking travelers, 46

United States. *See* Congress (U.S.); Constitution (U.S.); laws and regulations; right to privacy; Supreme Court (U.S.)

*United States v. Ropp*, 27, 32n7

Universal Declaration of Human Rights (EU), 231

Universite Catholique de Louvain, 13

University of Missouri, 121

University of Pennsylvania, 15

University of Toronto, 105

URL-content filtering for home network security, 201

USB thumb drives, 198

*U.S. v. Jones*, 106, 135

Utah Data Center, 39. *See also* National Security Agency

Verizon, 38, 106, 175, 221

Veterans Administration, 69

videogame-playing consoles, xiii. *See also* gaming systems

Video Privacy Protection Act of 1988, 5

Virtual Network Computing (VNC), 21

virtual private network, 201

virus protection. *See* anti-malware software

Vista, 32

Vizify, 64

Vodofone, 217

voice-recognition, 140, 214, 221. *See also* biometrics

voice print, 142. *See also* biometrics

Wales, 43

*Wall Street Journal*, 78, 86, 176

Walt Disney Company, 108

warrants, 237–238

*Washington Post*, 37, 185, 186

*Washington University v. Catalana* , 168,
   170n16
wearable computers and technology :
   for active solo sports, 217–218; for
   children and teens, 218; for health
   care, 218; new products and trends,
   214, 216, 217; used to track the
   wearer, 108–109; used to train police
   and soldiers, 216. *See also* Google:
   Google Glass
web browsers. *See* Internet browsers
webcams. *See* cameras
website checkers, 201
Webwatcher, 25
Wexler, Chuck, 57
White House, vii
Wi-Fi networks (home). *See* home
   networks
Wi-Fi networks (public): insecurity of
   free networks, 196–203; used to
   track mobile devices, 98, 117; in the
   United Kingdom, 196
Wi-Fi Protected Access V. 2 (WPA2),
   201

Windows 7, 32
Windows 8, 32
Windows Defender, 32
*Wired*, 39, 51
Wireless Sensor Data Mining Lab, 100
wiretapping: encryption to protect
   against, 207; and keystroke
   monitoring, 27–28; limits on law
   enforcement and government, 35;
   through spyware, 20, 25
Wi-VI, 179
World Wildlife Fund, 121

Xbox. *See* gaming systems

Yagan, Sam, 86
Yahoo, 43, 118. *See also* email; search
   engines
YouTube, 50, 176. *See also* social media

Zabasearch, 83
Zappos, 101
Zuckerberg, Mark, 83

# About the Authors

**Theresa M. Payton** has over twenty years of advanced business and security technology expertise and leadership at the highest levels of both government and in the financial services industry. From May 2006 until September 2008, she served as chief information officer at the White House, the first woman to hold this position. Since leaving government service, she has served as a key advisor to government and corporate leaders in their efforts to improve their security. She has received numerous security awards including "Top 25 Most Influential in Security."

**Theodore Claypoole** is an information technology and data management lawyer with Womble Carlyle, where he leads the Privacy Team. He co-chairs the Cyberspace Mobile Commerce Subcommittee of the American Bar Association's Business Law Section. His current work includes contracting for creative online payment systems, business use of gaming engines, testing radio frequency chip applications for wearable consumer products, drone development for military and civilian use, and helping build the business and technology architecture for the Internet of Things.